W9-CDK-544

ROCKET LAUNCH TO THE STARS

Atlantic Records president Ahmet Ertegun and I disagreed on which song to release as the single. . . . I decided to go out on a limb and prove to him I was right. They were already promoting "It's Gonna Rain" on the Atco label when I cut an acetate of "I Got You Babe" and offered it as an exclusive to KHJ, a red-hot radio station in L.A. that trumpeted itself as Boss City. It was sneaky as well as risky but, I thought, worth it.

The deejays loved the song and began playing it immediately.

It was like a rocket launch. The station's switchboard lit up instantly. Within a week, the song was tops in L.A., and Ahmet and Atco switched gears, pulled "It's Gonna Rain" and jumped on "I Got You Babe." By mid-July it seemed as if the entire listening world, at least from the United States to England, knew of Sonny and Cher.

Most Pocket Books are available at special quantity discounts for bulk purchases for sales promotions, premiums or fund raising. Special books or book excerpts can also be created to fit specific needs.

For details write the office of the Vice President of Special Markets, Pocket Books, 1230 Avenue of the Americas, New York, New York 10020.

SONNY BONO

AND THE BEAT GOES ON

POCKET BOOKS

New York   London   Toronto   Sydney   Tokyo   Singapore

POCKET BOOKS, a division of Simon & Schuster Inc.
1230 Avenue of the Americas, New York, NY 10020

Copyright © 1991 by Sonny Bono

All rights reserved, including the right to reproduce
this book or portions thereof in any form whatsoever.
For information address Pocket Books, 1230 Avenue
of the Americas, New York, NY 10020

ISBN: 0-671-69367-0

First Pocket Books paperback printing June 1992

10 9 8 7 6 5 4 3 2 1

POCKET and colophon are registered trademarks of
Simon & Schuster Inc.

Cover photo by Tony Costa

Printed in the U.S.A.

This is for my wife Mary, who entered my life at a most critical time. She brought with her a strength that has given me the focus and direction I had never before been able to achieve. And to the greatest gift a man could receive . . . to my children, Christy, Chastity, Chesare, and Chianna.

For his many years of tremendous dedication and loyalty, a special thanks to my best friend, Denis Pregnolato. For his kind assistance, I am grateful to Todd Gold. And for her passion and insightful editorial guidance, my deepest appreciation to my devoted editor, Judith Regan.

This story is not about right or wrong. It's just another story of a life and what one goes through, hopefully gathering wisdom as one travels.

PART I

NEEDLES AND PINS

1

SHE'LL MAKE ME CRY
UNTIL THE DAY I DIE

I have to say that I was expecting it.

Still, the first time that my relationship with Cher was mentioned in my campaign for mayor of Palm Springs, I stumbled. I was shaking hands outside a local senior citizens' center, where a long line of people were waiting to get their cholesterol checked. It was a few minutes after 7 A.M. on the second-to-last day of February 1988. The hot sun was covering the vast Cochella Valley like a first coat of paint. I sipped from a cup of coffee.

I noticed two gentle, grandmotherly-looking ladies point at me and whisper. I thought I was ready for them. After declaring my candidacy, I had telephoned Clint Eastwood for advice. Unfortunately, Clint was out of town, but I spoke to the woman who had managed his campaign. Her advice was simple: Drink lots of coffee and talk to everyone in town.

That's what I was trying to do. So, coffee in hand, I approached the two women.

"Hello, I'm Sonny Bono." I smiled. "I'm running for mayor."

"You used to be married to Cher," one of the ladies said abruptly.

"That's right. A long time ago."

3

"Well, dear . . ." She considered for a moment. "I've got to tell you, that hair of hers and those clothes—"

"When she wears them," her friend interjected.

"I don't know about her," the first lady said. "I just don't know."

"I don't know what to say," I replied. "I'm running for mayor, did you know? I hope you vote for me." I gave them my best smile and moved on.

If it seemed as if I was following Ronald Reagan and Clint Eastwood by trading celebrity for political office, the similarity was unintentional. The way I saw it, I was merely an outraged citizen, Joe Average, who was fed up with the old-boy network that had run city hall for years. A few silly bureaucratic battles over the remodeling of my house had pushed me to the breaking point. By running for mayor, I was simply standing up for my rights.

My opponents chided me for being the ex-Mr. Cher. They called me Sonny Bonehead. They labeled me Mr. Anti-Establishment, an upstart rabble-rouser and rock and roller. Ironically, I was a registered Republican who had voted for Reagan in 1984. They also criticized me for having no experience in government. Not even student-body president.

Nevertheless, I was the front-runner. The polls indicated a wide lead.

Like most of my endeavors, from meat packing to music and later from pasta to politics, I entered the race for mayor with little more going for me than good gut instincts, a sense of right and wrong, and total honesty—exactly what I wanted people to expect from Salvatore Bono, a hard-working guy with a strict, blue-collar Italian background. It was also, I found, the stuff that gives great irritation to full-time politicians.

I tried to slough off anything to do with Cher, since she was not the issue, though, in truth, she was partly responsible for my living in Palm Springs. My love affair with the jewel of desert cities began during the breakup of our love affair, which ended in divorce on June 26, 1975. Since then we had had little to do with each other, crossing paths irregularly, like sagebrush blowing across the sand.

Our daughter, Chastity (Chas), a film student, served as

a loving and trustworthy go-between. She kept us up to date on each other's personal, social, and business calendars. Cher was dating bartender-turned-actor Rob Camilletti, and my wife, Mary, was pregnant. Cher was starring in the movie *Moonstruck,* while I was running for mayor. That was as far as it went. No telephone calls, no Christmas cards, no requests for "Sonny for Mayor" T-shirts.

Then, in the midst of the campaign, I received a surprising phone call. But not from Cher. On the line was a producer from "Late Night with David Letterman." After some pleasant chitchat, she got to the point.

"We wonder, ah, if you would like to be a guest on the Letterman show," she said. Then there was a slight pause. "Ah . . . with Cher."

I loved it. Chas had told me that Cher was trying to revive her recording career and had a new album about to come out. If I guested on "Letterman" with Cher, it would draw a tremendous amount of attention to the show, and to her. For a brief moment, we would be Sonny and Cher again. I grasped the ploy immediately and thought it was a brilliant move. I also figured that Cher was behind it.

"If you have any hesitations, Mr. Bono," the producer said, interrupting the silence, "think about the exposure it will bring to your campaign."

Exactly. One of my primary concerns was gaining a higher profile for Palm Springs. Going on national television, on a show that promised to be a ratings bonanza, fit into my program nicely.

"Sure, I'd love to do the show," I said. "Just give me the details."

The show was several weeks away. The week after accepting the invitation, I received another out-of-the-blue phone call. This time the voice on the other end was familiar. It was Cher. There was no how-ya-doin', no what's shaking, no how's the campaign going. Instead, Cher was all business and got straight to the point.

"Son, I'm really concerned about this Letterman show," she said. "I don't know if I can handle it. I've been freaking out about this for the past few days."

"Woa, wait a minute," I said, remembering too well Cher's preshow anxiety attacks. "What do you mean freaking out? You've always had stage fright, and you've always gotten through it. Relax.''

"No, Son, you don't understand.''

Then Cher explained that the last time she went on Letterman's show, she and Dave got into a sarcastic tiff that ended with her calling him an asshole. I laughed. An asshole? On national television? And he wanted her back?

"That's why I'm worried,'' she continued. "I know his sense of humor, and I know yours, Son. I don't want both of you ganging up on me.''

Together for more than a decade, we developed a kind of telepathic understanding, an intimacy that didn't need to be articulated. Cher was keenly aware that I could needle her as no one else could. I also knew that she was equally adept when it came to hitting my jugular. Our routines were rarely scripted. The much-publicized, spirited digs we traded about her nose and my height were only one aspect of this intuitive connection.

I told Cher not to worry. I was hip to the game plan. I was going to be there to support her.

"Well, you can go out first, test the water,'' she offered. "You should go out alone and talk about running for mayor. Then I'll come out. It'll be okay.''

"That's what I'm trying to tell you.'' I laughed. "Don't worry.''

A few days later, I got the distinct impression that my private telephone line was becoming a clearing board for surprising calls. It was Letterman's producer again. Her voice was more tentative this time, lighter than before. She apologized for bothering me again, but said that a question had popped up since we had last spoken. Would I, she wanted to know, sing with Cher?

"Oh gosh,'' I hemmed, "I don't think she wants to sing with me. She wants to do her record. I think Cher's into her own thing now.''

"Let me ask you this,'' she said diplomatically. "If Cher will sing with you, will you sing with her?''

That was the big question. I can't even fathom a guess as to how many times I'd been asked that question. When our ill-fated, post-divorce "Sonny and Cher Show'' went off the air after one season in 1977, that was it. Cher and

I quit performing together. Still, our songs, such as "I Got You Babe" and "The Beat Goes On," continued on the radio, while the breezy, romantic image of Sonny and Cher never lost its appeal.

So will you and Cher ever sing together again? My answer never varied: I'd love to sing with Cher again. I had a great time doing it. I've always believed that something special happens when we're onstage with each other. But it would have to be a mutual decision. I've had my days of scraped knees. I'd only want to perform with Cher if she wanted to perform with me.

That's what I told the producer. If Cher was amenable, then I was too. Obviously, Cher was going to be asked the same question. Would she sing with me? I wouldn't know until it happened. The producer told me nothing was going to be planned. But if something did happen, if sparks flew, would Cher go along with it? She was the star. If anything was going to happen, it hinged on Cher.

It was early evening when my wife, Mary, and I arrived at our midtown hotel. That morning Mary and I had boarded a plane in Palm Springs, flown to Los Angeles, and landed at New York's JFK International Airport six hours later. A car took us into Manhattan. Mary, who was seven months pregnant, was exhausted by the traveling and dozed through the bumpy ride. I spent the bumpy ride staring at her with a mixture of love and awe and gratitude.

Meeting this bright, energetic, and outspoken woman, who also happens to be quite beautiful, had been the single most positive occurrence in my life since, well, since the late 1960s or early 1970s, and that was long before Cher and I split. I was an old-fashioned Italian at heart. I liked to impress my girl, and Mary believed in me in a way that no one had, including Cher. Mary gave me the spark that had been lost. She provided me with the fuel I needed to soar.

By the time the car stopped in front of our hotel I was ready to join Mary in a little snooze. However, the bellman's enthusiastic greeting reminded me that we were in New York City, not Palm Springs, and I was jolted awake by the undeniable awareness that this skyscraper-filled megalopolis was just waking up.

My daughter, Chastity, the most valuable legacy of Sonny and Cher, phoned that night and delivered an enthusiastic hello. She and I have had a pretty close relationship. Though she grew up living with Cher, I was Chas's pillar of stability. I might not have been as exciting as her mother, but I was always there. I had my place in her life. When, for instance, their mother-daughter arguments got a little too heated, I'd enter the picture. If she had a sensitive issue to discuss, Chas knew that she could always talk to me.

Chas rendezvoused with me and Mary at the hotel the next morning. As I saw her come bouncing into our suite I couldn't help feeling proud. Cher and I had shortcomings and failures as parents, but Chas had grown into a remarkable young woman. She'd survived the double whammy of having parents who were divorced *and* in show business— talk about the ingredients for a messed-up life—and landed solidly on her feet.

Chas was as excited as I was about her mom and dad's mini reunion. Over breakfast, she and I entertained Mary with Sonny and Cher stories from the road and our television series, not the best of times for us. However, it's funny how time makes the bad bearable and the hellish humorous. The three of us laughed straight through the meal. Chas also gave me the latest on Cher.

"Now, Dad, let me ask you an important question," she said. "What are you going to wear?"

"I don't know," I said. "I brought some casual clothes."

She wanted to see them. I opened the closet and showed Chas the jeans and sweater that I had brought to wear on the show. She didn't look too impressed with my selection.

"That's no good." She shook her head. "Mom's going to dress to kill. You know that. She'll be awesome. So you'd better have something nice too."

My hipper daughter insisted that I yield to her sharper sense of fashion. I didn't put up an argument, though I didn't know where to go. At Chastity's suggestion, the three of us cabbed it down to Greenwich Village and Chas took over as guide. She knew all the stores. I tried on shirts, pants, shoes, jackets. The works. Finally, I settled on a real hot silk shirt and a pair of baggy black trousers.

"And you've got to comb your hair back," she said back at the hotel. "Remember, Mom is going to look spectacular, like fireworks on the Fourth of July."

"Maybe worse," I joked, and all of us laughed.

A car provided by the show dropped Mary, Chas, and me off in front of the NBC building at Rockefeller Plaza, where "Late Night" is taped. Up until that point, I was really pretty calm. We had been talking about the show in the car as if it were an everyday sort of thing. Which wasn't true. But it didn't hit me until I strolled past the revolving door and into the lobby.

That's when I began to sense the full magnitude of Cher and me appearing together again. Up to that point, the fact that both Cher and I would be sitting next to each other on Letterman's show didn't seem like such a big deal. I'd be grabbing some national visibility while helping to draw attention to Cher and her new record. It was the kind of fabricated event television lives on.

However, as we moved through the skyscraper's lobby, I felt myself surrounded by the stares and whispers that charge a spectacle. The reality I was entering was much different than I had let myself believe, and I began to feel the sort of preshow jitters that I hadn't felt for years. Like everyone else, I found myself wondering, What is going to happen? Are Cher and I going to sing?

Suddenly my mind was flooded with memories. Sonny and Cher had meant a lot to other people. That had always been obvious. But I'd forgotten how much Sonny and Cher had meant to me. I'd blocked so much of that turbulent part of my life and now it was coming back in one enormous, overpowering tidal wave of emotion. It was yesterday all over again.

There was Cher, the skinny, homeless waif she'd been when we first met. Scared but strong. Certain that she wanted stardom. I pictured her hanging out in the studio with me and Phil Spector. I remembered having to calm her nerves during our first tentative attempts at recording. Then the release of "I've Got You Babe" brought the stardom and the craziness that seemed to stay with us throughout our relationship, no matter whether we were on top of the world or down in the dumps.

"Dad?" asked Chas. "Earth to Dad?"

"Huh?" I snapped out of it.

Mary and Chastity are two of the biggest Sonny and Cher fans I've ever encountered. In the elevator, the three of us suddenly fell silent and tense, then started to laugh.

"This might be a really big deal," I said. "Bigger than I expected."

The elevator ride became a metaphor for my tension. The higher we went, the closer we got to the source, the greater it became. I had learned that there's a huge difference between being in show business and being on top. It's the difference between turning a light on and sticking your finger in the light socket. Then the doors opened, and before we could step out, we were greeted by a phalanx of photographers. They formed a virtually impregnable wall, flashing lights and thrusting microphones in my direction. I thought of Muhammad Ali stepping into a ring before a fight.

Chas turned to me and said, "Oh, this is *big!*"

After a few moments of smiling and posing for pictures, we made our way down the hallway. The show's staffers seemed unusually nervous, the way they nodded and skittered beside us. Someone mentioned that Cher was already in the studio, rehearsing.

But as Mary, Chas, and I rounded the corner, we walked straight into Cher and Rob.

Cher's and my eyes locked. It was a hard stare that melted into a smile. Strained but genuine.

We were together for 11 years. But the Cher whose eyes I was looking into was a completely different person—redesigned, remade, redefined. Physically, we were the same two people—well, mostly the same. But all those shared emotions and events that had once charged us with passion and urgency were gone.

I felt strange standing face to face with Cher that day. Here was this mercurial woman I knew so well and yet there was so much about her that I didn't know at all. Cher too was uneasy being with me, and I knew why. She had no use for the past. She hated to be reminded. Cher had become such a beautiful creation, one that had taken her so many years to perfect, and she truly found it distasteful to have to confront any part of her background, least of all Sonny and Cher.

There was a moment of awkward silence, which Chas cut through with a bright "Hi, Mom!"

Then like that, we were all old pals. Or pretending to be so. Cher and I gave each other a hug. It was just that, a friendly hug, and nothing more. I'd met Rob briefly once before, and we shook hands. I've gotten along with all of Cher's boyfriends, at least those whom I've met, except for entertainment mogul David Geffen, whom I credit for destroying much of my and Cher's relationship. Mary and Cher talked briefly about being pregnant. It was easy, nice, and friendly.

Then, with a mixture of excitement and urgency, Cher pulled me aside.

"Son, come in the booth," she said. "You've gotta hear my new single. Listen to it."

Leaving the others behind, we walked into the engineer's booth, where Cher instructed someone to put on her new song.

"I want Son to hear it," she said.

In the old days I listened to everything. As far as Cher was concerned, my opinion was the acid test. Suddenly, after what seemed like a hundred years, here was Cher, doing the same old thing again—asking for my opinion. It was like a time warp. We were hanging out in the booth, Sonny and Cher, listening to her latest single, while Chas stood in the background.

I tried listening as objectively as possible but was overwhelmed by an emotional déjà vu. There we were—mother, father, child. Once a family. There we were—Sonny and Cher. We'd struggled together, created together, married, thrived, divorced, and gone our separate ways. There was a deep and complicated history there, and suddenly tears and sadness began to choke me.

I tried hard to figure out what I was choking back, since the sentiments I felt were both strange and bittersweet. Cher and I had loved each other, then fallen out of love and traveled our different paths. What we had, what we did together, it was locked away somewhere in the past. Gone. Then we found ourselves in this abnormal resurrection of Sonny and Cher. The nostalgia was impossible to sidestep. I don't know what it did to Cher, but it smacked me in the jaw real good.

I didn't miss Sonny and Cher. I was comfortable, delighted, and happy with my life. But it was like turning a corner and thinking that you've caught a glimpse of a long-lost friend. Maybe you have, maybe you haven't. You don't know. But you're still hit with all these mixed emotions.

"That was great, really great," I told Cher when the song finished playing. I had been able to listen enough to know it was OK. "I loved it."

"You did? Really?"

"Really," I said.

After watching Cher rehearse with Paul Shaffer, a long-time friend of mine, and his band, it was time to wait. The old schmooze and snooze. Mary and I hung out in my dressing room. Then, as the time grew close, we moved to the greenroom. I don't know who was more excited, Mary or I. If "I Got You Babe" comes on the radio, she'll crank the volume. I looked at her glowing face and felt so grateful that we shared a genuine and mutual love. Mary didn't know what to expect from the show, but, like everyone else, she hoped it was going to be special.

"Do you think you guys will sing?" she asked.

"You know, Mary," I said, "I don't have the slightest clue. I kinda hope so. But I don't know how Cher feels about it."

There was always a part of Cher that was impossible to read. As close as we were, as much as I thought that I knew this superstar whom I'd watched grow from teenager to woman to mother, she was always surprising me. In the greenroom, I recalled the time when we were headlining at the Sahara Hotel in Las Vegas in 1972. We were at our peak. Cars were lined up and down the Strip for blocks, waiting to park. Getting tickets to our show was as easy as breaking into Fort Knox.

To enter the stage, you'd have to pass through the hotel's kitchen. Cher and I always thought that was funny. She'd be dressed in her sequined gown, I'd be in my tuxedo and all around us would be food flying, waiters yelling at cooks, outright madness, which, in a way, reflected our lives at the time. So one night, we're surrounded by all this activity, waiting to step out before a sellout audience, and Cher turns to me.

"Son," she said, "I wish we were really big."

Well, you could've knocked me down with a feather.

Although I had met Letterman in the hall before the show, it wasn't until he introduced me to the audience—as the songwriter of ten gold records, an actor, restaurateur, and political candidate—that we had any real conversation. Letterman has an unpredictable, zany, combustible quality that I like. That's what makes his show so exciting. There's no telling what he's going to say or ask, which makes sitting across from him like catching bullets in your teeth.

He mentioned that I was on my fourth marriage, that I was running for mayor, and that I had left show business.

"Uh, I didn't leave show business," I corrected. "It kind of left me. It got hard for me after Sonny and Cher broke up."

"Oh, rub it in." Dave shook his head, alluding to Cher. "She had nice things to say about you."

Prior to airtime, there is a quick briefing when the producer provides the guest with a rough sketch of the questions Dave plans to ask, and for the first couple of minutes he stuck close to the script. We talked about the mayor's race, which was a nice plug. National television. Millions of people watching. Can't beat that exposure. Then I noticed that mischievous spark in Dave's eye.

"Enough with the politics." He chuckled. "Let's get to the good stuff."

Oh no, I thought. I knew what was coming. It was time to rag on Cher.

"What happened?" Dave continued. "Where did it all go wrong? You were responsible. You molded her. You had the look, the sound. You wrote the songs. You had the idea for the television show. . . . And then one day, bingo, it all goes south on you."

"I . . . I ask myself that every day." I laughed. "No,

13

not really. It's just too hard for two people to have a marriage and to be in show business. Comes a time when you lose the relationship and discover you're a business. I look at Sonny and Cher almost as two other people. I love them, like any other fan."

As smooth as my ten minutes with Dave went, it seemed obvious to me that we were simply killing time until Letterman brought Cher out. There was no sense denying reality. She was the headliner. The Academy Award nominee for her work in *Silkwood*. The big star. Still, I knew that my presence added an extra spark that Cher couldn't provide on her own. There was no denying that, either. Nonetheless, as Letterman introduced Cher, I got as excited as anyone in the audience.

Coming out as only Cher can do, she launched straight into a spirited rendition of her single, a nice but ultimately forgettable rocker. Yet the song didn't stand a chance against her outfit. Chas was right. Cher was dressed to kill. Her outfit was a quadruple homicide. It personified the difference time had placed between us. Sexy, black thigh-high stockings and boots were met by the underside of a black leather jacket that covered—well, how to describe what it covered?

That was Letterman's first question when Cher finished and sat down.

"What the hell are you wearing?" he asked. "Was there a fire at the hotel?"

"It can be anything you want it to be," Cher said.

The tension between Letterman and Cher was apparent in the care that they took in speaking. They were like two boxers feeling each other out in the first round. I had the best seat in the house. I knew Letterman was merely warming up with his comment on Cher's outfit. While she was singing, the genuinely surprised, and perhaps shocked, talk-show host had whispered to me, "Are those tattoos on her ass?"

"Uh-huh," I nodded. "Butterflies."

Naturally, then, Letterman started in on Cher's bum artwork. Shortly after our divorce, she had gotten the two butterfly tattoos. I'd seen them when she had sunbathed nude at my house, something she did occasionally when we were still on friendly terms. I didn't particularly care for them then, and didn't now, but I understood their shock value. Letterman had a field day with them. He feigned disbelief. He compared them to billboards, a Rorschach Test. He said, "Gosh darn," and acted stunned. He'd heard rumors about her tattoos, he confessed, but never realized they were so elaborate.

"I've got everything but the Late Night logo," she snapped.

"Well, let's get to work," Letterman countered.

I got as much of a kick from watching Cher work as I did from being onstage with her for the first time in ten years. When Letterman asked her how she felt being back together with me, Cher deadpanned that she felt nothing. She quickly recanted and said she was joking. But I didn't know. Cher had an icy, unemotional, calculating side to her. I hoped she felt something, but then experience had taught me better. I reminded myself to sit back and enjoy the moment.

"We have a very strange relationship that no one will understand," Cher said. "I don't understand it. Sonny says that he doesn't understand it either."

"Do you ever think of getting back together again?" Letterman asked Cher.

"In what capacity?"

"Married."

"I don't think Mary would like that," Cher said. "She's pregnant."

"Are you friendly with Mary?" he asked.

"Yes."

"And is Sonny friendly with—"

"Ah, with her husband?" I chimed in when Dave stumbled.

Quipped Cher, "I'm not even friendly with my husband."

The immaculate timing was still there. Ten years had passed and we didn't miss a beat. Ba-boom. The audience howled. Letterman laughed. But Cher felt on the spot. Letterman was pushing her into a place that made her uncomfortable—her personal life. She told Letterman outright that she felt he was just "bullshitting." To the audience, she then reprised her description of Dave by mouthing "asshole."

Finally, Letterman asked the question that everyone hoped he would ask. Was there any chance of our singing together? We looked at each other. I was game, but Cher clearly didn't want to. She was uncomfortable. I could see it in her eyes. A backward move, sliding into the old Sonny and Cher shtik. She was a movie star now. Above the din of the audience's encouragement, she professed to have a bad throat. Letterman led the crowd on.

"None of this has been discussed," he said.

"You're full of shit," Cher said.

"I can't believe the way she speaks." He turned to me. I shrugged.

"This is a dirty show," I said. "I'm leaving."

I stood up, looked at Cher, and gave her a nod that said, "What the hell." That did the trick. Her resistance to performing live caved in. Reluctantly, she rose from her chair and, backed by the audience's hoots and cheers, followed me onto the floor. Cher laughed to herself, as if someone had pulled a fast one on her, which, in fact, they had.

Paul Shaffer was already leading the World's Most Dangerous Band through the opening of the song most identified with Sonny and Cher—"I Got You Babe." A pair of microphones were handed to Cher and me. Suddenly we were standing beside each other, feeling out the music, shifting from one foot to another, drifting back in time—or trying to, at least. Once it had been second nature for us to sing together. Now . . .

Strangely, it was still second nature. There was no denying that Cher and I were different people. Nothing about me was attractive to her, I was sure, and vice versa. But put Cher and me together and you'll get an explosion. That's just the way it is. Once we got onstage, the magic was still there. That chemistry we'd once shared was still there, which made singing to Cher especially hard on me.

I had to force myself to look into Cher's eyes because what I saw wasn't real. In our married days, through good and bad times, the looks we exchanged onstage were the glue that held us together. No matter what was going on in our lives, those looks carried us through anything. They told of the life we shared, of the hurdles we overcame, of how much we achieved, of how we needed each other. Those looks said, "Don't worry. Screw whatever's happening in our lives. I'm here, you're here, let's do what we do best."

But on "Letterman," I looked into Cher's eyes and what I discovered wasn't I love you and you love me or I got you, babe. It was more like What the hell is going on? A Sonny and Cher reunion was an emotional event for me. But I found myself dealing with immense curiosity about the woman who had once been my wife. I saw this person with the tattoos, the leather and stockings, and I was dumbfounded. What the hell had happened?

Of course, I loved singing with Cher again and everyone else loved it too. I saw Chastity and Mary crying in the booth. It was impossible not to be affected. Actually, I was choked up and sad. I felt as if I were watching a timeless love story replay itself, except that the story was all screwed up, which added a slightly bittersweet taste to the sentiment. Ironically, Cher and I forgot some of the words, but we latched on to the cue cards and finished singing.

Cher: "I got you to hold me tight."

Me: "I got you to walk with me . . ."

Soon after the taping, Cher and Rob left the studio and disappeared in the midtown traffic in a stretch limousine. Mary and I said good-bye to Chastity, who was going out with her friends. Then we caught a taxi and went out for a nice steak dinner at Smith and Wollensky. Cher and I had exchanged no teary parting words after the show, nothing that might have indicated she'd been touched. It was just a simple "Thanks" and "So long." Still, Mary was anxious to relive every moment.

"How do you think Cher felt?" she asked.

"Honestly, Mar, I don't think she cares about those memories," I said. "I think if she could blow them all up, she would."

Mary was puzzled. The audience had been emotional. She and Chas had been emotional. I'd been emotional. She

17

couldn't understand how Cher alone could remain unaffected by the reunion.

"Cher said it all," I tried explaining, "when she went to court and changed her name to Cher. Period. Nothing else. No La Pierre. No Bono. No Allman. Just Cher."

"And you? How do you explain yourself?" She laughed.

"Me?" I shrugged. "What can I say? I'm Italian."

That night Mary insisted on staying up and watching the show again. I kept one eye open but fell asleep early on. I don't like watching myself too much. But the next morning the telephone started ringing off the hook. People I hadn't heard from in years were calling to say how great the show was. An old pal, disc jockey Sam Riddle, called and asked, "How does it feel to have the hottest tape in the country?"

"What do you mean?" I asked.

"Everybody I know taped last night's show," he said. "I even heard people are selling them."

New Yorkers aren't the shyest group, and all morning, as Mary and I shopped, I was stopped by people who wanted to tell me they loved seeing me and Cher together. I was really touched. Finally, though, it was time to return to the real world—Palm Springs, the campaign, my restaurant. After checking out of the hotel, the bellman hailed us a cab. We slid into the back and I told the driver where we were going.

"I thought that was you," he said, swinging around. "I heard the voice and said to myself, 'That's Sonny Bono.'"

"Yeah." I nodded. "How ya doing?"

"Great show last night," he said, pulling into traffic. "Lot of memories, man. But let me ask you this: What the hell happened to you guys?"

PART II

THE REVOLUTIONARY KIND

2

IT'S GOTTA START SOMETIME ... IT'S GOTTA START SOMEPLACE

Where to start? My childhood? My mom and dad? School? It's all so spotty.

I was staring at the first page of the diary Cher had given me as a birthday present, studying what I had written.

My thirty-third birthday had come several weeks after the release of "Good Combination," the last Sonny and Cher single to do anything on the chart. It was a sign of the painful, occasionally desperate downhill slide on which Cher and I were embarking. We didn't realize it, though. That day in 1968 was as hectic as any other. That afternoon I made a solo appearance on Rowan and Martin's "Laugh-In," just as Cher had done several weeks earlier. After, we guested together on "The Tonight Show" with Johnny Carson.

Later, we celebrated my birthday by having a quiet Italian dinner with friends, then returning late at night in our chauffeured limousine to our gated Bel Air Mansion. I remarked on our good fortune, and Cher agreed that we were living a dream.

"I don't know if I want to wake up," I said.

"Babe, you aren't even asleep yet." She laughed.

In the bedroom Cher finally presented me with a small, gift-wrapped box. I knew that she'd gotten me a gift; I just wondered when she was going to spring it on me. She waited anxiously on the edge of the bed while I held the package. I shook it, turned it upside down, and finally ripped off the paper.

Inside was the diary. My face lit up. I was thrilled. I sat back against my pillow and fanned the blank pages.

"A book waiting to be filled," I said. "I love it, Cher. Thanks."

"I knew you would." Cher smiled. "Promise me two things, though."

"Anything."

"First, that I can write in it too."

"Sure," I said. "My life is your life."

"And second, that I can read it whenever I want."

"I'll leave it in the bathroom." I laughed.

Satisfied, Cher curled up and went to sleep. I reached for a pen and started to write. My mind was suddenly spinning with ideas and thoughts; I was compelled to say something profound. "But where should I start?" I began scribbling, which is probably how everyone begins a diary. Staring at the first page is like looking over the rim of Niagara Falls.

It's all a jumble. So much to put down. I wish I could write faster. I have so much to say. Isn't it funny, every time you think you have all the answers, it dawns on you that no matter how old you get, you'll never have all the answers. But as long as you keep looking, you're okay. When you stop looking, that's when you're in a lot of trouble.

So I started with my mother and my father. Jean and Santo. Descended from Italian peasants. My mother was second-generation American, my dad came from Montelabre on the boat. As was traditional, theirs was an arranged marriage. My mom was fourteen when her parents ushered her into bridehood. She wasn't happy about it, but she wanted out of her family. My dad was an honest, hardworking man who always held a steady job, which made him successful.

They settled in Detroit and began having children. Betty was firstborn, and two years later Fran arrived. I was born three years later, on February 16, 1935. The first boy. Sicilian conventions dictated family roles. That's the trouble with being Sicilian. The book's already been written, and you just fall into place. My dad was stern, taciturn, glowering, and naturally I feared him. When my mom was calm, she was fine, all warmth and caring, but cross her, upset her, and she was like Vesuvius: she exploded.

I don't think any of us ever connected to our parents. None of us grew up bitter. We didn't sit around and complain about being mistreated. But we were more at peace whenever they weren't around.

I began attending grammar school in Detroit, where I remember starting each day by saying the Pledge of Allegiance. That was important to my folks, who impressed on me the value of being one of the good boys. Still, I didn't like school much. I used to pretend to be sick and spent an inordinate amount of time in the nurse's office, lying on a hard table that had a roll of crinkly paper on top.

Whatever ailment I brought in, the nurse reacted the same. She stabbed a thermometer into my mouth. As I sat there like a Butterball turkey cooking, I stared up at a poster tacked to the wall, which illustrated the four basic food groups. It had a picture of a fish, a quart of milk, a hunk of cheese, pieces of meat, and slices of bread. If the nurse left the room, I quickly removed the thermometer and held it against the heater.

For some reason, though, I never made the temperature rise. I wasn't a good liar. The nurse sent me back to class.

We didn't have desks in the classrooms. All the kids sat next to each other at long tables. Our final chore of every day was to put our chair on top of the table. One day, I thought I was extremely ill. To say I had gas was an understatement. All day I had thought of going to the nurse but was embarrassed to tell her what was wrong.

By day's end, I was still alive and ready to split for home, where I could deal with my problem in solitude and no longer risk embarrassment. I didn't think anyone knew about my condition. But when it came time to put our chairs on top of the desks, the kid next to me began sniffing my chair. Then, as if he were Sherlock Holmes solving the case, he called everyone over to smell my chair.

"It's Sonny's chair," he exclaimed. "He's been farting up a storm all day."

I was mortified and spent the next week as the most hated kid in school.

Not long after, I got into my first fight. It actually began as my best friend's fight. He was trading punches with another kid. A big circle had formed around them. I elbowed my way to the front just in time to see my friend get hit and start to cry. Before I knew what was happening, I took his place and started fighting. I have no idea why I did it but there I was, in a clinch, looking for an opening.

Then my opponent made a grave error. He turned his back on me, and I threw a punch as hard as any six-year-old could, which landed square on his head. He burst into tears, more out of shock than hurt, and ran off. I was the victor, the hero, and, much to my surprise, I had no trouble accepting any of the glory that went with winning a playground battle.

Somehow I also wound up in a school play. The play was a not-so-clever commentary on good and bad kids. I was one of a twelve-kid chorus line costumed to look like World War II defense stamps. We rehearsed daily. My part was walking onstage with a king-size stamp slung over me like a giant billboard. That was it. The part was so simple that I learned several other parts, too, including Big Chief Foot in the Aisle.

Now Big Chief Foot in the Aisle was an example of what good children were not supposed to do during class—namely, stick out their foot. The boy playing the part was given knee-high boots to wear, then he was to walk out and announce himself: "Me Big Chief Foot in the Aisle." Easy, right?

Well, the night of the performance, I decided to entertain my fellow thespians backstage by imitating the old Big Chief himself. I planted my foot surely in the boot, except that I put my left foot in the right boot. It was stuck. I couldn't get the damn thing off. No matter how I struggled, it remained firmly affixed to my foot. Suddenly it was time for me to go on.

My fellow stamps were calling for me to quit stomping and step to it. Panicking, I hobbled to the side of the stage, vainly trying to yank the wader off. No luck. Finally I gave up and followed everyone onstage. Once there, I took what I considered the wisest course of action. I crumbled to the ground and had a good cry.

The play was halted. One of the teachers scurried up out of the audience and pulled the boot off. There was a moment of readjustment, and the play resumed, finishing just as everyone had rehearsed.

Despite my tears, I remember how, when the teacher was helping me remove the boot, the entire audience focused their attention on me alone and how wonderful it made me feel.

When I was seven years old my parents started talking about moving to California. The reason was simple: better opportunities. My mom ran a beauty parlor out of our house and, the first time I heard them discuss the idea, the place smelled of the last permanent. My dad didn't seem to mind the odor. I hated it. But I was intrigued enough by California to put up with it and eavesdrop.

Talk of the move lasted for weeks, and it was finally decided that my dad should first venture out west by himself to case it out. We all moved in with my grandmother. Not quite senile, she still had her ways about her, which were humorous to a point. My mother's father lived across town in an old, musty house. When we visited him I had to drink wine, which I couldn't stand but drank out of respect. I always caught a slight buzz.

My mother's brother, Uncle Phil, loved to play with me. Phil was a joker, a man with a kid's heart. He used to clip his fingernails and hand them to me according to size. He told me I could redeem them at the drugstore for cash. The larger ones were worth a dime, the smaller ones a nickel. His brother, Joe, played with me too. His game was to tease me until I cried. Then he paid me off in coin. I loved both of them, but Phil was my favorite, the man who I wanted to be like when I grew up. It was hard to accept when he was killed in the war.

We got a big send-off from all the relatives when my parents finally decided to make the move. My dad, who was still in California, left the packing chores to my mom. I was giddy with excitement. Not so much because of the change of scenery. Instead, my mother told me that I could have all the hamburgers I wanted on the drive out. That was OK with me.

My mom's objective was to cover five hundred miles a day. Mine was to eat nothing but hamburgers. However, by the time we got to Cheyenne, Wyoming, two things happened to alter the trip. I turned into a fan of hot roast beef sandwiches, and the car broke down.

Prior to that, the drive was boresville. My mother's arm got seriously sunburned from hanging out the window so long; one of my sisters nearly caused an accident when a moth flew into the car and she started screaming hysterically; and we spent one night in a crummy motel so filthy that bugs were crawling up and down the wall as if it were their room instead of ours.

But the car breaking down was the final straw. It seemed as if we'd never arrive in Los Angeles. The bus we got on stank. The ride was interminable. But we finally pulled into the sprawling city, whose traffic signals impressed me. They weren't lights; rather, they were signs that went up and down. One said stop, the other go. That was cool.

My father, who had established himself as a truck driver and was hauling asphalt in his dump truck, picked us up at the bus station and drove us to our new home in Hawthorne, a blue-collar suburb south of L.A. Ours was a large—well, two-bedroom—and, I thought, beautiful Spanish home, much nicer than our old place in Detroit. It had a green lawn in front. Still, it didn't feel like home for quite a while.

I slept on a little couch bed in a room that I shared with my two sisters. Life followed a regular pattern. My mom opened a beauty shop, my dad drove his truck, and every Sunday at two, they fought. We used to dread it. It was always loud, very loud, and pretty energetic. It put the fear of God in us, and we used to cower.

My dad never communicated easily. Oh, he got his various points across, mostly through intimidation and fear. I don't remember him ever giving me a hug or a kiss. Things were done his way, no argument otherwise. Every two years or so he decided to paint the outside of the house, which meant that I was dragged into the drudgery as his assistant. It was like doing jail time.

Once he was mixing paint and drinking coffee. I tried cracking a joke. My dad responded by glaring up at me and saying, "How would you like a cup of coffee in your face?" Uh, no thanks. The next time we painted—the interior, this time—he kicked a bucket of green paint over, spilling it on the carpet. I was so delighted I had to take a break and leave the room.

But I also wanted desperately to please him. Shortly after settling into our new home, we got word that our car was repaired. My dad and I took a train back to Wyoming, where we picked up the car and started driving it back. Somewhere in the desert, we picked up a sailor who was hitching a ride. My dad told me to get into the backseat.

After a while I noticed the door wasn't locked, which I decided to correct. For some reason, though, instead of pushing the handle down, I pulled it up. The car was doing about seventy miles per hour. Because of the speed at which we were traveling, the door blew open. It happened so suddenly that I was still holding the handle, and I was yanked outside.

I hit the road like a sack of potatoes and went rolling over the gravel. The rocks punctured my body and cracked my skull open. Inexplicably, I didn't lose consciousness. And after I stopped rolling, I sprang up and started limping back toward the car. My dad had been driving so fast that it took him half a mile to stop, which made me think he didn't know I had fallen out.

"Daddy! Daddy!" I yelled. "Wait for me!"

Then I saw him turn the car around and come back toward me. I was relieved. The panic drained out of me. When my father stepped out of the car, he looked as if he'd seen a ghost. His face registered shock. I didn't realize the extent of my injuries, so naturally I assumed that I had done something bad and started apologizing.

"Please don't hit me, Daddy," I cried. "Please don't hit me. I'm sorry. Really sorry."

Without saying a word, my dad scooped me up in his muscular arms and carried me back to the car. I saw the bloodstains mottle his shirt, which is when I discovered that I was hurt more than I had realized. My father, showing more concern than I'd ever imagined he could, slid into the back with me still cradled in his arms and told the sailor to drive.

"Try to find a hospital," my dad instructed.

The sailor felt awful. He knew that if we hadn't picked him up, I wouldn't have fallen out. But he found a hospital. Admitted right away, I remember the doctors had trouble removing the gravel from my skin. It took a long time. When they finally sewed me up and bandaged me, I looked like a pint-size mummy, wrapped from head to toe. I even bled under each fingernail.

Thanks to the painkillers the docs gave me, the rest of the drive was a blur. When we pulled into our driveway, my dad checked me out, then told me to wait in the car for a minute. He wanted to explain to my mother what had happened before she saw me. Soften the blow a bit. My mom came running out of the house like a woman fleeing a fire, and headed straight for the car. By then, blood had soaked through my bandages, so when she glimpsed me, she went to pieces.

"My baby!" she howled. "What happened to my baby?"

My father got his chance to explain the entire incident. My mom went to pieces, though by the time she'd heard the tale, cooler heads prevailed. She watched my father carry me inside and put me to bed. They stood over me for a while. Thinking I was asleep, my mother asked my dad to repeat the story, and as he did, he began to cry.

"My boy," my dad sobbed, "he stood on the road and said to his papa, 'Don't hit me, Daddy, please don't hit me.' "

It was so difficult for him to say I love you, and right then he was paying the price for it. Years later, I made my share of mistakes as a father. But saying I love you wasn't one of them. Though he never said the words, I'm sure my dad believed his kids knew that he loved them. Anyway, that night he cried for a long time.

I never had a problem saying I love you. Not when it came to girls. About two years after we moved to Hawthorne, I was offered my first glimpse of heaven: a girl's vagina. I'd thought about it, puzzled over it, heard friends talk about it, and wondered what it looked like. Finally, the mystery was going to be unraveled—er, revealed.

The volunteer was somebody's sister. All the boys on the block were alerted to the event. I emphasize *event*. The procedure was detailed to us as a group. The girl was going to stand in a back bedroom, right beside the window. She would hold up her dress, sans panties. Did we understand?

All of us nodded, yes.

In a group, we marched down the street, across the lawn, and up to the side of a white row house, where we stood outside the window. The window was high. All I could see was the top of her head. A patch of black hair. I wondered if I'd really, truly get to see a patch of anything else. Then the time came. The word passed that she was ready.

We stood in single file. Each boy was given a boost up, so that the window was at waist height. He then got roughly thirty seconds to look, before dropping back to the ground and giving the next in line a chance to see. I was either last or next to last in line, but it seemed like an eternity before my turn came.

Finally, the boy in front of me scurried down the wall and nodded to me. My turn. I was given a leg up and pressed my body against the window. There she was. I smiled. Nervous, I wanted to get as good and as close a look at her thing as possible when she lifted her dress. So I pressed closer. In doing so, however, I brought my leg up on to the sill and smashed it into the window.

The damn glass shattered. The girl left as soon as she heard the crash. The gang below me sprinted off, running like hell through the neighborhood. I was left hanging from the window like a rug hung out to dry. It took a few moments to collect myself and drop to the ground. Then I, too, got my ass home as fast as possible.

What a letdown. Not only did I suffer the fear of having

broken a window, and feel completely humiliated. Even worse, I had been gypped of the chance to see the forbidden fruit. My moment had come and I'd blown it.

It seemed typical. No one in the family held out much hope for me. My parents always emphasized the importance of education. They drilled it into my head from early childhood. Go to college. My dad wanted me to be a lawyer. A doctor was okay, but better still was a lawyer. Unfortunately, scholastics and I mixed about as well as oil and water.

My lack of academic ability was always a popular topic of discussion whenever family gathered. One night, after a boisterous, filling Italian dinner, my dad offered up my dismal report card for inspection as if it were a remedy for indigestion. I accepted that I was doing poorly, but it was hell listening to a dozen adults confirm the fact.

Finally I reached the breaking point. I couldn't take it anymore.

"Who cares about school?" I blurted. "I'm going to be a movie star!"

Anybody who wasn't convinced of my stupidity was assured of it after that performance. But I meant it. I could never admit it to my parents, but college wasn't in my plans. Nor was becoming a lawyer. Or anything else, for that matter. I graduated from Inglewood High School in 1952, but the degree was only worth the paper it was printed on. I'd already set my sights on becoming an entertainer.

That wasn't the kind of thing you broadcast in a strict Sicilian household, but I didn't keep it a secret elsewhere. I'd discovered the wonderful effect saying I wanted to be a movie star had on girls.

By this time we had moved to a different house, not too far from the old one. Our new home was smaller, and there was the sense of living on top of one another. But that house is where I was finally shown one of the wondrous secrets of life—a naked girl. It happened just because I was shrewd enough at ten years old to mention to this particular girl that I was going to become a movie star and she was impressed.

Her name was Barbara. We were pals. One day she

showed me a muscle magazine. The pictures had these hulking, overdeveloped musclemen in G-strings. We paged through the thing, making funny comments about their skimpy suits.

"I wish they didn't have to wear them," Barbara said.

My heart skipped a beat.

"I'll show you a real one, if you want," I ventured.

"I have to think about it," she said, promptly getting up and walking out of the house.

I don't know where Barbara went, but fifteen minutes later, she returned and said okay. We met under the house. Both of us tingled with nervous anticipation. I unsnapped, then unzipped my pants and pulled them off. Then my underwear. Then she slowly removed her shorts and panties. We were naked. Staring at each other, wide-eyed, awkward, but not embarrassed.

"Can I touch it?" She reached out.

"Ah-huh," I said. "Can I feel yours too?"

Although willing, neither of us really knew what to do with the other's parts. We tried, though. We rubbed, fondled, caressed, poked, and prodded. Then Barbara started to worry that someone was going to catch us. She wasn't able to relax, and suddenly it was no longer fun being naked in the dank underside of the house. She put on her shorts and split. I slipped my pants back on too, but with a different, broader, more confident sense of myself.

In grammar school I made up skits, acted out sword fights and told jokes, anything to get a reaction—usually a laugh. Later I picked up a bit of music from my dad, who tried his hand at playing banjo and then accordion. His Sunday afternoon concertizing was absolutely dreadful. But his interest in popular music piqued mine. And by high school, my peers accepted me in the role of the entertainer.

But in the fifties, boys didn't sing. That was sissy. It wasn't macho. So if you wanted to be a singer, you had to go out on a limb. Take a real risk. But I wanted to sing and felt I had little choice but to do it, damn the consequences. So I sang. I sang in the same marginal, limited, nasal voice that graced Sonny and Cher records, the same voice that I have now.

I was looking for something, anything, that would spring

me into something approximating legit entertainment. My
break turned out to be the Friday-night high-school football
games. After buying a handmade conga drum from a pawn-
shop for five bucks, I teamed up with my buddy Corky.
Corky had two talents: fighting and playing the piano. He
was great at both.

When the football games ended, everyone gathered
across the street at the recreation center and danced to a
big band. The center also sported a tiny side room with an
upright piano. Corky and I set up there. Corky used the
keyboard like a lumberjack with a chain saw, cutting a
spirited boogie-woogie and a ball-busting, Jerry Lee Lewis–
type rock and roll. I sang and beat the congas. When we
realized that we were drawing a crowd away from the band,
we decided to play every Friday. Our repertoire was basic:
the ten most popular songs and, every once in a while, a
little blues and R&B.

In 1952 there were only a few radio stations that played
rock and roll. I used to mickey with the turning dial for
hours. I was able to pick up Hunter Hancock's show,
which featured R&B bands like Big Jay McNeely, whose
honkin' saxophone was the absolute coolest sound on
vinyl. I also listened to Johnny Otis. Actually, any little
station that played rhythm and blues and rock and roll. My
ducktail made me the rebel of Inglewood High, but I was
one of the few kids who knew music.

Not coincidentally, I was placed in charge of a school
assembly my senior year. My job was to hire a band. No
one told me who to book. Or what kind of music. So I hired
local saxophonist Jimmy Jackson and his band. Jimmy was
a wildman honker out of the Big Jay McNeely school. Blowing a gale of music, he worked up a monsoon-size sweat
onstage and then, while honking the same three notes for
fifteen minutes, seemingly stuck in an orgasmic frenzy, he
romped up and down the aisle, carrying on as if he were
having sex with his baritone sax.

The kids went berserk. None had ever seen anything like
it. Neither had the faculty, most of whom thought Jimmy
Jackson's antics more shocking than if I'd hired strippers.
It didn't help any that Jimmy and his band were black, the
only blacks besides the custodians in the entire school. As

thanks, I was suspended for three days. The reason—putting on a raucous concert.

My dad was convinced that I was going to be a failure, a fact that caused him no end of frustration. Although I was fortunate enough to attend school, he never thought I was cut out to do anything more than clean the streets—if that. But as sure as my dad knew I was going to fail, I believed that music—somehow, some way—was going to be my springboard to a better life. That was the only way I could think of going beyond my family's working-class legacy.

Nonetheless, I accepted the fact that I was going to be a failure. Everyone else believed it, so why not me, too? Rather than confront the dilemma, I just threw in the towel. I realize now that subconsciously, though, I fought it; I never gave up.

I was always thinking, always on the lookout for something. Anything. Any opportunity. I didn't have talent, of that I was convinced. I could barely sing. Couldn't play the piano. Couldn't do anything. The conga got me only so far. Then I got a ukulele and learned how to play three chords. That was a breakthrough. Three chords were better than a drum. With three chords I could write a song.

In early 1952 my idol was singer Frankie Lane. In my opinion, the man had no competition. He was my Bruce Springsteen. Whenever I sang, whether in the shower or at a school assembly, I did a Frankie Lane song. And when it came time to write a song on the ukulele, there wasn't any question about whose style I was going to adopt.

"Frankie Lane?" said my friend John Bloomfield, whom I enlisted as a co-writer. "Why him?"

"Because he's the best," I said.

That night, in about an hour, I wrote, with John's help, my first song. Titled "Ecstasy," it was pure adolescent wish fulfillment. "She would taunt me," the lyrics went, "then haunt me, then love me, then leave me . . . she was ecstasy."

Believing "Ecstasy" a certain hit, I auditioned to sing it on Peter Potter's "Search for Songs," a local TV show that was competing with the "Amateur Hour." The woman who interviewed me had excellent taste. I got on the show.

On the night of my performance, I invited everybody I knew at school to come and watch, since the winner was decided by applause. I think I knew almost every single person seated in the bleachers. Still, when the time came for me go on, my knees were shaking so badly that I practically limped to the center of the stage. The shaking continued through the entire song.

I won the competition anyway. I don't know if I was the best, but the applause meter shot off the scale. Nothing like playing poker with a stacked deck. My prize was a transistor radio. But sweeter than the victory was standing onstage and drinking up the rousing ovation my friends gave me. What a buzz. The rush rocketed straight to my head. It was like drinking 110-proof moonshine.

And that was it. I knew I had found myself. Sure, I was scared shitless of performing in front of people. But the recognition, the validation, the acceptance—they were overwhelming. I was instantly addicted.

3

WHY CAN'T I BE
LIKE ANY GUY

I graduated from high school in June 1952 and found myself with nothing to do and no plans. At seventeen, my life was horrible.

Both my sisters were married and gone from the family fold, leaving me at home with my folks. They were on the last leg of their marriage and battled each other constantly. That atmosphere made my existence a lonely one. Add to that the confusion I felt about the future, and it was no wonder that I felt lost.

The grisly summer received a breath of fresh air only when my aunt and cousin came to visit from Detroit. My cousin, two years older than I, was quite pretty. I hadn't seen her in fifteen years. She was like any other girl to me. Before long, we had the hots for each other and started a furtive love affair.

By the end of the two-week visit, she and I were desperately, passionately, ill-fatedly in love. Unable to stand the thought of her leaving, I followed her back to Detroit. On her home turf, reality proved more than either of us could handle. Within days, we detested each other.

I wanted to get back to L.A. as quickly as possible, but I had a problem. I was out of money. I was so broke that I couldn't afford lint for my empty pockets.

I looked for a job and went from one interview to another. Finally I was hired by the Sydney Hill Health Club. I wasn't the pool boy or the custodian—the only jobs for which I was qualified. No, I was the health club's new masseur. With no experience, I faked my way through several sessions, lasting just long enough to earn the hundred dollars I needed to buy a one-way plane ticket from Detroit to L.A.

I literally had one measly nickel in my pocket when I returned home, but by then my parents' marriage was completely bankrupt. My mom was involved with a neighbor, a jeweler whose store was next to her beauty shop. The two of them often lunched together, which ultimately led to their affair. My mom had tired of living a double life and had run off with her new love. My dad freaked. Never mind that they'd sparred with each other since before I was born. My dad lost his head when my mom told him she was leaving.

He owned a gun. A pistol. Every New Year's Eve he took it out, and at twelve o'clock, he fired off six bullets into the air. That was our celebration. That's what they did in Italy. Shortly after my mom left, he sank into a dark depression and I occasionally found him talking quite violently. That caused me to think about his gun. It seemed to me that, according to Sicilian traditions by which my dad lived, if your wife took up with another man, you could shoot one or both of them and sort of justify the act.

Well, chewing on that at night got me plenty worried. I was afraid of what might be going on in my dad's head. Finally, one afternoon I took the gun and hid it. Sure enough, my dad went looking for his pistol right after that. When he couldn't find it, he knew something was up. There was no chance that he had misplaced it. He kept it in the same place year after year. And I was his only suspect.

"Sonny," my dad snarled, "where's my gun?"

"What d'ya mean?" I asked.

"My pistol," he snapped. "It's gone. Where is it?"

"Ummm." I gulped, thinking hard. "I . . . I . . . I hid it."

"Tell me where it is," he demanded.

I refused. He asked again, and once more I refused. That

did it. My dad exploded. He grabbed my shirt and jerked me toward him, not certain what he was going to do to me but knowing that he definitely wanted to do something.

"I'm not going to tell you where I hid it," I gasped. "I don't want you doing anything to hurt yourself . . . or Mom . . . or doing anything crazy."

My dad tossed me back into the chair as if he were discarding a newspaper, then stormed out of the house. He never forgave me for hiding the gun. It was like a breach of tradition, I suppose. But I still feel I did the right thing.

Not long after that incident, my dad took a trip to Sicily to see his family. He was retreating. The situation at home was too heavy for him to go it alone. Or with me. Obviously, I was no help. So he returned to the Old Country, looking for comfort as well as a new spouse, which he did happen to find.

I was never able to let go of the fact that deep down my dad knew I was trying to protect him, even at the risk of getting smacked around. I expected that some time later he would come back and say he understood, perhaps even thank me. He never did.

In the meantime, I had the house to myself. No different than any other seventeen-year-old, I knew that spelled only one possibility—*party!* I threw one every night. The big drink then was a mixture of vodka and Manischewitz wine. I emptied the bottles in an oversize punch bowl, and everyone drank until they were blown out of their minds. Those few weeks were fun, an exhausting combination of hospitality and hangovers, but it was my last real fling with irresponsibility.

Shortly after that, I moved into my mom's house. I thought the change in scenery would make me feel less lonely. When it didn't, I decided to leave home altogether. It was time, I thought, to forge my future—whatever that was. Although I dreamed of getting into the music business, I found work bagging groceries at Better Foods, a local grocery store. In lieu of making records, I did a lot of singing in the aisles and whistling melodies while I was helping old ladies carrying their groceries.

At the time, Harry Belafonte's calypso was hot. One day

I noticed we'd gotten in a new brand of cookie, Coco Joes. Something about that name stuck with me. For days, I repeated *Coco Joe* to myself. Finally, one night I wrote a little calypso song about Coco Joe on my uke. The next day I played it for the store manager and asked him what he thought.

"Wow" was all he said. About a half hour later he sought me out.

"Sonny," he said, "I called the company that makes Coco Joes and told them about your song."

"Yeah?" I said, not knowing exactly what his thinking was behind the call.

"Yeah," he nodded, getting excited, which made me excited, even though I didn't understand why both of us were suddenly so thrilled. "I spoke to the district manager, who talked to his boss, and they want you to go down to their office next week and play your song for them."

The following week I traveled across town to an industrial area of south central Los Angeles. I walked into a large, aromatic factory, carrying my ukulele. A receptionist instructed me to go to a certain office, where I met a heavyset executive. He sat behind his desk. I played my song.

"Very clever. Very amusing." He smiled. "But I don't think we have any use for it."

"Well, I'm not exactly sure why I'm here in the first place," I said, somewhat disappointed. "But, you know, thanks for listening just the same."

Six years later, I pulled "Koko Joe" out of the mothballs and gave it to one of the hottest rhythm-and-blues duos in music. But that was later.

In the meantime, my personal life accelerated my progress toward premature adulthood. Soon after returning from my doomed affair in Detroit, I met a pretty blond waitress at Scribner's Drive-In. Her name was Donna Rankin. She was just the type of ornament, blond and beautiful, that I didn't believe I had a chance of getting, so I hung on to her with blind determination and pretty soon she progressed from Saturday-night sweetheart to serious girlfriend.

My life was moving faster than I could handle, but the

future was a fog to me. I didn't know where I was going or what I was doing so I kept in constant forward motion.

Because it was easier to act than to think, I followed in my father's footsteps. He was working at Douglas Aircraft, and that sounded right by me. I quit Better Foods and got a job at the factory driving a tug, an enormous, thick slab of motorized steel with an open cockpit. The job was miserable, a mistake. I had earned more money at the grocery store, and I wasn't treated like part of a herd of cattle. At Douglas, everyone funneled into a little gate like livestock. I was stuck in the middle of it. All I thought about was how to break out and not be part of the herd. It was dehumanizing.

For amusement, I began to drag race my tug against the other tugs, but one day I was racing another guy down a long, equipment-lined corridor when my foot got caught in the other tug. Suddenly our boss turned the corner. The other tug hit the brakes, while my tug continued forward. Unfortunately, my foot stayed behind. I spun out of the tug and was tossed to the ground. The mishap severed an artery in my foot and blood spurted everywhere.

Fortunately, there was an operating room right on the premises, and I was rushed into surgery. My dad came in as I was being prepped.

"You all right?" he asked.

I nodded.

"What the hell happened?"

"It was an accident," I tried to explain. "I was just screwing around, and it was an accident."

"You're lucky they didn't fire you," he snapped.

"Am I?" I muttered.

I proposed to Donna and she accepted. My mother insisted on a big Catholic wedding, which I didn't care for but went along with anyway. Donna and I were married in February of 1954. Neither of us recovered. A happy, extroverted girl when we met, Donna did a complete turnaround after the ceremony. Perhaps she realized it was a mistake. I don't know. But Donna sealed herself off from the outside world. She stayed in the house, didn't answer the phone, and seemed content watching television and living an insular, slow-paced life. A life headed nowhere.

I was just the opposite. With my dreams and schemes, I felt an overwhelming need to get out and let the world know I was alive. It's no wonder that I quickly became frustrated within the confines of our mismatch of a marriage. About the only thing we did have in common was Donna's sympathy for my unhappiness at work. I continued to think of myself as a songwriter, not the driver of a tug at Douglas Aircraft, and not surprisingly I jumped at the few chances I got to play my songs for someone of a certain influence.

Johnny Otis, a Greek whose entire life had been dedicated to black music, was one such man.

"What do you mean you got a song?" he asked.

I wondered how many times Otis had heard someone tell him that they had a song. A thousand? Ten thousand? Perhaps thousands more than that. That didn't bother me. I could handle it. But how many times, I wondered as I sat across from him, had the person doing the asking been a skinny, white Italian kid with a mediocre voice?

"What'd ya say your name was again?" he asked.

"Sonny Bono," I said.

It was early 1955. Donna had bid me good-bye that morning, expecting me to follow the well-worn path to work at Douglas. Instead, I veered off course and found myself in Otis's hot, unair-conditioned office at his personal label, Dig Records. Off to the side was his A&R (artist-and-repertoire) man, Plas Johnson, a big-time session sax player who did all the *Pink Panther* sound tracks. A neophyte, I still knew the rules of Otis's business. You sang your song to him, took your best shot. If he liked it, he'd cut a demo, then play it on his KFOX radio show. If the song got any response, he'd put out copies on his Dig label.

"My song is called 'Ecstasy,' " I added.

Otis leaned back. He had acquired his chops playing drums with big bands in the 1940s. When that era faded, he opened a nightclub in Watts (L.A.'s Harlem), the Barrelhouse Club, where he discovered numerous terrific singers, including Mel Walker, with whom he recorded many hit rhythm-and-blues songs. In the early 1950s, he launched the Johnny Otis Revue, featuring then little-known singers Hank Ballard, Big Mama Thornton, and Jackie Wilson. In 1954 he went on the radio.

Otis was the real thing—at least as real as any white guy could get to R&B (rhythm and blues). Here I was. Salvatore Bono. Another white guy. A teenager who was auditioning a self-described "hot" R&B number on his ukulele. My knees shook through the entire song, but Otis looked interested when I finished.

"That's okay," he said. "We'll schedule a session and see what happens."

I was ecstatic. It was my first record, and from there it seemed like just a short hop until I would be sharing the marquee with Frankie Lane. Otis played "Ecstasy" on his show several nights in a row, and I went out of my mind when I heard myself on the radio. Unfortunately, not only was I my biggest fan, I seemed to be my only fan. The song bombed big-time. Otis printed up two hundred records, but there's no telling how many of them sold. Not many, I'd bet.

At least I'd gotten on the radio. That was something a nineteen-year-old guy could hang on to for months.

However, that one thrill had to last a long time because nothing else was happening, particularly in my dismal marriage. My father-in-law recognized my frustration and offered me a job in his construction business. He was a good man, upbeat in outlook, and I had a better relationship with him than I did with his daughter. I think we shared a similar frustration with marriage. His own marriage to Donna's mother ended in divorce. Donna's mother was an alcoholic, a strange, troubled woman, who one night lapsed into a manic rage and started a fire that took her and her second husband's lives. When my father-in-law offered me the job, I quit Douglas immediately.

"It's not easy work, I promise you that," he told me of construction. "But at least you'll be working outside. That's gotta beat the factory."

"Count me in," I quickly said.

I poured concrete. That was my job. In those days, though, there weren't cement trucks. The concrete was dumped by the bucketful. I worked in Anaheim, building the bridges that lead to Disneyland, which was then only a glimmer of an idea. I rode the bucket—up a crane and then onto the bridge. At that point I hit a lever, dumped the mud, and then rode back down and loaded up again.

It was hard but physically satisfying work. However, about seven months after I started, I was fired. It came out of nowhere. I didn't know why. There was no precipitating incident. When I asked my foreman why, he shrugged. None of my superiors came forth with an explanation either. It was incredibly frustrating. I've never had the temperament for unemployment, and every day I spent doing nothing was torture.

Little did I know, but getting fired turned out to be just the break I was searching for.

After six months of job hunting, I got a job delivering meat for the L.A. Meat Company. It was late 1956. I was almost twenty-one, and I felt saved. The weekly paycheck relieved some of the pressure I had of supporting Donna and myself, and the time I spent riding around the city was perfect for creating songs. My route crisscrossed the entire city, but I eventually negotiated for the Sunset Boulevard route in Hollywood. I wanted that route because of the stretch of Sunset that was loaded with independent record labels. It was L.A.'s version of Tin Pan Alley.

I'd made that discovery by accident. Not long after I started delivering meat, I began taking singing lessons from a guy in Inglewood, who had a small studio in a back room. He recorded me singing "Ecstasy." Back then, everything was recorded straight onto disc. The whole sound went directly onto the needle. I loved watching it. There was a big brush, and as the grooves were cut, the little threads of black vinyl were brushed away. When it was finished, you had a demo.

I took my demo home and wondered what to do with it. I'd written it with Frankie Lane in mind. Why not try to give it to him? I got out the telephone book and looked up the phone number of Lane's record company, Crystal Records. I called.

"Frankie's not here right now," said the man on the other end. "Can I take a message?"

I paused, not knowing what to say.

42

"Ah, well, ah," I stammered. "My name is Sonny Bono, and I'm a songwriter. I have a song that would be great for Mr. Lane."

"Good, very good," he said. "I happen to be Mr. Lane's brother, and I run Crystal Records for him. Why don't you come down here and play it for me?"

I snatched the offer like a man starved for opportunity. Then the next day the phone rang. The woman at the other end told me to hold for Mr. Lane.

"Hello, this is Frankie Lane," he said in a voice I immediately recognized.

I couldn't believe it. The day before I'd talked to Frankie Lane's brother. Now Frankie Lane himself was on the phone for me, inquiring about a song I had written. The probability of this happening seemed downright impossible. I told him the title of the song, and he seemed to like it.

"How's it go?" he asked. "Can you sing a little?"

"I've got a demo," I said. "How 'bout I play some?"

"Go ahead."

I held the receiver up to the hi-fi and played about thirty seconds of the song. Frankie interrupted me.

"Sounds fine," he said. "Come on into the office tomorrow."

I hung up the phone, spun around, and snapped my fingers. Frankie Lane had asked me to come to his office. To meet with him. I couldn't imagine a better break.

I showed up the following day after work, parking the truck a few doors down so nobody would know that I wasn't a real songwriter. Nervous, I walked inside holding my demo, trying hard to keep from shaking. Frankie wasn't there. But his brother was, and after listening to "Ecstasy," he asked me to bring in more songs. I admitted that I delivered meat full-time, but that I'd be back in a few days with a new batch of songs.

Of course, what I didn't mention was that I first had to write them, which seemed like such a small detail now that my foot was in the door.

In the meantime, Donna's father, having heard that I played my song for Frankie Lane, called me up with a confession.

"It was my doing," he said.

"What was your doing?" I asked.

"Getting you fired from the construction job."

"You're kidding," I said, astonished.

"I knew that your heart was in music," he explained sweetly, "and that you'd never go anywhere if you stayed with the company."

We both had a good laugh.

In those days, the record business was a very distant cousin to the multimillion-dollar, bureaucracy-laden corporate labels of today. Back then, the record biz was exciting. The labels were small, independent, and owned by a single person, who ran the business like a game of craps. A kid like me could walk in off the street, talk his way into an audition, and several weeks later have a single out. If it sold, you were a star.

I wrote songs fast, at least one a day, usually while I was making my meat deliveries. I rushed through my route to hang out at the Crystal office. Why not? Schmoozing with the Lane brothers was infinitely more exciting than my regular paying job. Though Frankie never cut "Ecstasy," he and his brother approved almost everything that I wrote, which was encouraging.

"I've got this kid you won't believe," I overheard him say to someone on the phone. "The kid writes songs like you don't believe. He's hungry like I haven't seen."

In those days, I didn't have the luxuries songwriters have now. There were no advances. You didn't get an office. No expense-account lunches. Nothing but the chance to make dreams come true. That was enough, though. Having someone approve my songs was enough to make me write like a prisoner trying to sing his way out of jail.

Crystal Records had a young rhythm-and-blues singer for whom they had great expectations, a real brash twenty-year-old who never made it. But he had great pipes. I was given the task of writing songs for him, and it turned out to be a valuable lesson in patience. I remember one night when he and I were shooting the breeze at the office, talking about the only thing we had in common—not having any money.

"I just want to make it before I'm twenty-one," he said.

"Yeah?" I cocked my head to the side. "I don't get it."

"I want to make it, you know, big-time, before I'm twenty-one," he repeated.

"I know. I heard you," I said. "I just don't get the part about before you're twenty-one."

Why wouldn't he just want to make it, period, I thought.

Closer to the business than I ever imagined possible, I felt I was learning something new every day. The way the independent record companies were lined up on Sunset reminded me of a bank of gumball machines. All you had to do was put in the right coin and they were ready to pay off. There was Liberty, Imperial, Dot, Crystal, and Specialty. Their doors were all open to anyone with new product and the guts to audition.

Oddly, it was black music that got me into the business. I couldn't sing or play that well. But I was accepted. Why? Because I liked the music. I was accepted for that. They let me love the music with them.

From Crystal, I eventually wandered into Specialty Records. Specialty was owned by Art Rupe, a small, dictatorial man who ran Specialty as a mom-and-pop business. That was standard practice then. Lou Rudd did it with Imperial; Randy Wood did it with Dot. These men had a sound in mind, and they wanted their artists to sing and produce that sound without much variation. Their motto was: If it sells, it's good. Art gave me credibility. He admired my love of the music and my desire.

At Specialty, I met singer Sam Cooke and Bumps Blackwell, an A&R (Artists and Repertoire) man. I dropped by the office nearly every afternoon and passed the nighttime hours with Bumps and Sam. Sam was still singing with the Soul Stirrers, and unknown to the other Soul Stirrers, Sam was making plans to leave the gospel-tinged group.

The first clue of Sam's new direction came with the release, in 1956, of his first pop record, "Lovable," a reworking of the Soul Stirrers' hit. Sam was disguised as Dale Cook. Specialty's owner, Art Rupe, hit the roof when he learned who Dale Cook really was. He didn't want to lose any of his coveted gospel market and refused to entertain the notion of Sam crossing over into pop. But Sam's obsession with the ruckus caused by sensations Elvis Presley and Gene Vincent only grew, and in one conversation after another, he confirmed his intention to cross over from soul to pop.

"Blues and gospel are getting hard to sell," I mentioned one evening.

"They're getting hard to sing too," Sam bemoaned. "Too much money's going the other way."

"Sonny, you listen to Sam's new stuff," Bumps said. "He's gonna be big. Real big."

Even though Art Rupe was opposed to any changes, they knew what was what, and they were prepared to fight.

That problem was put on the back burner, and in the middle of 1957 a big, intimidating black guy with a deep, overpowering voice started hanging out at the office. Larry Williams's dilemma was no secret. He didn't know whether he wanted to be a singer or a pimp. Bumps had discovered Larry playing piano for Percy Mayfield and other local rhythm-and-blues artists. In addition to singing, though, Larry was also clever. He wrote songs with funny rhyming or alliterative titles, such as "Short Fat Fannie," "Bony Moronie," and "Dizzy, Miss Lizzy," songs that had as much to do with the women he knew as the music he loved.

"Hey, truck driver," Bumps said to me on the phone one evening. "You got a session tomorrow night."

"What d'ya mean?"

"I'm putting your song on the B side of Larry's new record."

It was amazing how fast things happened. Only days before, I'd played "High School Dance," a new song, for Sam and Bumps on the office piano. A couple days later, there was Bumps producing Larry, who was singing the hell out of it. The A side, "Short Fat Fannie," became a smash, hitting number five on the pop charts and number two on R&B. Then the lucky combo was given another shot when Larry recorded "Don't Bug Me, Baby," to back "Bony Moronie." Lightning struck again. "Bony Moronie" went to number fourteen. I was elated.

About the same time Bumps told me that Sam had written a song that was going to knock me out, but I had to keep quiet about it around Art. Sam told me the same thing, then sang me an early version of what would become his big hit, "You Send Me."

"Ah, it's sweet, man," I said. "Very sweet. I can see why you don't want Art to know about it."

"It's my breakout," Sam said. "I'm leaving the group with this one."

Little Richard was the king of Specialty Records. His sound dominated everything, from sales to sounds. Flamboyant, raucous, boisterous rock and roll with screaming saxophones and balls-out piano playing. Because of Richard's success, Art developed a pet saying: Everything is bunk, except funk. He even had that printed on a sign in the middle of his desk. That was his basic philosophy. And you didn't buck it.

However, in late 1957 Sam and Bumps informed Art of their plan to record "You Send Me." With that mellifluous voice and light guitar, I knew it was a sure bet. Our entire clique was mad about the song. Everyone except for the boss. Art finally heard Sam's demo and thought it was dreadful. But Bumps and Sam were adamant about releasing it as a single, and a stormy confrontation followed. Depending on which side you talked to, it ended with each side firing the other.

In any event, I was summoned into Art's office one afternoon when I showed up after my deliveries.

"There's an opening here," he said.

"For what?" I asked.

"A&R," said Art, referring to the Artist and Repertoire job, which included being talent scout, producer, psychiatrist, and babysitter.

"I'll take it."

"First you've got to interview for the job," he said.

"When?"

"It just finished."

My starting salary was seventy-five dollars a week—plus a gas card. That was the clincher. My first job was a cover-your-ass kind of thing. Sam and Bumps signed with Keen Records and released "You Send Me." In December Sam performed it on "The Ed Sullivan Show," and the single exploded on the chart like a stick of dynamite, going number one and selling a phenomenal 1.7 million copies. Those numbers were unheard of then. Art began drilling me. He wanted to know what Sam had left behind.

It turned out that we had seven unreleased Sam Cooke tapes, songs that he had been auditioning. I found an extended sample of mono tape with just Sam playing guitar. Nothing else. Another had him singing "I'll Come Running Back to You." That song was the closest in sound to "You Send Me." So I took the mono tape of Sam on guitar into the studio, doctored it up with instruments, and then duplicated it with Sam's vocals. Not only was I an A&R man, suddenly I was also a producer.

But those were only two of the many hats I wore at Specialty. My real job covered whatever was necessary.

For instance, Art was battling with the label's biggest star, Little Richard. Richard had scored big on Specialty with classics like "Tutti Frutti," "Long Tall Sally," "Lucille," and "Good Golly, Miss Molly." Then, at the pinnacle of his success, he quit. Just back from a tour of Australia, he reported that a vision of the apocalypse had come to him in a dream, and he had seen his own damnation. He told another story that had him on a plane whose engine caught fire and he prayed to God, promising to mend his ways if the plane landed safely.

Not surprisingly, the office heard a different story of Richard's retirement from the one printed in the papers. We heard about Richard's fight with Art. Richard claimed that Art owed him back royalties as well as an increase in his percentage. The label owner took a hard line, refusing to negotiate. That's when I remember Richard quitting the business, going to school at Oakwood College in Huntsville, Alabama, and surfacing as an ordained minister. Art never bought Richard's proclaimed devotion to the ministry.

"The hell he is," Art told me. "Nobody quits, especially Richard. Go talk to him, Sonny."

This was the late 1950s. I was a nothing, an ex-delivery man and would-be songwriter. Little Richard was a star. He lived in an enormous house in Hancock Park, a wealthy, genteel section of Los Angeles, which I approached with bulging eyeballs. Richard's living room was teeming with musicians who were hanging out, waiting for the star to make his appearance downstairs. I joined the wait. Naturally, I didn't know what the hell I was doing there. I was Art's messenger, a last-ditch effort to coax his money-maker out of retirement, but Richard didn't even know who I was. Nor did he care.

Richard finally came downstairs, descending like grand royalty in a silk bathrobe, his eyes sweeping across the room, taking everything in.

"I need to talk with you," I said after introductions were made. "Preferably alone."

"There's no need to be alone," he said, taking a seat on the sofa. "I'll give you all my attention."

And he did. Talking to Richard was like getting your eyes examined. He was there, 100 percent.

"You've got to fulfill your recording obligation," I said, not having the slightest clue what to say.

"There's another obligation that needs to be filled before I can do that." He smiled. "Mr. Rupe owes me."

"Listen," I said, getting into the discussion, "you signed a contract. The contract is valid. You're committed. An obligation is an obligation."

"I understand."

"And you're way past deadline," I continued. "You're not in the studio and your record is due out now."

"This is something to think about," he said, grasping my hand in a gesture of utmost seriousness. "Okay."

"Okay?" I said, confused.

"Yes, okay." He shook his head. "Let me go talk to Jesus."

What was I going to say? Richard stood up, smiled at me, then disappeared upstairs. I continued to sit in the living room. One hour went by. Then another. Finally he strolled back downstairs, repeating his earlier, rather florid descent. He sat down next to me and attempted to make polite conversation. But I was through being tested. I wanted an answer. Something to take back to my boss.

"So?" I asked. "Did you talk to Jesus?"

"Yes," he said sweetly.

"And what happened? What'd he say?"

"Jesus said, 'No.' "

Then he spelled it. "N-O."

49

*   *   *

Not long after that, I came home one night and Donna told me the opposite: Y-E-S. Yes, she was pregnant, and in July 1959, she gave birth to our daughter, Christy. I look back and wonder why we had a child. The marriage was doomed from the beginning, though we were too inexperienced to know it, and after five years it was obvious our marriage was going nowhere. It wasn't horrible, but it wasn't good. It wasn't anything, and that was the problem.

Christy was adorable, but she ended up suffering the brunt of our error in judgment. After Donna and I split up I rarely saw Christy. To this day I regret that I knew so little then and was unable to care for her. But I'm happy to report that Christy has admirably overcome her parents' legacy. It took her a long time to get back on her feet, but she did. She now owns a restaurant in Venice, California.

Christy was just a newborn when I convinced Donna that we needed to move from boring Gardena, a working-class suburb, to Hollywood. I was intoxicated by the glamour and flash of the music business and wanted to be closer to the action. We couldn't afford the move, but Art Rupe owned an enormous plot of land smack in the middle of downtown Hollywood, something like five acres that had been home to a nursery, and in the center of the overgrown foliage, tall grass, and out-of-control bushes and trees was a little house. Art let me rent it cheaply.

It was a cool environment, a secluded patch of Mother Nature in the middle of the city. An Italian market was located across the street. Harold Battiste, a brilliant saxophonist who was Specialty's New Orleans A&R man, moved out to L.A. and loved to play his horn in the hothouse that was attached to the nursery. The jazzy sounds he made there covered the property with a sonic cloud, wafting across the lot and disappearing into the steamy Hollywood night like the sound track to a movie.

"This place would make a helluva coffee house," Jack Nitzsche, then Phil Spector's arranger, used to say as he and I talked about music and listened to Harold play.

Unfortunately, I didn't spend much time at home. I was in limbo. Donna and I were just going through the motions of being husband and wife, and barely that. I was an incurable romantic. I enjoyed falling in love and lived a double standard because of it. I expected Donna to stay home and care for Christy while I played around. At the time I thought I was entitled. My Italian blood was on perpetual simmer. I lived for the impetuous craving for fiery romance that had once driven me to chase my cousin to Detroit. I stayed out as late as I could get away with. I lied. I cheated. I was awful. I did all the things that lousy husbands do.

Was I proud of that? No. Not at all. I cringe when I think of it now. But I was twenty-five years old. I was a kid on the make. Marriage seemed like some kind of accident, and I did my best to forget about it.

4

A COWBOY'S WORK IS
NEVER DONE

It was the worst song I'd ever heard, but these two young songwriters, Herb Alpert and Lou Adler, were incredibly enthusiastic about it. Either that or they were delivering one terrific sales pitch. It was hard to tell. Herb was a smooth, supremely talented musician; Lou a tough-talking, streetwise hustler. The song was called "The Round," and we played it several times. Both Herb and Lou were telling me what a tremendous hit it was going to be.

"But I don't like it," I said. "It's not for us."

"How can you say that?" Lou rallied. "We wrote it specially for you."

"Specially for Specialty, eh?" I laughed.

We jawed back and forth like that for half an hour—probably because none of us had anything better to do. There was no difference between us. We were all simply trying to realize our dreams. Herb went on to a superstar recording career, as well as to cofound A&M Records, and Lou became one of the most powerful manager-producers with the Mamas and the Papas. Both were incredibly sharp.

I was as frustrated in my job as they were in trying to sell their awful song. Specialty wasn't getting any records played, and I felt stagnant.

As a result, not long after the meeting with Herb and

Lou, I started moonlighting as a producer. I kept it very quiet from Art. I didn't want him to know I was competing with Specialty. Actually, what I was doing was a side business more than starting up an independent label. If someone wanted to cut a record but didn't know how, I offered to produce it for a fee. Then they'd go on with their demos or whatever they chose to call them.

At the time, I developed a close friendship with Jack Nitzsche, an extremely talented musician who went on to have a fine career as a writer and producer. Back then, he was struggling. He walked in off the street, a funny-looking guy who looked the part of the academically trained musician he was. I admired his ability tremendously.

In those days, when someone came in to audition a song, they rarely brought a lead sheet. They just sang. So I hired Jack to write lead sheets for three bucks a piece. He was thrilled. Married and struggling, he was happy to have work. But Jack was equally important to me. Full of ideas, he had an expanded, exciting vision of music, which we spent hours discussing. Even more important, he liked my song writing. He validated my ability to write and arrange.

We were both struggling, but he looked up to me. I was now an A&R man, up to a whopping one hundred seventy-five dollars a week, which wasn't bad then. With my gas credit card, I was doing great. What I lacked in the confidence department, I made up for with a zealous drive to succeed. Whenever I saw any kind of opening, I took it. That's how Art found out I was moonlighting. I was too sloppy, too ambitious, and failed to cover the tracks I was leaving around town. Word got out, and Art heard.

"Got some bad news for ya, Sonny," he said to me one day in the office.

I was just hanging up the phone, arranging a session for myself for later that night. Jack was waiting for me to call him with the time.

"What's that?" I asked.

"Cutbacks," he said. "I have to make a few cutbacks. I'm going to have to let you go."

"You're firing me?"

"Call it what you want," he said. "But you ain't got a job no more."

*   *   *

Nor did Donna and I have a place to live. After firing me, Art would no longer let us rent the little house on his property. Hampered by a shortage of funds, we moved to El Monte, a cheap suburb about an hour outside Hollywood—nowheresville, as far as I was concerned. I saw the move to the suburbs as a defeat. It was as if I had dropped out of the fast lane, given up my chance at the pot of gold.

The move didn't upset Donna. As always, she was content to stay at home. I wasn't, though, and that became the final problem in our marriage.

I had wanted out of the relationship for quite a long time but didn't have the guts to call it quits. Donna and I didn't fight often. We didn't talk much, either. In fact, we didn't communicate, period. We lived our separate lives and bided our time, an arrangement that kind of worked itself out because neither of us knew any better. I take most of the blame. I think men are mostly inept when faced with unhappy home lives. I wanted it over but then I would start worrying whether I could handle being alone.

It's cowardly to stay in a bad relationship, but I was a coward then. I wanted an easy way out and waited for Donna to make the move. I didn't have to wait long. After moving to El Monte, a friend of mine, Tom Wright, moved into the same block. Tom and I had driven tugs together at Douglas Aircraft. He was married, and the four of us occasionally hung out together.

One day I drove home from work and found Donna and Tom together. They weren't doing anything. But when I saw them I spotted a look that told me something had happened. No one said anything, but it was obvious. I would've bet dollars to doughnuts they were having an affair. Guilt was plastered across their faces. I never called Donna on it. How could I? I'd had more affairs than I could even remember. I couldn't blame Donna for wanting the same.

But both of us were finally ready to face the truth. The marriage was over. After so many years, it was finally time to call it quits.

I moved in with Lee LaSeff, a friend of mine who worked as a promotion man for Record Merchandising, and saw

Donna sporadically. I had great intentions of staying involved as a parent but I failed to keep them. Then Donna moved to Montana and we lost contact altogether. It wasn't until years later that I realized what I had lost by letting my daughter go.

Lee LaSeff had enjoyed some success and was living in a nice apartment in Hollywood, where I stayed for several weeks until I bummed a place to sleep with Jack Nitzsche and his wife. That was a mistake. With my marriage gone bust and no job, I dropped a few notches in Jack's eyes. At the same time, he was starting his ascent, working as an arranger for Phil Spector.

"The guy's a genius," Jack used to tell me. "He's out of his mind, but he's a true genius. The Albert Einstein of music."

It was tough listening to Jack recount the nightly excitement of working with Spector at Gold Star Studios, the hub of Phil's operation, when I was sliding downhill as quickly as he was shooting up. I moved into my own apartment as soon as possible and set out to test the knowledge I'd gleaned from the past couple of years.

Hooking up with a small studio located at the end of Western Avenue, I started my own independent record company, Gold Records. The catchy name was more wishful thinking than anything else. I entered into a record deal with the studio that called for me to solicit business or cut records, and then split the profits with them. Later, I discovered they were teetering near bankruptcy.

One of the first calls I paid was to Clint Eastwood, who was then co-starring on the television series "Rawhide." His apartment was next door to a friend of mine, and one afternoon we started talking out front. Not yet the big star he was to become, Clint was pretty humble pie back then, and he wanted really badly to sing. We talked several times about what material he wanted to sing, getting him to the studio, and scheduling, but nothing ever came of it.

That was pretty much the story of Gold Records. I went to my office every day and mickied around, pretending to be arranging recording dates. But the phone never rang. I had no one to call. My savings were being drained. I spent hours doing absolutely nothing. I got so bored and desperate, I produced myself singing a handful of songs under the pseudonyms Sonny Christie and Ronny Summers, records destined to become collector's items.

In late 1961, when my bank account got lower than my car's gas tank, I closed the door to the musty office that I called Gold Records and took a promotion job with Record Merchandising, an independent distributor owned by Sid Talmadge. The promo biz was fast-track hustling then, the link between the artists on independent labels and the radio stations.

Disc jockeys were kings then. They ruled the airwaves, determining what records got played and what didn't. It was the job of the promo man to sway their opinions. In some cases, this required a payoff of some sort—cash or merchandise or both—though the scam was kept extremely hush-hush. It wasn't company policy, but it was OK to take a dee jay to dinner or give a dee jay a present on a holiday. One Christmas I flew to Philadelphia to give Dick Clark a movie projector. Art Rupe was hoping the present would persuade him to play a few of Specialty's records on "American Bandstand" and spring us out of our rut.

Dick was then the king of kings, so popular that I had to stand in line to hand him the present. It was like paying tribute, since airtime on "Bandstand" meant an instant hit. A few weeks later, I received a thank-you note in the mail. Years later when I recounted this story to Dick on the air, it didn't go over too well.

Promotion was all about schmoozing, getting enough to the deejays to hang out with them. If you could take them to dinner, great. If you could buy them a new suit, a television, even better. If you got close enough to slip somebody a wad of bills, that was hitting the jackpot. But it wasn't thought of as payola. It was more like Here, let me do something real nice for you.

The stable of artists I pushed was pretty good, acts like Chubby Checker, Little Richard, Gene Pitney, and my pals Don and Dewey. Unfortunately, I was a terrible promo man. Once a week, everyone at Record Merchandise received a stack of records, the latest batch of potential singles to peddle. The problem was that there was such an overwhelming amount of product, there was no way in the world everything was going to get on the air.

The standard practice was to flip through the stack, figure out which were the one or two good records, and then dump the rest. Before long, however, I was tossing all of my records in back-alley garbage bins and then heading off to Hollywood Lanes, which was the record industry's hangout and the place where everybody picked up news on what was happening and who was hot.

At the time, there was one name on everybody's lips—Phil Spector. I knew of Spectra, Phil's first label. How could I not? The guy was a legend at twenty-one. He had more hits than a Sonny Liston fight. Spectra was also distributed by Record Merchandising, and the guy who handled the account always seemed to be smiling.

"What's bothering you, Son?"

It was Red Turner, one of my fellow promo guys, and we were talking on the phone. He knew I was frustrated. I'd been spiraling on a downer for weeks. It was April. The promise of spring was in the air, and I was depressed.

"I can't believe Spector," I said. "There's no end to the guy's work—'To Know Him Is to Love Him,' 'He Hit Me,' 'He's a Rebel'—all smashes."

"So," Red said, "he's a genius."

"Right. But I wanna be writing and producing too. And what am I doing?"

"It's what you aren't doing," Red interrupted. "You need a broad, that's what you need. How 'bout me arranging something over the weekend?"

I knew Red was seeing a girl about whom he was nuts. He was always talking My girl this and My girl that. He had mentioned that she had a few interesting friends. So I thought, Why not, and told him I was game.

We met a few days later at Aldo's, an Italian restaurant in Hollywood that was the big promo hangout. A low-lit joint, I walked into Aldo's like a gunslinger coolly sauntering into a bar, and spotted Red in a good booth. He was sandwiched in between two girls. Both were especially attractive. Red first introduced me to his date, a tall, skinny girl with long, dark hair, a teenager's bad complexion, and the most intense, dark eyes I'd ever encountered in a female.

"Nice to meet you, Cher," I said, checking her out.

Then I turned my attention to my date.

"And this is Melissa," Red said. "Melissa, this is my good friend, Sonny Bono."

Cher was gorgeous, but Melissa was a knockout too. I was attracted to her instantly. The four of us chatted over drinks for about an hour. The conversation never dragged. Red suggested a double date the next night, which struck everyone as a fine idea. I'd be with Melissa, Red with Cher. A funny feeling gnawed at me, though. Throughout our drinks, Cher had been staring at me. She had this look, which she still has, that locks on to you like radar, and I couldn't figure out what it meant.

"I like your outfit," she said to me as we headed out the door. "Black on black. It really looks good."

"Thanks." I smiled. "See ya tomorrow."

Red was right about needing to get out and find some female companionship. I went home that night with a lightness in my step I hadn't felt for a long time. Cupid had fired a bull's-eye. I couldn't get Melissa out of my mind. Whenever I closed my eyes, I saw her sultry smile and had thoughts that made me feel among the living again. Later that night I told a buddy of mine, "I've met the girl I'm going to marry. She's beautiful. Her name's Melissa."

The next evening the four of us met at Aldo's. The girls looked sensational. Melissa was a brown-haired seductress. Cher, with her black hair pinned back, looked flawless—except for a big nose, which I thought gave her character, something perfect-looking women lack. The red wine flowed. Sparks flew. Everybody laughed. After dinner, Cher and Melissa suggested we go dancing at a club they promised was lots of fun.

"What's it called?" I asked.

"Club 86," said Cher, who then flashed Melissa the grin of a Cheshire cat.

Melissa and Cher spoke about Club 86 with great familiarity, as if going there were a nightly occurrence.

"I've never heard of this joint," said Red, who, like me,

was no stranger to Hollywood nightlife. "How 'bout you, Son?"

"Naw," I said. "But if the girls say it's hot, I'm game."

The club had the nondescript exterior of every club. A gray facade and a huddle of people around the door. The interior, though, was darker than the restaurant where we had eaten dinner, darker than a back alley. But Cher and Melissa led the way to a table. As we ordered drinks, I looked around. Suddenly uneasiness crept over me, a feeling that we had walked into the wrong place. I glanced over at Cher and Melissa. They were fine.

But as I looked out at the crowded dance floor and studied the people at the other tables, it became uncomfortably and painfully obvious that Red and I were the only men in the entire club. Something was not kosher.

"You're sure this is the right place?" I asked, casting Red a sidelong, get-a-load-of-this look at the same time.

"Yeah, this is it." Melissa nodded.

She smiled at Cher. I wondered about our dates.

My curiosity was piqued even further when Cher and Melissa got up and danced with each other. Watching from the table, I was confused, and I flashed Red a look that asked What's up? He shrugged.

"I don't know from nothing," Red said. "They're kids."

"You sure they aren't something else too?" I asked.

"Like I said, I don't know from nothing."

When Cher and Melissa came back to the table, I knew from the vibes that none of the things I hoped for were going to happen between Melissa and me. The dreams I'd had the night before were just that, dreams. Melissa's interest wasn't in me, that was for sure. And Cher? She was unreadable. I didn't know what to make of her. She seemed to be as comfortable with Melissa as she was with Red. No matter. Red and I made it clear that we wanted to get the hell out of the club.

Cher got up and let Red help her with her coat. But when I stood up and made a move to help Melissa with hers, she refused.

"Thanks, but I think I'll stay," she demurred.

I didn't know what to say. I made a slight move to kiss her on the cheek. Then I thought better of it and shrugged.

On the ride back home, Red and Cher took the front seat of his car and I sat in the back seat, a disappointed jackass. My fragile male ego had been bruised. Cher cut the tension by talking the entire way back—to me. She turned around so that she was able to see me. Again I felt Cher's hot stare reeling me in, and didn't know what to make of it. Was she flirting? Playing a game? After this Club 86 escapade, I didn't know. But I definitely felt something flying in on the runway.

"That's a damn shame about what happened," I said as they let me out. "I could've made her happy."

"Well, don't worry." Cher laughed. "I'm not that way."

"Goddamn, I hope not." Red was also laughing. Then he waved. "So long, Sonny. See ya later."

"Yeah, see ya," Cher said.

Three weeks later I was looking out the window of my apartment, which was in a sprawling complex on Franklin and Vine, and, lo and behold, I saw Cher staring out the window of a neighboring apartment. Her face registered the same look as mine—total surprise. It was what in the movies they call "meet cute." We exchanged smiles and waves, then each motioned to meet outside.

"What are you doing here?" I asked.

Cher kind of bobbed her head from side to side.

"I ran away from home—sort of." She smiled. "And I'm living with some girlfriends—but not really. You know?"

"Sort of. But not really."

I didn't know what to make of this girl. She was a hot-blooded paradox. I knew she was young, under twenty for sure, but she looked and acted an experienced thirty-five. Our conversation revealed her maturity, yet I sensed a vulnerable part of Cher. She tried hiding that softness with a tough exterior. Her mouth was as salty as a sailor's. The filth streamed out in every sentence. But I knew she was doing that for effect.

"You got a job?" I asked her.

"See's Candy Store," she said. "I'm working there. At least I was."

"Well, which is it? You are or you aren't?"

"I just quit."

"And you're living with the girls there?"

Curiosity got the better of me. I had to ask. I knew the three girls in whose apartment I had spotted Cher were gay. Despite Cher's denial the night of our double date, the situation made me wonder about her. Was she or wasn't she gay?

"Ah, they're friends of mine," she hemmed. "I—ah—I don't really have a place of my own."

Standing in the airy courtyard, under the shade of swaying palm trees, our friendly chance encounter developed into an exciting, flirtatious conversation. It was fun. My heart started to beat a little faster. Cher was a real player, coquettish and streetwise. Her patter kept pace with mine. She smiled and batted her eyes as if they were connected to strings that made me dance inside like a marionette.

I decided to throw the dice, let 'em fly.

"If you really don't have any place to stay, would you like to stay here with me?" I asked.

"No, I couldn't," Cher said. "Thanks, but no."

"Why? No funny business. No strings attached."

"I don't have any money. I can't afford the rent."

"Don't worry." I smiled. "We'll trade. You clean the house, make sure there's food, stuff like that, and you can stay here."

There was no question that Cher had stars in her eyes, but for the life of me, I didn't know what she had in her head, especially after our first night together. I was already deeply smitten by the time we finished lugging her clothes and belongings, meager as they were, up to my apartment. I wasn't able to keep myself from staring at her. Cher was not only physically attractive; she put out an alluring, intoxicating aura, a magnetism, that pulled me closer and closer.

For a kid, she possessed incredible strength. I heard it in the way she talked. I picked up on it in the ballsy way she bounced around town. Yet Cher was also full of fear, a deep, disturbing and chronic fear. I didn't discover that troubled, anxious side of Cher until our first night together when we crawled into bed—separate beds.

There were twin beds in my bedroom, and when it came time to turn in, we each climbed into one. Both of us understood it was a bogus arrangement, a temporary one at best.

There was too much electricity racing back and forth for it to be anything but temporary. But we pulled up the covers, said good night, and then I turned out the lights.

"I can't sleep," Cher mumbled a few minutes later.

I was turning in my bed.

"What? Did you say something?"

"I can't sleep."

"What's the matter?" I asked.

"I can't sleep without the television on."

"But I don't have a television in the bedroom."

"Then I can't sleep."

"OK, what'll do it for you?"

"Nothing except the television."

"But the television's in the living room," I said, exasperated.

"Then I guess we'll have to sleep in the living room."

Finally I got out of bed and brought the damn television into the bedroom. Wedged it right between the doorway and Cher's bed. There was just one problem: the bedroom didn't have an electrical outlet. So I spent the next half hour disconnecting and then reconnecting all the extension cords in the apartment, rerouting them so I could plug the television in in the living room but show it in the bedroom.

That's how we left it. Cher slept like a baby, and I stayed up and watched the tube.

The next morning I learned that Cher had run away from home and told her mother that she was living with a stewardess. She explained that she and her mother, Georgia, were having difficulties, an understatement, it turned out. I soon learned that they were always having difficulties. Cher and her mother loved each other, but they related like cats and dogs.

Cher's mother was an aspiring actress, a pretty, youthful party girl who circulated on the fringe of Hollywood, measuring her success by the men she dated and the cars she rode in. Georgia circulated in the fast lane, and Cher made it clear that she suffered for it. As a child, she was often handed over to relatives or friends while her mother went out on the town. Cher felt herself a burden and later, as she matured into a real beauty, her mother began to see her as competition.

The doors of Cher's complex makeup opened slowly. The stewardess story was the first phony story Cher revealed to me. A second came right away. I was startled to learn that she wasn't eighteen as she had said earlier. In reality when I had first met her, this mysterious girl, whose real name, Cherilyn Sarkasian LaPierre, as complex as she was, was sixteen years old. She was born May 20, 1946.

"I'm actually seventeen," she insisted.

"How do I know?" I asked skeptically.

"Because I am," she said. "I'm telling you that I am." In a short time I learned from the girls next door that Cher's birthday had indeed just come and gone. I knew her age was cause to put me behind bars. Nothing had happened between us yet. But I was falling for Cher and I worried that her mother would eventually find out where she was living and have me thrown in the slammer.

I couldn't keep myself from falling, though. Cher's eyes were as deep and as dark as tunnels. The longer I stared into them, the stronger their pull on me became. Her personality was magnetic and it drew me toward her. I tried to keep a wary distance. Cher was full of mystery, and I was constantly being surprised.

For instance, not too long after Cher moved in with me, she went out with her girlfriends for a night on the town. Ordinarily it wouldn't have been a big deal, except for the incident at Club 86 and that I knew her three pals were lesbians. My heart sank. I thought, Oh no, here we go again, another Melissa. Until then, Cher and I had only flirted with each other. Our relationship was all tease and play.

Suddenly I wondered if I was being conned by a slick fast-tracker. Was it all a rose-colored ruse by a girl who needed a place to live?

Our arrangement at the time was informal, so my worries were purely selfish. Both of us were entitled to our independence. I was free to date and so was Cher. That was our understanding from the start. I was just hoping something more was going to develop.

The next morning I didn't say anything, but I watched Cher hanging around with her girlfriends. Something mysterious was going on, though I didn't know what or with whom. But I definitely knew I was the outsider. Even with Cher. I sensed an intimacy between Cher and the girls that excluded me. I felt threatened by it. If something was going to happen between me and Cher, I first had to find out whether or not she liked men or women. We slept in the same room. We were developing an intimacy of our own. But I'd be damned if I had a clue about her sexuality.

Finally I couldn't stand the pressure that was building inside me and I confronted Cher.

Cher was genuinely taken aback when I asked, point-blank, whether or not she preferred girls to boys. She was even embarrassed. Or so it seemed. Perhaps it was because I was so serious.

"What do you mean?" she asked, startled. "Sonny, I don't understand why you even have to ask."

"I see who you're hanging out with, Cher," I said. "Come on. I'm naive, but I'm not blind."

Sitting opposite one another on the sofa in my tiny living room, Cher and I were equally awkward. We owed each other nothing, yet there was a sense that we did. In these first few weeks of living together, Cher was full of confessions and revelations, though as far as our future together was concerned, this issue was perhaps the most important. As she spoke, Cher's voice was marked by more tension than I had ever heard in her.

Intimately and sincerely, Cher told me that she had already lost her virginity. Between the ages of fourteen and sixteen she had been searching for comfort and affection and had latched onto whoever gave her those.

Cher assured me it wasn't anything to worry about. Among her more recent dalliances, she said, was a handsome young actor named Warren Beatty. I hadn't yet heard of Beatty, but I remembered his name. Ironically, years later, when Sonny and Cher were on top, we got a call from our agent at William Morris. Warren Beatty was making a gangster movie, *Bonnie and Clyde,* and he wanted to test Cher for the part of Bonnie.

By then I knew of Beatty's Lothario reputation all too well and said, "No way." The movie turned out to be great and I deserved the shots I took from Cher about discouraging her from auditioning. Deep down, I was insecure, and I just wasn't thrilled with the idea of her and Beatty together.

Cher's past experimentation didn't thrill me, either.

"It's just something I passed through," she said. "How do you feel about it?"

"I don't know how I feel about it," I said. "I don't know that it's important either way. Considering."

"Considering what?" Cher asked.

"Well, considering that there's nothing between us."

"What makes you say that?" She smiled coyly.

If Cher was fishing, I was biting. Within seconds, we were kissing, tasting each other like two friends sharing their dessert. Our first physical encounter was exploratory, a passionate first step that extended our relationship without making it too serious.

But I fell fast after that. Cher and I weren't sleeping together yet, but we shared the same dream—stardom. We were broke, insecure, and full of doubts, but both of us craved the spotlight. I wanted to write and produce records, and Cher wanted to sing. We talked of little else. Cher loved to sing. She wasn't much of a conversationalist, but she was always singing, imitating whatever style was popular. That's how she expressed herself best—through song.

I saw in her a tremendous desire to be a performer. She didn't admit it outright. But people were always paying compliments to Cher about her dancing. She was a hot dancer, and when she danced, it was more a performance than a turn on the dance floor. Whether she was singing in the shower or in the kitchen or dancing at a club, she gave notice of an obvious need to be the center of attention. There was no doubt in my mind that Cher was a performer—even if she didn't know it or wasn't saying it.

These are some of the most touching and tender memories I have of our time together. Cher and I were innocent, romantic, two people in love, crooning songs and entertaining each other. The ten-year gap in our ages didn't matter. We were equals. We had a need for each other, and we were reaching for that. When people are down or confused, they always search for a relationship. That becomes the immediate answer. We were locking on to that.

Cher and I were survivors. We admired that quality in each other. I also gave her stability. Until then, she'd been with guys who were a lot older than I was and they'd been just playing around. From the outset, my position was clear. I wanted to do good for her. She wanted someone to make her dreams come true, and I was willing to dedicate myself to helping her achieve that.

Basically, we were two lost kids who found direction in each other.

Of course, in those first few weeks both Cher and I were playing a mating game. We knew what was going to happen. It was just a matter of time.

We'd been living together slightly more than a month when I finally made the first move that both of us were anticipating. I slipped into bed beside Cher. I wish that I were able to say I saw banners and fireworks the first time Cher and I made love, but I didn't. The physical part was fine, though I wouldn't equate it with a religious experience. More important than the sex was the love story that started to unfold between us.

I like physical lovemaking, but I don't think Cher and I were ever that outlandishly physical. Maybe her other relationships were different. But it never really meshed with us. In the most intimate moments, Cher was reserved and protective. There was a part of her—and it still exists—that no one can get to. It's the source of her mystery and strength, the vulnerability she won't reveal. On the other hand, we cuddled and hugged and sat in bed and talked till the television stations went off the air.

Those memories are nice. The romance between us was real. It was heartfelt. It was honest. It was rooted in friendship, need, trust, and sincerity. That's where the allure of Sonny and Cher developed. I wanted to pull off something fantastic for Cher. I wanted to be the boy who walked the fence to impress the girl.

And Cher believed I could do that.

5

JUST YOU

In all the years Cher and I were together, there was no more romantic period than these first few months. Our life was simple. Having little money, we lived on our dreams and talked of the future. Cher wanted so much. From the few hints she dropped, I realized that she was desperate to forget a childhood in which she'd patched holes in her shoes with cardboard and watched her mother buy her new clothes and then return them in a fit of anger. Cher was determined to create a new life for herself. I understood that.

What I didn't understand, though, was her sense of urgency. I kept asking what the hurry was.

"I'm not going to live very long," she admitted with great reluctance one day.

"What?" I said, shocked.

"I've had these premonitions," she said. "For a long time. I probably won't live very long."

"How long are we talking?" I asked.

"Thirty," she said. "I don't think I'll live past thirty. If I even make it that far."

"Don't talk like that," I said. "I don't want to hear you say those things."

We had that discussion often, which bothered me every time. I didn't know if Cher really believed she wasn't going to live past age thirty, if that was just her way of voicing her fear, or if she was saying it for effect. I learned early on that part of Cher liked to create high drama. It was her way of building excitement.

I fell for it too. I bought into her hurried timetable.

Cher and I used to eat out at little restaurants—dives with atmosphere. On Western Boulevard, there was one homey little Italian restaurant, a favorite of ours, where we were able to fill our stomachs with a delicious meal for three or four dollars. The laughs were free. The old Italian who owned the place was a loud, crusty character whose tongue was as sharp as the spices he put on his pizza.

The whole world seemed to sit down for a dinner served over the restaurant's red-and-white-checkered tablecloths. This fascinating joint was a hangout for old actors and Gypsies, a fringe crowd that lent Hollywood some of its color. One wrinkled and bent Gypsy woman came in every night, ordered dinner, ate half of it, and then left the remainder for her kid. When her son came in later, the owner pulled out the same half-eaten dinner and set it on the table.

Another regular was obviously a character actor from the old studio westerns of the thirties and forties. Wearing boots, a bandanna, and a cowboy hat, he sauntered in as if he were checking out a crowded bar scene. He had a big handlebar mustache painted above his lip. Midway through his dinner, half of it disappeared—part on his napkin, the other part floating atop his second or third glass of beer. By the time he staggered out, he was clean-shaven.

"Babe, don't let this happen to me when I get older," I said to Cher.

"Don't worry, Son," she said. "By the time you and I get old, somebody will have invented waterproof makeup."

One evening we were at our table, eating our plate of dollar-and-a-half pasta, garlic bread, and red wine, when an apparently well-dressed man barged through the front door in a panic. The place was as big as a medium-size living room. Naturally, everybody turned to look. The restaurant owner came out from the kitchen. He seemed to know the guy.

"Hey, Joe," the man yelled. "Where's the toilet?"

"Toilet?" the owner replied, puzzled. "You know I don't have no toilet here. Go over to the gas station."

"Come on, Joe," he pleaded. "They ain't got a key over at the gas station. Where's the toilet?"

"Outta here, right now," the owner shouted. "If you gotta go, find your way to the gas station."

Cher and I were seated by the front door, on the front line of the argument. Finally, the man turned and walked out the door in a huff. Our plates shook as the door slammed shut. We watched through the window as the guy walked across the street. Then he turned back again, stood directly in front of the restaurant, and relieved himself. When he was finished, he stuck his head back in the door.

"Hey, Joe," he yelled. "I found the toilet."

Cher and I enjoyed these nightly mini dramas more than television or the movies. Real life was so interesting, vibrant, and, above all, satisfying. It even got a bit tastier when I finagled a line of credit at Martoni's, another Italian restaurant, which served as the unofficial clubhouse for the music industry. It was *the* place to be seen and to schmooze.

"Being able to sign a tab—is this the greatest or what?" I said to Cher one night.

"This must be what it's like to be rich," she replied.

"Oh baby, someday I'm going to pull something off for you that's going to be outrageous. Something big."

I meant really BIG, which showed how rapidly my definition of success was changing. I felt I was inching closer to the major leagues. In early 1962, immediately before he started writing charts for Phil Spector, Jack Nitzsche and I wrote the song "Needles and Pins." Whenever we hung out, Jack used to play the piano, and I have to say, he came up with more brilliant hooks than anyone I had ever met.

One night I began singing whatever words came to mind to Jack's guitar playing, and by the time he left, we had "Needles and Pins" in pocket. Jackie DeShannon, whom we knew well, recorded it for Liberty Records and made it the B side to one of her singles. Ironically, "Needles and Pins" did better than the single, reaching number eighty-four on the charts. Two years later, of course, the Searchers covered it and the song became an international hit, soaring to number one in England and reaching thirteenth place in the United States. But when Jackie's version charted, I considered a soft hit a pretty good achievement.

Still, I was itching to get to that next level, the place where I could pull off something BIG for Cher. I just had to figure out how. With the modest success of "Needles and Pins" clawing at my frustrated ego, I determined to forge a plan that would spring me from the blahs of working at Record Merchandising. My thought process was this:

Okay, I wanted to write and produce. A few years earlier, I had wanted to write R&B songs, and I had gone about that by hanging out with guys like Don and Dewey and soaking up as much of their expertise as possible.

Firsthand experience. That's the only way I knew how to learn things.

At the time, there was one sound that was blowing me away, and one man was responsible for it. I got his telephone number from my compadre Jack Nitzsche, who had gone to work writing charts for him.

"I'd like to speak to Phil Spector," I said to a secretary with a thick New York accent. "My name is Sonny Bono."

"Uh-hah," she said. "So? Would ya like to know mine?"

"Jack Nitzsche told me to call," I said.

"Hang on a minute," she said.

The receptionist put me on hold. I listened to the silence for five or ten minutes. Maybe longer. I wasn't going to give up until I got no for an answer. If I had to hustle, then I had to hustle. I knew what I had to do.

"Yeahhhh?" said a thin, nasal voice that sounded like a child who was either whining or utterly bored.

"Phil?" I asked.

"Yeahhhh?"

In a rush of words that came out of me with the force of an explosion, I introduced myself and our mutual connection. Spector respected Nitzsche, which is why he was still listening when I finished my opening spiel. So I got right to the point. I begged for work.

"Yeah, and what do you wanna do for me?" he asked.

"Anything," I said. "Anything."

"I don't know if there's an opening under that job description," he said. "I'm in the record business, you know?"

As if I didn't know. But that was pure Phil.

By mid-1962, the string of top ten records crediting Spector as producer made it clear to anybody with ears that he was breaking all the old rules and setting standards that were higher than ever before. Coming-of-age productions like "There's No Other (Like My Baby)" and "Uptown," early hits by the Crystals, confirmed his revolutionary status. But by the time "He's a Rebel," with Darlene Love singing lead, went number one, in November 1962, his Wall of Sound was hitting high gear and no one questioned the twenty-one-year-old producer's genius.

What I really wanted from Spector, more than employment, was a tutorial in record production. I was dying to know what the hell he was doing in the studio. But that's not what I told him on the phone.

"You need a West Coast promo man," I said. "Philles Records is too big, too strong, too vital to be with a company that handles lots of different labels. I'd be representing just your label."

"Yeahhhh," he mumbled. "Yeahhh. I like the idea."

Another few minutes of heavy schmoozing and the wunderkind producer awarded me the job that I had just created. The transformation in my life was amazing, faster than an overnight sensation. With one fortuitous phone call, I was suddenly working for the hottest record label in the music business. I was thrilled. My attitude skyrocketed, my confidence grabbed a first-class seat.

However, that was only step one in the effort to reverse my fortune and pull off something spectacular for Cher. The next move was easy. I resigned from Record Merchandising. It was good riddance to the weekly stack of records I usually tossed in the alley Dumpster. Within minutes I was shopping my new connection as Philles's West Coast promo man like the sure thing it was and ended up at Jack Lewerke's independent distribution company.

Why there? Simple. I was driving a dinky-ass Chevy Manza at the time. Cher and I hated that car. It was symbolic of our struggle. Jack offered me a convertible Cadillac if I brought the account over to him, and I really wanted to impress Cher. Her uncle drove a Caddy.

It was afternoon when he handed me the keys to the car. The sun was hanging overhead as if it were a single, overly ripe orange in a sky-blue tree. I felt juiced. I had a great job that offered me status and prestige. I was sitting in the front seat of my own Cadillac, with the top down. The radio was blasting as I pulled into traffic and headed for my apartment. I never thought life would get that good.

Driving home, I decided how I was going to play the windfall in front of Cher. I'd be Mr. Nonchalant and act as if it had been just another hum-drum day at work. However, Cher spotted me through the front window as I pulled up curbside, and came sprinting out the door. Her eyes were like the dots under large question marks; her mouth was agape.

"What's this, Son?" she exclaimed. "What's going on with this car?"

"Ah, it's nothing," I shrugged, trying to contain my smile. "It's just a Cadillac."

Even before I really watched how Spector worked and learned that everybody in his system was interchangeable, except for himself, I wanted him to produce Cher. I was convinced that this shy, skinny, teenage girl with bad skin, a big nose, and an unusually deep voice, was star material. All she needed was someone to channel her hidden talent. Spector, the Midas of the moment, had that ability.

In those halcyon days, everything Spector touched turned to gold, and as the West Coast promo man for Philles Records, my job was sweeter than the icing on a double chocolate cake. Disc jockeys embraced me as a favorite friend when I brought around new Spector-produced records—a dramatic turnaround from the days when I pushed new and unwanted product at Record Merchandising.

But before I could hook Cher up with Phil, I first had to go through the process of getting close to the legendary producer. It turned out to be easier than I thought. Whatever dark and troubled thoughts swirled in his turgid mind, Spector controlled the activity in Gold Star's Studio A, the calm in the center of a storm. No matter who was singing or playing, there was no doubt in anybody's mind about who was the main attraction.

Like a spoiled child, Phil needed to be center stage, the focus of everybody's attention. He stood in the center of a chaotic session like no one I had ever seen. He was dressed entirely in black. Sunglasses shielded his eyes. His longish hair was a variation on a beatnik's bowl cut. Physically, he was short and unimposing, but he gave off a heavy vibe that warned you not to screw with him.

In short, Spector had presence. It was impossible to deny or ignore. Like any showman, he knew how to use it. I was completely overwhelmed by this strange, brilliant, and enigmatic man.

Phil was never an easy person to communicate with. He used silence to control people. Everyone around Phil constantly wondered whether they were in or out of favor. His moods shifted with quixotic unpredictability, jubilant and excited one minute, depressed the next. He also expected the people around him to be in the same mood. For instance, Phil once called me in the middle of the night. I'd been asleep for hours, but that didn't matter. He was awake and restless.

"Sonny, it's Phil," he said. "Want to go get some cole slaw?"

"Oh sure, I'm glad you called me, man," I replied, groggy but knowing better than to disagree. "That's just what I feel like doing. What time is it?"

"Four."

"Great. Okay, I'll see ya."

If you wanted to be on Phil's good side, you followed his lead like a good soldier. So I picked him up at his hotel, then trudged off to Denny's and ate cole slaw. Now the most irritating part of that routine wasn't being awakened from a sound sleep. Nor was it having to ingest a bowl of mushy cole slaw, which, having been prepared the previous afternoon, threw my stomach into a noisy upheaval. No, the absolute worst part of that particular escapade was sitting in a booth across from Phil in total silence. He apparently didn't feel like speaking. Not a single syllable passed through his lips.

He wanted to be thought of as interesting, and he was

by nature. But he did strange little things to prove it all the time. He even practiced the coolest way to sit in his car, studying the various angles. He would put one arm on the window, try steering with one finger, all sorts of different poses. Then he would have me stand outside the car and ask how he looked.

When Volvo came out with a sports car, Phil immediately rented a little coupe.

"What do you think of Jackie DeShannon?" he asked one night when we were cruising around Hollywood.

"Very nice," I said of the singer.

Jackie was hot in those days. She had never popped big-time, but everybody in L.A. believed in her and Phil had a thing for her.

"If she saw me driving, do you think she'd like me better with my glasses on or off?" he asked.

"Gee, Phil, I don't know," I answered. "That's something only Jackie would know."

"Okay, we've got to find out where she's driving," he said.

After a couple days of snooping around and making phone calls, we found out Jackie's schedule, and figured that at a certain time she was going to be driving on Sunset Boulevard. So we went there too—Phil drove and I rode shotgun—and waited. Sure enough, Jackie came zipping down the Boulevard, and when Phil, a jangle of nerves, saw her, he was hardly able to contain himself.

"Sonny! There! There she is!" he cried.

Speeding through traffic like a Grand Prix racer, Phil inched the Volvo right behind Jackie's car, steeled his nerves, and then made his move. As we slid alongside the cute singer, Phil positioned himself so that he was sitting almost completely sideways. Most of his back was toward the window. He was, he thought, looking as cool as possible. From Jackie's vantage point, though, he was barely visible.

It didn't matter. We drove parallel to Jackie for a good mile and a half, and that whole time Phil held his pose, offering her maybe a sliver of a glance from behind his sunglasses.

It's doubtful that Jackie even knew the guy in the other

car was Phil Spector. She probably thought it was some wacko fan. At any rate, I remember her giggling for a while and then turning off in another direction. Phil was crestfallen.

"Damn," he said. "The sunglasses probably scared her."

Phil didn't need to appear interesting just to the people he knew. Strangers also counted. We passed the wee hours of too many nights walking around the farmer's market, pretending to shop while we repeated in absurdly loud voices the half-dozen phrases Phil had learned to speak in French and then taught to me. If nobody heard us, then we repeated the circuit, trying to impress people with our worldliness.

Looking back, Phil's behavior was more idiotic than interesting, though at the very least, he was creating interest within himself. There was value in that, I realized, especially for someone like me, who wanted to absorb every aspect of Spector's tremendous power to turn heads. Of course, both Jack Nitzsche and I began imitating our guru. We grew our hair, donned shades indoors and out, and attempted to dress as weirdly as possible.

But the one place where it was impossible to emulate Spector was the studio. Phil was the Wagner of pop music—larger than life, grandiose. He brought a whole new way of thinking to recording. Rather than thinking about an entire album, Phil focused 100 percent of his energy on a single song. He wrote it and produced it. Then he crammed the studio full of musicians—four or five guitars, three drums, three pianos—and pushed all the sound up into the distortion range.

The first time I saw it, I thought, What the hell is going on here. He was breaking every rule. And to my knowledge, Phil invented the technique called bouncing. He got two two-track recording machines and bounced the various instruments back and forth, which enabled him to squeeze even more sound onto the tape. Nobody had ever done that before. Call it clever, call it genius, it was unique.

So watching him was like opening a door to an entirely new world. He worked in enormous strokes, stirring everybody's emotions as he concocted what was an entirely new sound at the time, and what eventually came to be known as Phil Spector's Wall of Sound.

The more I saw him work, the more I understood. His method wasn't based on madness, as he would have liked people to believe. It was due to something much more complicated—utter simplicity. That was essential to him. He had an incredible ear, one that could pick up every single note in his dense Wall of Sound. If there was a goof, he heard it. He listened to a song over and over, and when it finished, he used to say, "Hey Sonny, is it dumb enough?"

"Dumb enough" was a catchphrase for a lot of things that simply boiled down to the song's appeal. Was the hook infectious enough to grab the listener? Were people going to remember the song after hearing it on the radio? It took me some time to understand that when Phil asked, "Is it dumb enough?" what he really meant was, Is everybody going to get the simplicity of this? Will the simplicity of the hook cut through everything and grab them?

Spector knew when he had a song that was going to strike pay dirt. His ear seemed infallible. I was standing beside him as the final playback of "Da Doo Ron Ron" finished. Phil pointed to the speakers and flashed me a sneaky smile. Trying to impress him, I said, "Man, that sure is dumb enough."

"No, Sonny," he said. "That's gold. That's solid gold coming out of that speaker."

And of course it was.

Phil was a perfectionist in the worst and best sense. He paid painstaking attention to detail. As a result, a Spector-produced recording session dragged on for hours—sometimes days—which was opposed to everything I had been taught about cutting records as quickly as possible. But Phil didn't care how everybody else made records. He wasn't concerned with budgets and union scales. Whatever he had to do to make the song the way he heard it in his head, he did.

The recording studio was Phil's theater, the one place where he was able to perform, where he was happiest. In that atmosphere, a larger-than-life person emerged from this tiny man, and magical things happened. For one, he made me a percussionist. Not that it was strange for me to participate in his sessions. I sang backup on nearly every Spector hit, including "Da Doo Ron Ron," "You've Lost that Lovin' Feelin'," all of his Christmas albums, and most of the Crystals' LPs. He used to refer to me as his "funk."

"I like that voice you got," he said. "It's so bad it's good, ya know?"

By then I understood what he meant. When Phil handed me a tambourine and instructed me to play percussion, I realized another important lesson in record making: It was perfectly okay to fake it. In fact, Phil legitimized faking. He didn't care whether or not I knew how to play something. Nor did it matter that I was scared to death of screwing up and incurring his wrath or triggering his explosive temper. He cared only about getting the right sound.

There was a downside to that singular perfectionism. If you entered the studio at four or five in the afternoon, you knew perfectly well that the session might not end until six or seven the following morning. This was understood by the singers and musicians, but it didn't stop us from grumbling, "Christ, I wish he'd hurry up with this thing."

Phil either didn't hear this or, if he did, it didn't faze him. He spent hours listening to playbacks, adding one ingredient at a time as if he were carefully following a recipe, which, in a sense, he was. Spector tolerated the griping of only two individuals—Darlene Love, who had the balls of a buffalo and didn't take crap from anyone, and Phil's mother. Mother Bertha was the only person who outright bullied him and got away with it. She sat right in the booth, evaluated every record, and in the process drove him nuts.

Ronnie Bennett Spector was Phil's girlfriend—they married in 1968—and she had her own methods for controlling him. She threw him a stern look here, a gentle smile there, and played him as a lion tamer does his ferocious beasts. All of us heard the rumors about their relationship: that Ronnie had to use a separate toilet because she was black; that Phil forced her to eat meals from separate plates and silverware; that he locked her in the bedroom and kept her prisoner for days.

What we actually saw was altogether different. We saw Phil baby his hotshot girlfriend as if she were the queen of Egypt, lavishing her with fabulously expensive clothes, jewelry, and the sort of praise that none of us ever heard but would have killed for. Cher envied the hell out of Ronnie, not so much her voice or stardom but that she was dripping in stylish clothes. Ronnie enjoyed strutting her stuff too. She played up the fact that she was the boss's girlfriend.

No matter how he treated Ronnie in private, Phil reacted with insane jealousy if anyone showed her attention in public. One night Ronnie, her sister, and her cousin—the other Ronettes—were sitting around the studio. Ronnie said she wanted a hamburger. The other girls were hungry too. Since I was Phil's number-one flunky, I naturally assumed it was my duty to make sure everybody was satisfied and took the girls and saxophonist Nino Tempo, who was Phil's best friend, to Dolores's Drive-In.

The studio was full of musicians when we left, but Phil was busy mixing. He kept the musicians sitting around in case he needed to add an instrument. Otherwise, he didn't want to be bothered. He was in his own world. None of us wanted to sit around the studio, since there was no telling how many more hours Phil was going to work, so we took our time eating hamburgers and shooting the breeze.

Less than an hour later, we returned to Gold Star, a gaggle of happy campers. But it was like walking into a murder scene. Phil was irate, brooding in a corner. His arms were crossed, tied in knots. He refused to look at any of us, preferring to sulk in a black cloud of silence that was message enough for everyone. His engineer was also silent. Nobody talked, in fact. When Phil was happy, everybody was happy; when he was depressed, everybody else was scared shitless.

"Oh man, what's wrong?" I whispered to Nino. "This is deep shit."

"The deepest," muttered Nino

Thirty minutes passed and Phil just stood there, propped up against the wall. I thought that if he dared move, he might actually crumble to the ground. The rest of us stood or sat, waiting—rather, hoping—for a signal. It didn't come. More time passed and Phil shuffled head down like a sulking child into the mixing room and sat in the dark, brooding.

Finally, Darlene Love got too antsy to sit there any longer. She didn't take anything from anybody, and she hated Phil's games anyway. The rest of us were frightened of him, but she didn't care.

"Phil, when the hell are we going to record?" she blurted.

He didn't respond. Didn't acknowledge that Darlene had spoken. Didn't even blink.

"Man, I've got to get home," she said. "If we aren't going to work, I'm outta here."

Again there was no response from Spector.

"Fine, baby," she said, and then walked out, leaving us less courageous folks to wait out Phil's tantrum.

Finally Spector picked up the telephone and called his psychiatrist in New York, not an odd occurrence. He was constantly in touch with his shrink, who regularly pulled him out of these harrowing abysses. Sometimes Phil placed several calls a night. Anyway, when he hung up the phone, everything was better. He offered neither apologies nor explanations, but Phil emerged from the dark room and resumed work as if there hadn't been any lapse in time.

Nobody was fooled, though. Phil had been overcome by jealousy as soon as he discovered that Nino and I had gone out with Ronnie. He couldn't handle it. He never lashed out or yelled. He never made any accusations. Instead, he blamed Nino and cut his closest friend right out of his life.

The situation wasn't always that dire. Phil's favorite pianist was Leon Russell. Leon was an incredible musician. During the session for "Baby, Please Come Home," Phil was so touched by a little concert line Leon played that he took out his checkbook and wrote the pianist a check for $100. Leon kept to himself. He showed up at the studio dressed very properly and never said a word. He just did his work and left. That was his deal and everyone respected him.

However, one session Leon wobbled into the studio apparently drunk. Not only was that unheard-of behavior among professionals, it was especially unheard of around Phil. It was also extremely out of character for Leon. Normally he never said a word. But Leon came in plastered, making all sorts of smug and sarcastic remarks and continually interrupting the session. No one had ever heard Leon talk so much, let alone seen him drunk.

Phil finally lost his patience, stormed out of the booth, and confronted Leon.

"Have you ever heard of the word *respect?*" he snarled.

"Yes," drawled Leon in his 100-proof voice. "Have you ever heard of the word *fuck?*"

Phil wanted to kill him. Instead, he didn't say another word the rest of the session.

But that was the way Phil operated. He just disconnected. If he felt betrayed or crossed or sensed that someone wasn't as subservient as he desired, then he promptly detached and treated you as if you never existed in the first place.

The flip side to Phil's strange behavior was his willingness to put just about anybody on a record. If Darlene wasn't around, he substituted Ronnie. If the Crystals weren't available, he used Darlene, which is exactly what happened on the group's only number one, Gene Pitney's "He's a Rebel." Billed as the Crystals, the song actually featured Darlene singing lead and backed by a group of L.A. session singers called the Blossoms.

The point wasn't lost on me. Phil was the star—the song was his vehicle. The artist—be it Ronnie or Darlene or the Righteous Brothers—was merely a passenger on Mr. Spector's Wild Ride. With this formula Phil could make anybody a star. Whomever he decided to record had a pretty good shot at becoming a hit artist. Not surprisingly I wanted this Svengali of the airwaves to record Cher.

I wanted it badly. The idea had been in my mind since I started working for Philles, and I entertained myself daily with the same fantasy: Cher and Phil would connect, he would record her, the song would rocket to the top of the charts, and the potential I knew Cher possessed would explode like fireworks on the Fourth of July.

Yet when Cher and Phil finally got together in early 1963, there was absolutely no chemistry. The two of them stood opposite each other in the antechamber of the studio and eyed one another like a cat and a dog.

"Sonny tells me you want to sing," said Phil, his voice more nasal and whiny than ever.

"I like to sing," replied Cher.

"She's incredible," I interjected. "Man, Phil, you should hear her."

"Uh-huh," he said, giving me a not-you-too look. "I suppose I will."

This was Phil's famous cold-shoulder routine, and the cause, I suspected, wasn't Cher's lack of talent, even though Phil was never privy to Cher's natural ability; the closest he came to witnessing Cher dancing and singing around our apartment were my lengthy descriptions. And the times Cher came around to Gold Star she was quiet and withdrawn, especially compared to such extroverted characters as Darlene and Ronnie. But Phil had a sixth sense when it came to spotting talent, and I am certain he knew Cher had the stuff to make it.

No, the problem was personal. Phil didn't pay serious attention to Cher because she was my girlfriend, not his. He was jealous.

Phil was drawn to beautiful women of every shape, color, and style. Like many a small man with a complex, he imagined himself cut from the same leading-man cloth as Cary Grant. Power and influence made Phil Spector a drawing card at any party, sure, but he was no matinee idol. And not only did Cher not find him physically attractive, she was so in awe of his prodigious talent that whenever she was around Phil, she shriveled up like a snail withdrawing into its shell.

Obviously not a combo that was going to make beautiful music together.

However, I believed wholeheartedly in Cher. Only later did I realize that my belief in her was in inverse proportion to what I felt my chances were of making it by myself. It was more gut instinct than premeditated plan, but I realize now that by throwing myself behind Cher as powerfully as I did, I was also giving myself an excuse to feel the same about me. If I could give Cher all the stuff I dreamed of for myself, then I would benefit too.

Ironically, I started having some luck by myself. In the waning part of 1963, the Righteous Brothers came under the guidance of Phil's label. They were two young white kids trying to sound black. Emulating the sound of my old Specialty buddies Don and Dewey, they rummaged through a trove of mothballed and forgotten tunes before recording my earliest composition, "Koko Joe," which had been written in 1951 and covered by Don and Dewey in 1959.

The song turned out pretty well and became a local hit, a boost to both the Righteous Brothers and me. That led me to write and produce a couple of tracks for the Standells, including "The Boy Next Door," a song that still pops up on oldies radio stations occasionally. I was involved in a lot of behind-the-scenes hustle, and for a flunky, I was doing okay; my résumé was growing. But all that paled compared to my hope that Phil would record Cher.

She did eventually join me, Jack Nitzsche, Jack's wife, and legions of others who happened to be visiting or hanging out at Gold Star, in singing backup on a number of Spector classics, including the Crystals' "Da Doo Ron Ron," the Ronettes' "Be My Baby," and the Righteous Brothers' "You've Lost That Lovin' Feelin'." Cher wanted to be accepted as a peer just as everybody else did, and participation got you to that position. But as soon as it was time to sing, Cher tightened up something fierce. Nobody had ever seen anything like her.

It was downright bewildering. Here was Cher, this beautiful young girl, who was full of this obvious desire to grab everybody's attention, who wanted to perform, who seemed to have a natural claim to the spotlight. Not yet out of her teens, she was able to walk into a room and turn heads with an aura of strength and privilege just as women adorned with cocktail dresses, furs, and jewels do. But ask her to sing and she wilted. The indomitable strength disappeared. Her voice went into vapor lock.

Such a scene occurred after one of the "Lovin' Feelin'" sessions. Phil pulled out some additional background vocals, and he asked Cher to sing a solo part. She refused. With tears in her eyes, she ran into the hallway. She was trying to hide her shame from everybody as much as she was trying to hide herself from whatever demons didn't allow her to do what her heart wanted.

"What's the matter, baby?" I whispered, having chased her into the hallway.

"I'm so scared," she cried.

Cher's skin was cold, goosebumpy. I felt her trembling.

"But this is your big shot," I said. "What's the big deal? You know everybody here."

"I can't do it," she whimpered. "I want to. But I can't, Sonny. I'm too damn scared."

"It's okay," I consoled. "Stop crying. If you don't want to sing now, don't sing. It's not a big deal. Your time will come, babe. I'm sure of that."

PART III

I GOT YOU BABE

6

I GOT YOU, I WON'T LET GO

Quite a bit of time passed before Cher's mother discovered she was living with me and not a stewardess. Once that happened, though, life changed. A storm might as well've ripped the roof right off our house. Georgia's wrath and meddling were such that I felt like a disaster victim.

To appreciate fully the kind of damage she was capable of inflicting, it's important to understand Cher's mother. She defined the phrase "a piece of work." When I met her she was as striking as she was beautiful. She worked as a Hollywood extra but strutted with an attitude that told people she was a star.

Motherhood wasn't high on Georgia's list of priorities. She liked men, parties, fast cars, and fancy restaurants. She preferred the high life. That she had a daughter, Cher, who turned heads on her own was almost too much for her to handle. There was room for only one beautiful woman in her life—Georgia. That explains the volatility of her and Cher's relationship. It explains why Cher was so rebellious and anxious to get out of her mom's house that she dropped out of school after the tenth grade and set out on her own.

It was a long time before I heard Cher say anything nice about her mother, but for some odd reason, I found myself defending Georgia to Cher. That was before I met her. That was before she found out about us.

For a while Georgia believed Cher was sharing an apartment with a stewardess. The few occasions her mother visited, we gathered up all my clothes and belongings and tossed them in our neighbor's place. That was a nightmare.

But it wasn't nearly as harrowing as when Cher decided to lift the complicated veil of secrecy under which we were living and introduce me to her mother. It didn't matter that our relationship was flourishing. Nor did it matter that I was a responsible, mature twenty-seven-year-old man. I was a target, a big one, and that made me as nervous as a teenager going to pick up his date before the prom.

Cher was no better. She knew her mom was going to get me; she just didn't know how. But she was primed for a fight.

In silence born of worry and anxiety, Cher and I drove from our Hollywood apartment to her mom's house in Encino, an upper-middle-class section of the San Fernando Valley. The man Cher's mother was married to at the time was a loan officer at a bank, and they were doing well by the look of their nicely manicured lawn, blooming flower beds, and the Cadillac parked in the driveway.

Cher ushered me into the house. Georgia wasn't anywhere apparent. Cher went to find her. Capitalizing on this unexpected time alone, I gave myself a quick once-over. I realized that my look wasn't the norm. Of course, not everyone could pull off long hair, a colorful paisley shirt, jeans, and sunglasses. But the overall package was darn good, and I was a nice guy.

Finally Cher walked in, her face stoic, her eyes smoldering. Her mom followed close behind—only Georgia didn't just walk into a room; she made an entrance. She swept in as if walking on a carpet of air. Her eyes glanced from side to side as if she were flanked by swarms of photographers at a gala premiere. Her clothes were a mite snazzy for the time of day, but then her entire wardrobe was geared for after six. I wondered if she even saw me.

Then she shot me a piercing glance. The smile on her lips evaporated as quickly as a drop of water on a hot griddle. Perhaps it was only a twitch. Whatever. Several more darting glances came my way as Cher and her mother made uneasy small talk. Then Georgia rose.

"Can I speak to you in the other room?" she said to Cher.

They moved into an adjoining room. Cher stood like an angry child just inside the doorway. Her back was to the wall. I wasn't able to see her mother, but I heard both of their words clearly.

"What the hell is that in the living room?" asked Georgia in a tone of voice as taut and restrained as a violin string.

"That's Sonny," said Cher.

Her mother's head peered around the corner. I saw her brows furrow and a look of disdain cross her mouth. Genius wasn't required to know what she thought of me.

"I don't like him," said Georgia. "He's not for me."

"No, he's not," countered Cher quickly. "He's my boyfriend."

After another brief exchange, they returned to the room, trying to pretend that nothing harsh had been said. Their charade didn't play well. There was too much tension for any of us to have a conversation. Finally Cher informed her mother that we had another appointment. At the door I was forced to say good-bye to Georgia, who offered her hand.

"It was interesting meeting you," she said.

"Likewise." I smiled. "I hope we can all do this again soon."

"Indeed," she said.

In the car Cher fumed. I didn't know whether to be angry, insulted, rejected, or what. I was mostly confused.

"Well, that was a disaster," I said, breaking the silence.

"No, that was my mother," said Cher.

Unfortunately, Cher's mother's opinion of me seemed chiseled in granite. As the weeks passed, her displeasure increased. One day she simply announced to Cher that they were going away together on a two-week vacation to Arkansas. Suddenly she wanted time alone with her daughter, whom she had allowed to leave home at age fifteen.

"A vacation?" I laughed when Cher passed on the news. "From what?"

"According to my mother," she scoffed, "it's a vacation from men."

But that was being kind. Their use of the plural, *men*, was as transparent as the overall game plan. Cher's mother wanted to get her daughter away from me. I read into her wariness. Georgia looked at me and saw an older man, not to be trusted. She wanted to protect Cher from this weirdo with long hair who said he was in the record business. She didn't care two whits for our sincerity. She'd been down this road before in her own life and was convinced that she already knew the outcome.

Her plan was to whisk Cher away from home and talk sense into her in an environment where Cher couldn't slam the door and run away.

They traveled to her mom's hometown in Oklahoma, but the plan backfired. Cher and I wound up missing each other more than ever. We telephoned each other dozens of times every day. I pasted eight-by-ten glossy photos of her all over the apartment.

During the two weeks Cher and her mother were gone, this girl Mimi who'd once chased me around found out where I lived. One night she showed up at my place and we had a one-night affair. I'd never liked her enough to date her, but with Cher out of town I was vulnerable to a pretty girl. We only did it that one time, but it was a bull's-eye.

A couple of months later, Mimi said that she was pregnant and claimed that I was the father. She had a little boy, Sean. I didn't argue and made a settlement. That was the last time I saw her. Mimi dated Jack Nicholson for a while, then drifted out of sight, and Sean moved out of state.

I was up front with Cher and told her everything. She didn't have much to say about it either way. She didn't get angry. She didn't lecture me. It was strange. Our relationship wasn't overly physical anyway, so maybe she felt some of the pressure was off her to perform. Years later I read a comment from Cher in which she told women not to worry if their husbands cheated. It was no big deal.

In any event, Cher's mother's vacation plans were a bust. It seemed obvious to me that Cher's mom was unfairly blaming me as the source of the many problems that plagued their relationship. In me, her mother saw all the wrongs she'd allowed men to do to her. She wanted Cher to learn from her mistakes. She wanted Cher to achieve what she hadn't been able to. In fact, that's why their relationship broke down. Georgia tried to control Cher too much.

At Georgia's insistence, Cher was enrolled in an acting class. She was ambivalent about the craft and never showed much interest in attending classes. But her mother pushed it on her as if she, Georgia, were going to derive a benefit. She implored her to study and socialize. Acting class was a safety net to fall back on. Cher went, not because she had a love of acting but so her mother wouldn't pester her about it.

"If you don't like it, quit going," I counseled one night over dinner at Martoni's. "You know that the only reason you go to that damn class is because your mother wants you to go. And half the time you skip it."

"Yeah," said Cher. "So?"

"So you have to live your own life," I said.

"But what am I going to do if I quit?" asked Cher.

"You want me to tell you?" I replied. "I can't. It's not as if I have a crystal ball."

"Yeah, I know," she said. "What do you want me to do?"

"What do I want you to do?" I asked. "Or what do I think you should do?"

"Both," she said.

"How interested are you in acting?" I asked.

"Not very," Cher responded.

"And singing?"

"I like it."

"Hmmm." I smiled. "I think you just decided the issue for both of us."

But before she broke the news to her mother, Cher bowed to pressure and moved into a Hollywood hotel for women. It was similar to New York's Barbizon Hotel, including strict curfews and rules of conduct. Cher's mom footed the bill. Cher hated the place from the first morning she woke up there, and moved out less than two weeks after checking it. Her mother hit the roof when Cher delivered her double whammy: one, that she was quitting her acting class; and two, that she was moving back in with me.

"Sonny promised that he would concentrate on my career," Cher explained to her mother in a telephone conversation I overheard.

There was a long pause while her mother argued her case. Cher steamed as she listened.

"What does he know about show business?" she asked. "For one thing, he knows a helluva lot more than you do."

Once Cher made up her mind she stuck to her decision. Ordinarily she was not very aggressive in plotting her future. Cher preferred things to happen to her rather than to take action herself. But she didn't always drift with the current. Occasionally she kicked her feet, which is what happened when she quit acting class.

In making that decision Cher was following her instincts, instincts honed for survival. She believed in me as strongly as I did in her. It was a two-way street with us. When she realized that I was committed to her welfare, she placed her trust and her future in my outstretched hands, and fully expected me to run as hard and as fast as possible. I was dedicated to her, and she knew it. For as long as we stayed together, that was the crux of our relationship.

Cher's resolve was tested right away when her mother—who else—demanded that Cher visit a psychiatrist. If she was so determined to stay with me, her mom reasoned, she must be mentally ill. Fine. We got a laugh out of that. However, Georgia didn't just want Cher to visit the shrink, she also asked that I go along. Actually, she *insisted* that I go. Okay, Cher and I agreed. We felt good about ourselves. So we figured that we would see the doc, talk, and he would share a few giggles, then tell us to get lost and stop wasting his valuable time. But . . .

"I'm going in too," announced Cher's mom, who surprised the hell out of us by walking into the waiting room as we were passing time before our appointment.

"What?" asked Cher.

Then her husband entered too.

"That's the whole idea, darling," explained her mom. "I

suggested a psychiatrist so the whole family could get together and discuss our differences."

"But . . . but," sputtered Cher.

"Cher and I don't have any differences," I answered.

"We'll see," she harrumphed.

But the only discrepancies that surfaced throughout the fifty-minute session were between me and Cher's mother. Taking the shrink's first question as her prompt, Georgia began talking as if jolted by a surge of electricity. She levied one criticism after another at me: my looks, age, profession, apartment, savings account—or lack of one—were all called into question. I felt as small as the hind leg of an ant.

"He's all wrong for you," said Georgia.

"For whom?" interjected the doctor. "It seems as if you and Sonny are not compatible. But Sonny and Cher, that's another situation."

Cher and her mother exchanged looks as different as could be. Cher's was a victorious smile. Her mother's was a venomous frown.

"Oh shit," said Cher's mom to the psychiatrist. "What the hell do you know?"

Cher and I were bound by a strong and determined love and passion. Though there weren't fireworks in our bedroom, we thought of ourselves as uniquely compatible. It was us against the world. We respected one another, shared responsibility, and relied on each other for strength and direction. We were comfortable together. We didn't analyze our relationship the way people do today. We didn't ask questions. We just lived. We hung out together. We were best friends.

One day at Goldstar studio Glen Campbell, then a hot session guitarist who played most of Spector's hits, struck up a flirtation with Cher. He hit on her several times at the studio, and she played along. Everybody knew she was my girlfriend, which is why at first I treated it as innocent fun, more like teasing. But Cher was trying to make me jealous. It worked, too. After several days my Italian pride and temper boiled over. Cher and I had it out, and then it was over.

Cher was always a tough read, and I had to learn pa-

tience rather than worry about our commitment. I learned
that if I gave her mood enough time, I usually found out
what was troubling her. Not long after Cher turned eighteen, for instance, she began acting strange. She was irrita-
ble. She didn't feel well. She didn't want to talk much. She
didn't want to go outside. I was concerned but didn't say
anything. That was the pattern we developed. It was hard,
but I waited for her to give me a hint of whatever it was
she was wrestling with.

"Son," she said matter-of-factly one morning.

"Yeah."

I was getting out of bed. She was still lying under the
covers.

"I'm pregnant."

The news stunned me. I was buckling my pants. Without
thinking, I reversed gears and took them off.

"Wow. Pregnant," I said. "That's great."

"You aren't mad?" she asked.

"Are you crazy? How can you say that? You're going
to have a baby!"

"Yeah," she smiled. "I've got a baby in me."

Although she never confided in her mother, Cher, I
thought, was fine on the idea. She rarely, if ever, expressed
abundant happiness or joy. The same held true with disappointment and anger. Cher was very complex. So I lived
with the assumption that if she was content, if there were
no problems, then Cher was happy. I was more volatile,
more expressive. However, both of us simply let life unfold
as if we were starring in an unscripted movie.

The pregnancy was just one more turn of the plot. We
stood behind it. We talked of a baby, dreamed of its future,
considered ourselves as parents, and laughed and cuddled
over the prospect of being a trio: Sonny, Cher, and . . .
well, that was a question mark.

Then Cher miscarried. It happened suddenly. She was
nine or ten weeks into the pregnancy, a couple months
along. Then without warning, she started feeling pains, and
the pains quickly grew more intense. We rushed to the
hospital. A nurse hustled us into a small, sterile room and
helped Cher up onto the table. Then a doctor came in and

quickly examined Cher, who was reeling from the spasmodic pains.

A trooper, Cher was trembling as the nurse helped place her legs in the cold metal stirrups. Tears welled up in her big eyes. I held her hand tight, stroked her cheek with my fingertips, anything to comfort her, as the doctor told us what was happening. Cher was having a spontaneous abortion. We didn't know how to react. Cher was in pain and everything happened so suddenly. The doctor performed a D&C, and I stood by, holding Cher's hand.

"Hang on, honey." I tried to soothe her. "It's going to be okay. It'll be over soon."

That real-life drama was the most intense thing that had happened to either one of us. I felt totally connected to Cher throughout the ordeal. Strangely, there wasn't a great deal of discussion between us afterward. I wanted to talk. She didn't. The dialogue, while heartfelt, went mostly unspoken. But that's Cher. If she's in pain or suffering, she doesn't talk. She retreats inward. All she wanted from me was to be there. I saw her bleed. I watched her cry. But as well as I knew her and as close as we were, it was impossible for me to know how deep her pain went.

"Can you put more emotion into it?" I asked. "Forget the mike. Sing with feeling."

It was Cher's first time in a recording studio, and singing into a microphone was bothering her. But after several takes, she adapted. We were recording two songs, "The Letter" and "Love Is Strange." My old Specialty pal Harold Battiste was producing. The session was professional, but in no way did it resemble the extravagance of the Spector productions we had worked on. No, this was bare-bones record making.

By this time, late 1963, Cher and I felt our first serious shot at stardom was long overdue. In our apartment we constantly harmonized on songs as diverse as "Walkin' the Dog" and "Old Man River" and everything else that was popular. From the week we met, I began racking my brains for some type of act Cher and I could do that would click. Then I got the idea of covering several Don and Dewey hits, music I knew, which eventually developed into this session.

Conscious that every act needed a gimmick in order to catch on, or so it seemed at the time, I dubbed us Caesar and Cleo. How did I arrive at that? The movie *Cleopatra* was out at the time and gathering some notice. Cher's long, straight hair and dreamy eyes reminded me of Cleopatra. And the best description of my haircut was a Caesar, with bangs. Ergo, Caesar and Cleo.

Vault Records released "The Letter," and Cher and I played our first gig at a roller rink. Our second performance was at a bowling alley. There wasn't a third. On record and in person, Caesar and Cleo turned out to be a gutter ball.

But we didn't get discouraged—at least I didn't. There was no time, not between promoting Phil's records, singing backup, playing percussion, doing whatever other chores Spector needed taken care of, and trying to crank up some kind of vehicle for me and Cher. I was on a nonstop merry-go-round.

I really wanted to do something big for Cher, though. It was my way of proving myself.

Cher didn't make it easy, either. Not that she complained, which she didn't. Nor did she put any pressure on me. No, I just reacted to her habit of dreaming out loud. From the time I met her, she had enormous goals. She wanted to be a star as desperately as I wanted to make her one. Before she met me, her idea of climbing the ladder was to date men who had already gotten there. Nino Tempo. Warren Beatty. She didn't have any idea how to make it on her own.

But Cher had dreams and notions. She wanted people to ask for her autograph. She practiced her signature. She practiced smiling at fans. She stood in front of a mirror and pretended to tell hordes of admirers how she didn't have the time to sign everybody's paper.

At the same time stardom didn't seem that out of reach. One afternoon we saw Sandra Dee in a store buying clothes. One outfit after another. There was no limit to what she was able to buy. Cher hated and loved seeing that display. Her knees wobbled with envy. She suffered the same reaction when Ronnie Spector was around. Ronnie was a retailer's best dream, a chronic, non-discriminating shopper. Cher couldn't stand seeing all her various outfits.

Watching Sandra Dee just underscored Cher's fervid desire to shop without regard to price. It wasn't long after we stumbled across Sandra Dee that Cher added clothes buying to her dream of stardom. The two became synonymous. Oddly, it wasn't too different from her mother's idea of stardom.

But Cher and I weren't in that league, which was hard to live with. There was no denying it—we were struggling. Still, I wanted Cher to feel equal to anybody, and unknown to her, I scrimped and saved until I had scraped together one hundred dollars. There were several pawnshops around Sunset and Vine, right near the Brown Derby restaurant. In one shop I happened upon what I thought was a striking ring—a one-karat diamond. The price was an even one hundred dollars.

I snapped it up. It was a splurge, but there was a method to my madness. The ring would please Cher. It would also satisfy Cher's mother, who believed I was dragging her daughter down into an abyss of mediocrity. The diamond was pure, unflawed, and set as a solitaire. It was a symbol.

Cher flipped when I gave it to her. Then she showed her mom. Her mother oohed and ahhed, quite impressed. I scored major points on that one. I was proud. But I failed to learn the obvious lesson: that happiness, at least when it concerned me and Cher, came with a price tag.

By mid-1964 only corpses and codgers were unaware that music was changing. The reason was explained with four seemingly ordinary names—John, Paul, George, and Ringo. Yet the Beatles was no ordinary group. Their musical impact was as immediate as it has been lasting, and their songs registered a powerful impression on the man who was directly affected by the Fab Four's arrival, my boss, Phil Spector.

Radio was never the same, and Phil knew it. He loved the Beatles. He listened to their records obsessively. Phil analyzed songs by competitors with the same scrupulousness that the Pentagon studied the Soviet Union. He was bowled over by the Beatles' simplicity and razor-sharp

97

craftsmanship. They triggered his competitiveness and sent his ultracommercial mind spinning.

"I got an idea, Sonny," he told me.

It was late at night and we were cruising through Hollywood in his Volvo, searching for a place to eat. Actually, though, Phil had no intention of eating. Driving me around was an excuse to listen to the radio and not be alone.

"What's up?" I bit.

"Can't tell you yet." He snickered. "But I think you're going to dig it."

Okay, if Phil wanted to play games, I had to play. Prying the info out of him was impossible. So I waited, and several days later he called.

"Hey, Sonny, I got a song I want to put Cher on," he said.

"Great, Phil," I replied. "What do you need, a deep backup?"

"No," he drawled, "I think I want to make it her record, you know. Have her sing lead."

The song was called "Ringo, I Love You," and I was beside myself because Phil finally decided to pluck Cher from the background chorus. The song was a novelty. Phil wrote it in an attempt to capitalize on the Beatles' enormous popularity. However, if it hit, novelty or not, the song could serve as a springboard to the stardom Cher and I coveted.

When I broke the news to Cher, she tried her best to take it in stride. But then her smile turned into a laugh, and that laugh erupted into a happy dance around the apartment.

Phil and Cher in the studio together made a potentially volatile combination. He was a perfectionist; she was an explosive package of nerves. I worried about what might happen, but with a smoothness that was contrary to both of their tendencies, "Ringo, I Love You" was recorded quickly and released on Spector's Annette label. Cher was credited as Bobbie Joe Mason, another of Phil's ideas.

Unfortunately, the entire package was not one of Phil's better projects. In fact, it was a total flop. There were numerous reasons. First, the song wasn't that good; second, Beatles fans loved Paul more than Ringo; and third, Cher sang in a voice so low that many people mistakenly thought she was a guy singing a love song to another guy. Needless to say, that wasn't the stuff that made AM radio hits.

If Cher was disappointed, though, she didn't show it. I took the loss harder than she did. I figured the Big Guy who controlled destiny allotted a person only so many swings before he began pitching to somebody else, and I couldn't even count how many times I had whiffed.

It was depressing, especially when the crowd I was hanging out with at Gold Star were all happening. Spector, Ronnie, Darlene, songwriters Jeff Barry and Ellie Greenwich, Jack Nitzsche. It took all my powers of concentration not to ask myself the question Why isn't the lucky hat falling atop my head? Why?

Only one thing gave me hope—Cher.

Many days and nights my spirits dropped so low I could have used my chin to shine my boots. But then I would catch a glimpse of Cher dancing around our apartment, singing, grooving to the radio, her long hair flying like a hot wind. I stared in wonderment at this exotic, rail-thin beauty who ended her days curled up beside me in bed like the letter S in the word sex. And it was in these private, precious moments that I found myself convinced more than ever that this leggy feline, who had popped into my life with the grace, mystery, and independence of an alley cat, had the unique spark of a great performer.

"So what do we do for an encore?" Cher wanted to know.

"Try again, babe," I answered.

The reply was glib, but it was the truth. Whatever we were missing, it wasn't for lack of effort. I knew that if we continued taking our shots, sooner or later something was going to hit.

In the meantime I was becoming uneasy about our situation. We were getting known around L.A., not through any great commercial success but through our expanding social circle. The right people were beginning to know our names, and that was good. However, in 1964 it was still taboo for unwed couples to be living together as Cher and I were doing, and that made the conservative, image-conscious promoter in me nervous. But it was impossible for us to marry.

My divorce was not yet final. I hadn't rushed to file the papers. I'd seen Christy only a few times, usually at school functions, and Donna even less. For image's sake, I downplayed my past. Once the papers were filed, it took a while to finalize the procedure.

In the interim, Cher and I fabricated a romantic tale that had us eloping to Mexico. People believed us and the story became part of the Sonny and Cher lore. It wasn't true, though. Actually, when the subject of marriage arose Cher decided that a complicated legal ceremony wasn't necessary.

"I'll marry us," she announced one afternoon.

"You'll what?" I asked, taken aback.

"Marry us." She smiled. "You'll see."

She took my arm, led me out the door, and into the street. We dashed to an Indian souvenir shop near Sunset and Vine. Rummaging through the counter bins, Cher found a basket of gold-plated rings. The store inscribed names on them for an additional 25 cents. We bought two and had our names etched on them. Then we went back home, where Cher had decided to perform the honors in the bathroom.

In blue jeans and T-shirts, we stood opposite one another in the bathroom, gazing romantically into each other's eyes—at least when we weren't checking ourselves out in the mirror. Our hands were clasped. And instead of the solemnity of a traditional wedding ceremony, bursts of laughter punctuated our vows.

"Do you, Sonny, promise to love me?" asked Cher seriously.

"I do," I said.

"And now you ask me the same question." She smiled.

"Do you, Cher, promise to love me as I do you?" I asked.

"I do," she answered. "Okay, now the rings."

We slipped rings on each other's fingers. There was a lengthy, sentimental pause while we exchanged deep, meaningful looks. Both of us were smiling.

"Can I kiss the bride now?" I asked.

Cher shut her eyes and tilted her head slightly.

"You can," she said in a feather-soft voice.

From that point on we considered ourselves married. We told people we were husband and wife and that is how we thought of ourselves. Connected, if not yet legally, in body, mind, and spirit, forever.

The same couldn't be said of my long relationship with Phil Spector. By December 1964, I knew the sound Phil pioneered with unequaled success was enjoying its last hurrah. I understood this even before he did. How? With his latest single, "Walkin' in the Rain," in hand, I delivered it straight to L.A.'s hottest AM radio station, KFWB.

As Spector's top promo man, I had followed this routine for nearly two years and ordinarily the disc jockeys grabbed the single with the eagerness of a salivating dog. It was a practice both sides had grown accustomed to. However, when the deejay played "Walkin' in the Rain," he gave me a less-than-enthusiastic look—actually, a grimace.

"You know, the thunder and the tricks and the Wall of Sound," he said, "it kinda sounds tired."

"What do you mean?" I asked, stunned.

"I mean, it's not impressing anybody anymore," he explained. "Have you heard what McCartney and Lennon are doing?"

"Yeah, I dig them," I said.

"I know. Everybody does," he said. "It's rock and roll, Dad-dy-o."

As if dazed by a sucker punch, but not really, I left the radio station, walked directly to a telephone booth, and called Phil. I didn't know what to say and at the same time I didn't want to waste any time breaking the news. I felt a responsibility to my mentor. It took half a second for Phil to get on the phone. He was anxious to hear the deejay's reaction to the single.

"Am I making money?" he asked.

"Ahhh, they're not adding it right away," I replied after a pause to collect myself.

"What?" he asked.

"It didn't get on this week," I answered.

"What'd he say?" said Phil.

That's when I made my fatal mistake. Instead of just answering Spector's question directly, and with as few words as possible, I said:

"Phil, I, we"—and I purposely used the word *we* to make what I was about to say less personal, and thereby soften the blow—"I think we should change our sound."

In retrospect I can tell myself, Okay, who were you to tell Phil Spector to change his sound? But I was his trusty confidant, his right-hand man, his connection to radio stations, which were the bread and butter of his operation. He often requested my opinion, and even when he didn't I usually gave it anyway.

However, there was too much lag time between my statement and his response. Much too long a break in conversation. Minutes of silence. And rather than hang up, I had to wait for him to say something, but the ensuing silence told me everything I needed to know.

I was out.

But that's the way it was with Spector. That morning I had been as close to Phil as one could get, part of the inner circle. Then, like others who dared to cross him with a difference of opinion, I was going to suffer the consequences. He might as well have stuck needles into a voodoo doll; I limped out of the phone booth, doomed.

The breach in our relationship was as uncomfortable for him as it was for me, but it was time for me to start moving in another direction.

7

ECSTASY

Charlie Green and Brian Stone, who became our first managers, were two of the biggest characters ever to cross my path. They had the makeup of con artists and I liked them instantly.

We met at a session someplace, and they impressed us right off as energetic guys, and they spent all that energy trying to impress us. Their moxie was matched by a prickly sense of humor. They claimed to have heard of Caesar and Cleo and expressed surprise that we didn't have a recording contract. They pumped us with so many platitudes that it was almost possible to believe that our one record had been a smash.

"You do know 'The Letter' bombed?" I asked them. "I mean, our families didn't even buy a copy."

"Oh yeah, I know," nodded Charlie.

"Then why are you giving me this pitch, which you know is total BS?" I asked.

Brian stood to the side, shaking his head.

"Forgive him," he said of his partner. "Charlie's a chronic liar. I'll tell you the truth. I heard your record. It was awful. But you two showed lots of potential."

Humored by their antics, we signed them up as our managers, then learned that these guys were scammers of the highest magnitude. Every time I went to their office, the

103

waiting room was packed with people waiting to see them. Often there were more people than places to sit. If Cher and I walked in, their secretary took us directly into their office.

"How many out there?" Charlie asked his secretary.

"Ten," she said.

"Ten?" he repeated. "Good."

Then Charlie pulled a deck of cards out of his desk, which he and Brian cut. Whoever pulled the highest card lost, requiring him to deal with one of the people waiting outside. Of course, all the people who were waiting to see them were creditors. Every one of them hoped to collect money owed them; they rarely did. Once the creditor was inside, Charlie and Brian stalled and scammed, and the same creditors returned days and weeks later to wait with the others.

Both Charlie and Brian understood where I was coming from when I talked about my goals. Cher wanted to be a star, I explained, and I wanted her to happen in a big way. They laughed when I told how she practiced her autograph and rehearsed what she was going to say when fans mobbed her. It was so naive that it was cute.

In recent years Cher has given a different interpretation of this period. She's painted me as a controlling Svengali, which really hurt me. My charge was to see Cher realize the dream that we shared. Period. If I didn't pull it off, we wouldn't last. She knew that. It was like an unspoken contract between us.

However, Cher liked portraying herself as a victim (and still does). It was her defense mechanism, an apology as well as an excuse. In the event she failed, it wasn't her fault. In reality, she never, ever came close to being victimized—at least when I was with her. She simply preferred letting somebody else chart her course, and that somebody at that time was me.

If nothing else, I knew this: When you sit in the driver's seat, you better not be afraid to drive. I wasn't.

In early 1965 I wrote "Baby Don't Go." At the time I was listening to lots of popular folk-inspired rock, including Dylan, the Byrds, and Donovan, and the song was of that genre. Inspiration stemmed from my feelings for Cher. And I had in mind that it was going to be her vinyl debut. No pseudonyms or gimmicks. Just Cher. Her voice. Her name. My role was to sit in the background and steer.

Actually, I was the producer. With Charlie and Brian, I helped scrounge up one hundred thirty-five dollars to pay for studio time and musicians. I persuaded a bunch of musician friends whom I knew from Spector sessions to work for a charitable fifteen dollars. And I brought Cher to the studio, which was not as simple as it sounds. A bad case of nerves had her insides as twisted as a strand of rope—before a single note had been struck.

"What's the matter?" I asked on the way to the RCA studio.

"I don't think I can do it," she said.

"That's silly," I said calmly. "You've sung before, you can do it again. Your voice is one dynamite groove."

"But I'm scared," she said.

"There's no reason to be scared." I smiled. "Pretend we're at home and you're singing in the living room."

It did no good. The tracks were laid without a problem, but when it came time for Cher to sing, her confidence just disappeared and her voice did likewise. A big nothing. The poor thing was so scared she vapor locked. Her throat tightened so that not a sound worth recording came out. Head bowed, knees wobbling, Cher walked out of the studio and came into the booth a defeated girl.

"I can't, Son," she said. "I can't do it alone."

"What'll it take?" I asked.

"I don't know," she answered.

"How about if I come into the studio with you?" I asked "Fine."

So we tried that. I sat in the studio while Cher sang. Or tried to sing. But that didn't work either.

"Sonny, sing with me," she suggested.

"Okay," I said.

My participation wasn't in the plan, but the money we raised was only enough to cover a single day's expenses. In other words, getting "Baby Don't Go" on tape was a now-or-never deal. Consequently, I sat in the studio and sang background to Cher's lead. Anything to finish. So she sang to me; our eyes were locked on each other, mine reassuring hers, coaching her, telling her not to worry.

"How'd I do?" asked Cher afterward, which she did after every session throughout our time as Sonny and Cher.

"Great," I said. "I'm really proud of you."

But then I wanted to know how I did. Before releasing "Baby Don't Go," which went from a Cher solo to another Caesar and Cleo record, I sought an outside opinion, one that I respected above all others. With trepidation, I played the record for Phil, who had the sharpest ear of anybody. He was uncanny when it came to spotting a hit.

"What do you think?" I asked when the needle reached the end of the acetate.

He nodded. "Pretty good."

For Phil, that was tantamount to mopping the floor with his tongue. He wasn't one to hand out compliments easily, however minuscule. But that wasn't enough for me. I wanted him to go on record. I wanted honesty, not loyalty. I wanted validation as an artist in my own right.

"You want to buy half the publishing?" I asked in an I-dare-you tone of voice.

"How much?" he said, without hesitation.

"Five hundred."

Maybe half a grand wasn't much to a millionaire like Phil Spector, but it was a lot to me. And if Phil, a shrewd businessman, really thought the song was okay, he would put up the dough.

"It's a deal," he said, taking out his checkbook.

"Jesus Christ," I exclaimed. "You really think it's a hit?"

"I hope so." He smiled. "I own half of it."

Upon its release on Reprise in early 1965, "Baby Don't Go" failed to rocket up the charts, but it didn't fade into the aural woodwork either. Unlike our previous records, the song received substantial airplay, especially in L.A., where it was a legitimate soft hit. Equally or more important, I noticed that people took an interest in Cher and me. One of the reasons was the way we looked.

The look, heavily influenced by Spector, was not as

honed as it would be six months later, though it was obvious that Cher, who wore a T-shirt and jeans as if they were Bob Mackie originals, had a natural flair for clothes. My long, stringy hair and the colorful, prehippie, neorebel outfits we wore, especially the fur-lined bobcat vests and Eskimo boots, definitely turned heads when we walked onstage.

Though "Baby Don't Go" was only a soft hit, it was enough to get us work at about two hundred dollars a night, a small fortune in those days. Working ensemble shows practically every weekend as Sonny and Cher, we performed with up-and-comers like Herman's Hermits, Chad and Jeremy, Gary Lewis and the Playboys, and guitarist Mason Williams, but our first big gig was with Ike and Tina Turner in Sacramento.

As husband and wife duos, Ike and Tina and Sonny and Cher were a striking contrast in style. Tina was already a fire-spewing dynamo onstage—mile-high legs flying, wild hair whirling, and her voice crackling like the business end of a bull whip. Ike was a tyrant. Dominating Tina onstage, he made certain the other performers knew he was talented offstage. Cher and I, meanwhile, were just learning how to do it.

In those early gigs I often had to forcibly drag Cher kicking and protesting onstage. Before one show at the Long Beach Civic Auditorium, she stood in the wings and screamed, "I can't go out there." Her body was stiff as a board. We had already been introduced and the band was playing the intro to our first song for the second time.

"What's wrong?" I demanded.

"I'm sick," she said.

"Don't you think it's a little late for this, Cher?" I asked, pissed off.

"I'm sick. I can't go out there."

"Cher, you're going out there if I have to throw you out there."

Then I grabbed her arm, led her to the middle of the stage, and she was fine. It was always a struggle to get Cher to perform, though. Throughout our performing life, she was severely frightened by the audience. She hated confronting all those faces. Look at our old performances:

Cher worked toward me, not the audience. A long-standing joke between us was when she confessed her idea of an ideal show to me.

"The audience would quickly walk by the dressing room," explained Cher, "and say hello. I'd ask what they thought of my dress, then they'd leave the money in a cigar box and get the hell out of there."

Ironically, it was I, not Cher, who succumbed to debilitating nerves in our first important gig. We were booked into the Purple Onion, a small Hollywood club owned by Cher's uncle. Charlie and Brian had convinced Nesuhi Ertegun, the brother of Atlantic Records president Ahmet Ertegun, to scout us as a possible act on the label. Lots of friends and family watched too.

It was our first showcase. I was so keyed up that I took a shot of whiskey. I never drank before shows, and I rarely drank, period. But I didn't feel anything from the first one, so I downed another. Same reaction. Then I repeated the procedure a third time and walked onstage. That's when it hit me. Fighters say the legs are the first to go, and so it was with me. Drunk, my legs wobbled like a bowl of Jell-O, and midway into the first song, I collapsed.

The rest of the performance followed suit, and needless to say, we didn't get signed. Afterward, I sat in the dressing room, sweating and horribly depressed. The opportunity was there and I blew it. Cher stood outside the dressing room, talking with her mother, who then came in and flashed me an I-told-you-so look.

"Well?" I asked.

"A lot of people said you were good," she said. "But if you ask me, Cher doesn't need you."

"Thanks," I sighed. "Thanks a lot."

I was crushed. But I learned a lesson. That was the first time I ever took a belt, and I never did again.

Neither Cher nor I was ever into drugs or booze. For me, I never liked the feeling of being out of control. Cher was even more adamantly opposed to substances than I was, but her reason was more personal. Her father, Johnny, was a drug addict who had left home when she was very young.

Cher never forgave him, though after we established ourselves, Johnny occasionally worked for us as a road manager. Whenever he was clean, we hired him. Though Johnny and Cher's relationship was as cold as an iceberg, I found him a funny and entertaining man. He had done time in jail, so he was often accompanied by a probation officer. Unfortunately, his was a real hard, insensitive brute, who seemed to delight in humiliating John. It made you feel for the guy and understand why he would think about using again.

Anyway, Cher has always described her dad as an ogre, while painting herself as a victim. But she hardly saw him, even during those times when he was traveling with us. At his worst he was unstable, but he never did anything bad.

John had suffered many ups and downs too, but somewhere along the way, he straightened himself out and married a wealthy woman in Santa Barbara. Even in the mid seventies after our divorce, he and Cher remained estranged. But he kept in touch with me. He called occasionally and invited me to ride horses or just chew the fat.

What John really wanted, though, was to know how his daughter and Chastity were doing. He missed them, and Cher never took or returned his calls. Then one day he called with bad news.

"I've got cancer, Sonny," he said. "I'm going to die."

"Gee, John," I answered. "I'm awfully sorry to hear that, you know. Is there anything I can do for you?"

"Yeah, if you can," he said. "I really want to say good-bye to Cher and the baby. Can you help me out?"

"I'll try, man. I'll try."

I did try relaying the message too. Many, many times. But Cher didn't want to hear the message, so she didn't respond. By that time Cher and I were on the outs, and if she doesn't want to talk to somebody, it's impossible to break through all the protective barriers that buttress her from the outside world. That's the way she was with her father. Despite his efforts, I believe, he died without getting to say good-bye to either Cher or Chastity.

In spring 1965 we were going someplace, even if it was

only up and down the California coast. During one stretch, we performed thirty shows in forty-five days, touring with groups like the Dave Clark Five and the Animals. It was a vibrant, exciting period for rock and roll, and everybody on these tours spent their free time checking out everybody else's records. The best part, though, was payday. Cher and I were now taking in three hundred to three hundred fifty dollars a night, banking roughly two or three grand a month.

We were rich.

Rich enough at least to move from our tiny Franklin Street apartment into a funky hillside house in Benedict Canyon. I bought an old upright piano at a used furniture store for fifty dollars, then stuck it in the garage downstairs. It was too damn heavy to lug into the house. The arrangement was perfect, though. After Cher went to bed, I snuck downstairs to the piano and wrote, which was good since I didn't like Cher to hear anything until it was finished.

There was no bigger thrill than writing a new song during the quiet of the night and then playing it for her the next morning. Cher was an appreciative audience, and I treated these freshly brewed previews as if I were presenting her a little box with a diamond inside.

Though each song was a little gem—or so I thought—I was baffled by the lack of buyers. Sure, there was a slight buzz. After "Baby Don't Go" charted locally, Reprise, the label on which the single was released and a subsidiary of Warner Brothers, had us record a four-song demo. Two of their hotshots, Mo Ostin, who now heads Warner, and Joe Smith, currently president of Capitol Records, produced. I expected them to sign us soon after. They didn't.

Then one morning Charlie Green called. This wasn't long after I had blown our showcase for Atlantic's Nesuhi Ertegun.

"You gonna tell me Capitol's ready?" I asked a bit over-confidently.

"No," said Charlie.

"Oh." Then I didn't know why he was calling. "What do you want?"

"I was speaking with Ahmet Ertegun," he said. "He says he knows you. That so?"

It was. I'd met Ahmet, the president of Atlantic Records, while I was at Specialty. At that time, Atlantic was essentially a rhythm-and-blues label, though when they struck pay dirt with Bobby Darin, Ahmet immediately started to sign more white acts. We were recipients of Ahmet's philosophic turnabout. Charlie told me that the label chief liked "Baby Don't Go" and recognized me as Caesar and thought Cher had talent.

"I told him that you guys don't have a contract with Reprise," said Charlie. "Ahmet couldn't believe it. He wants to put you on Atco."

"He wants to sign us?" I asked. "With no demos? No hits?"

"Just your personalities." He chuckled. "And, of course, mine and Brian's."

Then Ahmet flew out from New York to meet us. He was full of encouragement, and we were impressed—as much with him as with the five thousand-dollar advance he offered. He wanted to release product immediately. Fortunately, we had several unused masters to hand over. Ahmet liked "Just You," which became our first single for our new label. It was also our official vinyl debut as Sonny and Cher.

The song was not quite a bomb, more like a bomb that didn't explode—merely a dud.

We were disappointed but not dejected, because we knew this wasn't a one-shot deal. Ahmet was prepared to try again, and quickly. At the same time, several other labels, including Liberty and Imperial, approached us. I knew everybody in the business then, and for some reason Cher and I were hot. When informed by Charlie and Brian that we were already signed, Imperial returned with a clever offer.

"Let us sign Cher," said Bob Skaff, the label's president.

"What do you think, Son?" asked Brian.

"Are they offering money?" I said.

"Five gees," he said.

"Then what are you asking me for?" I laughed. "Take it!"

Cher was more confident, though not by much, than when recording "Baby Don't Go" and insisting I sit in the studio with her and sing backgrounds to her lead; her solo debut, a cover of Bob Dylan's "All I Really Want to Do," went fine. Singing the high and the low parts, Cher's rendition generated an immediate response—not from the record buyers but from Atlantic's president.

"You're on that record, aren't you, Sonny?" asked Ahmet, who, like many others, believed I was singing too, and was thereby in violation of our contract with him.

"No I'm not," I said.

Ahmet laughed. "Look, I'm not going to do anything about it, but you're on the record. Right?"

"I swear to God, Ahmet, I'm not. Cher sang both the parts."

I still don't know if Ahmet, one of the sweeter, more honorable men in the music industry, ever believed me. It didn't matter. The point was moot, especially compared to the difference of opinion that developed on the eve of the release of the second Sonny and Cher single.

In a session done shortly before signing with Atco, I wrote and produced Cher and me singing "It's Gonna Rain." I never believed much in the folky tune, so I kind of stuck it on the shelf and forgot about it. Something made me play it for Ahmet, though, and he thought "It's Gonna Rain" was the greatest record he had heard in years. I was baffled, but he wanted to release it as the A side of our next single.

"I think it's a mistake," I argued. "I like the B side much better. Everybody does."

That was an understatement. There are times when all the desperate strings of the tapestry you are trying to weave come together magically. It is impossible to explain why. You aren't doing anything different than before, but for some inexplicable reason, everything gels. At those times, it is best to be either at the crap tables or the piano, which is where I was when I wrote "I Got You Babe."

Actually, the song came quickly, in one energetic spurt, as did most of my songs. Sitting at the kitchen table, I began absentmindedly scribbling lyrics on the back of a sheet of cardboard I plucked from some laundry just back from the cleaners. When it was about half done, I went downstairs and completed the song in about an hour. Then I sprung it on Cher, who grabbed the cardboard from the piano and grinned, "I'm going to save this forever."

Occasionally you write a song, don't think much of it and then, surprise, it explodes. But other times you know, absolutely, without a doubt, the song is solid gold waiting to happen. That's the type of enthusiasm Cher and I had about "I Got You Babe." We knew. We couldn't race to the studio fast enough to record it.

The electricity flowed at an even higher voltage at the sessions; everybody from Charlie and Brian to Cher to our pianist, Leon Russell, was blown away by what was being created. That's the amazing part of the recording process—when everybody from the artists to the songwriters to the musicians on down to the studio's receptionists can't control themselves from dancing and singing and pinching themselves at hearing a hit song as it's first created. That was the case with "I Got You Babe."

But then Ahmet and I disagreed on which song to release as the single. He really loved "It's Gonna Rain." I liked "Babe." I tried persuading him otherwise, but nothing I said caused him to change his opinion. He was the boss, after all. Still.

Unsuccessful in arguing with Ahmet, I decided to go out on a limb and prove to him I was right. Atco was already promoting "It's Gonna Rain" when I cut an acetate of "I Got You Babe" and offered it as an exclusive to KHJ, a red-hot radio station in L.A. that trumpeted itself as Boss City. It was sneaky as well as risky but, I thought, worth it.

The deejays loved the song and began playing it immediately.

It was like a rocket launch. The station's switchboard lit up instantly. Within a week, the song was tops in L.A., and Ahmet and Atco switched gears, pulled "It's Gonna Rain," and jumped on "I Got You Babe." By mid-July it seemed as if the entire listening world, at least from the United States to England, knew of Sonny and Cher.

In three alarmingly streamlined, whirlwind weeks—a scant twenty-one exciting days that flew by like calendar pages blown by a gale-force wind—"I Got You Babe" sold more than three million records around the world and ricocheted straight to number one on the charts both at home and abroad.

To say that Cher and I were beside ourselves doesn't even begin to describe the experience of instant fame. No, it descended on us more like a lethal injection. My goal had always been success; Cher's had been fame. Suddenly, overnight it seemed, we had both.

On the one hand, we were no different than we had been just days earlier. We lived in our little house in Benedict Canyon. We didn't have much money. We did our errands, went out for meals. Yet we were different. The wave we caught was a monster. A commotion followed us around the clock. People knew us, gawked, asked for the autographs Cher had been practicing for so many years, and generally added to a euphoria that rose seemingly without limits.

There was one night after an extremely hectic, disruptive day when Cher and I collapsed, utterly exhausted, on our bed. Both of us stared up at the ceiling, listening to the quiet as if it were the first time we had heard it. We inhaled deeply. There's no single prescription for coping with instant success. You just go with it. You try to keep your head, but it blows your psyche. No way about it. Confidence oozes. Your ego boomerangs. Suddenly I thought I had a handle on the formula. I knew how to do it—to produce and write—and what was happening was the validation I had been searching for since the day I gave "Ecstasy" to Johnny Otis.

However, in the silence of our bedroom, lying on the bed, Cher and I turned to each other and smiled. It was a moment of confession and honesty, a moment of bared souls. We were fortunate. We were experiencing something remarkable, a dream come true, and we had each other to share it. We started to hum, then sang, the lyrics to our song.

"I got you babe."

I looked at Cher. She grinned at me. We started to laugh.

"We did it," I said. "We pulled the wool over their eyes."

"Yeah," said Cher. "We did."

We snuggled closer and listened to ourselves sing. The music drew us closer. It was a moment of extreme tenderness, togetherness. We listened to the lyrics. We hummed the music.

We really loved each other.

8

WE GOT US, BABE

It was mid-August 1965. With "I Got You Babe" topping the charts, we flew into New York City for a week-long media blitz, hitting Manhattan with the subtlety and force of a thunderstorm. A rabid, screaming, hysterical mob greeted us at Kennedy International airport. People stared at us, in our jeans, fur-lined vests and boots, and long hair, as if we were sideshow freaks. The excitement was thick and palpable. Hundreds screamed, "Sonny! Sonny! Cher! Cher! Oh my God, they're real!"

It was real and then it wasn't, but it was really neat. Having long felt we were living our own private movie, we enjoyed being on display.

Cher and I were whisked into a long, black stretch limousine. Our managers followed. The plan was to drive to the city, check into the hotel, and then begin the rounds of television, radio, and print interviews. Charlie and Brian had hired a publicist, who sat in the back of the limo, briefing us on the itinerary. As was our pattern, I paid close attention, while Cher stared out the window.

After a twenty-minute drive into Manhattan, the limo pulled up in front of the Americana Hotel, attracting several uniformed doormen as if they were ants drawn to sugar. Cher and I climbed out, anxious to check in to our room and take a nap before climbing aboard the PR whirligig.

We anticipated a frenzy of fan reaction at the hotel but not the reception that waited for us. For one, the older doorman practically recoiled in disgust as we got out of the car. The bellmen snickered. But the lowest, absolute worst was the arrogant manager behind the front desk. As we attempted to register, Charlie and Brian giving our names as well as our reservations, the tweedy little man studied his records and then looked up at us, completely mystified by our presence at the hotel.

"I'm sorry"—he grimaced—"but I can't seem to locate your reservation and—"

"It was made two weeks ago," interrupted Charlie.

"And, as I was about to say"—he cleared his voice—"we are completely booked up."

I started to laugh. The situation pissed me off, but at the same time I found it humorous.

"What's the real problem here?" I asked. "I mean, come on. You guys don't lose reservations to a two-hundred-fifty-dollar-a-night suite. So level with me, huh, Pierre?"

For a moment his face turned into a tight, pensive, impenetrable mask. He blinked, closing his eyes for so long I wondered if he had fallen asleep. Then he gave me and Cher the longest once-over in history. Cher, not one for any type of confrontation, withdrew into herself, while I nearly burst out laughing.

"We have rules," he finally said. "Here at the Americana, we serve a certain class of people."

"Look," I said, losing my temper. "I've—no, we've all—been perfectly nice and understanding. We've taken your stupid insults about the way we look with a sense of humor. But we made a reservation weeks ago. We're tired. Just give us the room, we'll give you money. OK?"

"It would be, sir," he huffed, "if I did have a reservation. But, as I said before, we don't, and the hotel is booked."

We climbed back into the limo and stayed at Ahmet Ertegun's that night. When I thought about what had happened, it was remarkable. We had been thoroughly entertained, and we had been in the city only two hours.

But as they say: When you're hot, you're hot. Within

hours of getting the boot at the Americana, our publicist was on the phone with every newspaper columnist and TV station in the city. That night Sonny and Cher were at the top of the news. The following morning we were headlines. From nowhere, Sonny and Cher exploded into the public's consciousness. Suddenly we weren't merely pop music's flavor of the week, we were *the* class couple for the love-bead generation.

Later, Charlie and Brian were accused of having staged that entire incident as a publicity stunt. All I can say is, they should have been so clever. It was a sign of the times. How do I know? Because the same thing happened again.

No sooner did we return from New York than Cher and I were scheduled to make our first visit to England. Thanks to Liverpool's Fab Four and a troupe of followers, including rock's naughtiest band, the Rolling Stones, who mounted the biggest invasion of the States since the Redcoats in 1776, London was the center of everything hip in music. You weren't "in" unless you made it there.

Cher was more than nervous about going; she absolutely didn't want to make the trip. A white-knuckle flier who sickened at the faintest thought of being airborne, she wasn't particularly keen on the notion of spending nine hours in a plane, half of that flying over the ocean. Neither was she especially excited by the prospect of being in Europe. Not only was Cher a stickler about control, and hence her fear of airplanes, she was frightened by anything about which she wasn't familiar, such as a foreign country.

"Why don't you want to go?" I asked.

"I just don't," she replied tersely.

"Come on, Cher," I snapped. "That's not a reason. Give me a reason why you don't have to go to London. I mean, for Christ's sake, we've got a top-ten record there. How bad could it be?"

"Well"—she gulped—"I have this feeling . . ."

"I know," I interrupted. "That you're going to die."

"It's possible." She turned away.

Frustrated, I didn't know whether to laugh or scream at her. Cher was still totally convinced that she wasn't going to live past age thirty. Why thirty, I don't know. But she was a blend of hypochondria and fatalism. Disease or disaster, it didn't matter; Cher saw herself as the consummate victim, and thus had no problem imagining herself felled by a gruesome, painful, and above all else, dramatic death—tumors, cancer, hemorrhages, heart attack, car accident, or plane crash.

"We're going," I said with a finality that didn't allow for any discussion. "I'm going, and *you're* going, too."

Cher acquiesced, but not without first being tranquilized into a blissful state. The smile plastered on her otherwise expressionless face foretold that everything was OK. That was fortunate, because the scene at the Los Angeles airport was beyond our wildest imagination. The traffic was stopped. Mobs filled the terminal so full that the police and fire officials had cordoned it off. Because of us, business had ground to a halt.

"What's going on?" asked a mystified Cher as we were ushered by muscle-bound bodyguards through the screaming throngs.

"It's wild, huh, Cher?" I grinned. "A total groove, don't you think?"

"It's too much," she said. "It's scary."

"This is what you wanted, babe. This is what you've been dreaming about. These people love you."

"I can't handle it, Son. It's too much."

The intensity was a bit much, but calm descended on us once the plane departed. Then it was nine hours of somnolent, overseas flying and trying to catch our breath. The landing was a bumpy one, though. Whisked through a frenzied crowd at the airport, we arrived at the Hilton in a confused state of euphoria and exhaustion. The travel, the time change, the tranquilizers, the fans—we didn't know which way was up or down, and then the Hilton, like the Americana, refused us a room.

That was all Cher needed. She wanted to go back home. Immediately. She was scared. She was tired of being stared at. "The hell with England," she kept saying.

"It'll get better," I reassured her. "It's all gonna work for us."

No soothsayer, I was, however, right. Unable to check into any other hotels, we camped out in the luxurious London flat owned by Ahmet Ertegun and immediately began doing the town. Our days were consumed by interviews and TV shows, while the nighttime was spent in mod clubs. One night we hung out with Rod Stewart and the Small Faces. Another night we were chumming around with Twiggy. There was talk that in one club John Lennon hit on Cher, but the truth is we never met any of the Beatles on that trip. They were busy promoting *Help!*

At every corner, it seemed, my eyes bugged out in genuine excitement. Cher, on the other hand, hated the entire experience. The barometer of her unhappiness: she couldn't even muster up the enthusiasm to go shopping. Still, with the trip intended to be business as much as pleasure, she didn't have time to sulk in our flat. If our publicists didn't have us running around London, I did. For thirty-five thousand dollars I hired a documentary film crew to follow us everywhere—from pubs to Buckingham Palace to train stations to London Bridge to our bedroom. I didn't know what use we would put the film to, maybe a TV special, a movie, something. I liked the idea of turning our songs into little movies, the same idea that spawned MTV two decades later. But music videos still weren't a commodity and somehow the film was lost. To this day, all that film, thousands of feet of Sonny and Cher romping throughout England, remain unaccounted for.

In the meantime, "I Got You Babe" shot up on the English charts, taking over the number one spot for two weeks. Surprisingly, especially in light of how tame we really were compared to other groups, Sonny and Cher, for a certain period, were as controversial as they were hot. Nancy Sinatra, of all people, called us clowns. But she wasn't alone. Our look was so costumey that we were outraging people. We were called hippies. I was labeled a fag, some idiots tagged us commies. It was crazy. Somebody remarked to Charlie, our manager, "That's a nice circus act you've got."

"Yeah," he replied, echoing our overall sentiment, "I'm going to make big stars out of those clowns. Make a lot of money off them too."

Them weren't just fighting words, they were true. Not only were Sonny and Cher recognizable, name-brand stars but I realized after returning from England that we were also worth a good sum more than pocket change. We were holed up in the Hampshire House, one of the finest hotels in New York, which was an interim stop for us between London and L.A. Our feet still hadn't hit the ground since "Babe" exploded. The crazed fans, popping flashbulbs, meetings, interviews, TV shows, meetings with celebrities, hearing our song everywhere, it added up to one big blur.

While Cher half-dozed on the bed, I sat at the table in our suite, sipping coffee and staring out the window at the bustle of Manhattan below me—honking taxis, rivers of people pounding the sidewalks. Central Park, and needle-like skyscrapers puncturing a clear blue sky. As I looked down on all this, what amounted to daily life parading right by me, I was overwhelmed by a pleasantly detached feeling of position and power, and it somehow brought everything Cher and I had experienced the past month to a crystal head: We were on top of the world.

"Hey, Cher, you sleeping?" I asked, turning toward her.

"No, not really," she said.

"You know what I just figured out, babe?"

"What?"

"With royalties and money owed us, we're worth more than a hundred thousand dollars."

"What did you say?" said Cher, who bolted up in bed, smiling.

"One hundred thousand dollars!" I smiled too. "That's how much money we've got."

To us, that figure might as well have been twenty million dollars. I kept repeating it, and Cher kept listening. Suddenly we imagined ourselves being so rich. With that much money in the bank, it seemed as if your troubles were over for life. One hundred thousand dollars. It was too much to fathom in one quick shot, and so, rather than rush out and buy something extravagant just to prove we could, Cher and I lounged in our plush hotel room, savoring the smell of real money as if it were the bouquet of superior red wine.

Our restraint lasted less than twenty-four hours. The next afternoon Cher was in the stores. Her longtime aspiration was to buy clothes and sign autographs, and it took her about half a minute to create utter havoc along Fifth Avenue. Not only did she parcel out her signature, she achieved her goal by spending the previously unheard-of sum of five hundred dollars in one store. I had never seen Cher so elated as when she returned to the hotel, her arms holding numerous shopping bags and her head full of memories of being besieged by autograph hounds.

That was everything she had wanted, and everything I had wanted to provide for her. If she wasn't happy, Cher was at least content. I felt as if I had hit a home run.

Returning to L.A. in a state of euphoria, we decided to splurge, big-time. Cher wanted a house, and it was my desire to give her whatever she wanted. Within days of our arrival, Cher turned the long, painstaking process of house hunting into a single-day's effort. The house she found and then described to me as *the* house that she *had* to have was, not coincidentally, located in Encino, a couple blocks away from her mother's house.

"You sure you want to live there?" I asked. "So close to her?"

"That's the house," she affirmed. "I can't see us living in any other."

"But your mom," I hinted.

"She'll love it," smiled Cher.

I understood what was unspoken. Cher and her mom were intensely competitive, which was part of their problem in the first place. By purchasing a home around the corner from her mom, Cher wasn't just announcing her arrival, she was driving the point home with a row of exclamation points. We were delighted, though. Owning a home was a big win, and owning one in an affluent neighborhood made Cher and I feel of equal or better status than all those who ridiculed us for looking different than the norm.

The house was our parcel of the American dream.

Yet there were times when I got the distinct impression that Cher and I were perceived as more nightmare than dream.

Shortly after we laid stakes in our new home Cher and I went to Martoni's for dinner. The industry watering hole was our longtime stomping ground, the only place in L.A. that had allowed me to sign for a meal when I didn't have the cash flow to cover dinner out. We hadn't been there for months, the craze of "Babe" having kept us off the regular circuit. When we got there, I was delighted to find my old charge account was still good.

Going to Martoni's was like attending a club meeting, a very prestigious club, the Spago of its day. Everybody in the record business was there, and the gossip was as plentiful as the Parmesan cheese. Sammy Davis might be at one table, Sinatra at another, the rest of the place crowded with managers and promotion and A&R guys. I saw Sam Cooke eating dinner there the night he died.

"Hey, Sonny," he said, stopping by my table on his way out, "ya doin' all right, man?"

"Can't complain," I said. "Working for Spector."

"Top cat," he said.

Several hours later Sam Cooke, a huge star, was dead. Shot by the manager of the Hacienda Motel under circumstances that have remained murky to this day.

Cher and I had experienced our share of taunts and run-ins there. One night Christine Jorgenson, the first person to undergo a sex change operation, was there with two sleazy kids. As she passed by our table, she sneered. We overheard her tell her companions, "Look at those two phonies. Hollywood's full of them." However, those incidents were an exception, and almost every one occurred before we were widely known.

Yet this one particular evening, having just returned from promoting "I Got You Babe," we walked into the joint dressed in our usual attire of bell-bottoms, vests, wild, patterned shirts, jewelry, and boots. It shouldn't have been a big deal, since we had been dressing in that style for as long as we had been eating at Martoni's. But the enticing smell of simmering garlic and butter wasn't the only greeting we received as we walked into the restaurant.

"I didn't know they served fags here," said a man, though I was unable to see exactly who he was.

I heard similar comments nearly every day, and it was my practice to let them go. We heard jeers so often that eventually they didn't mean anything. Actually, I also knew that there was some value to causing such a ruckus, and I didn't want to let that go. But this was different, I could tell.

After Cher and I were seated, the name-calling began again. There was an angry, violent tone to it. Cher was uneasy. I looked around, trying to locate the source. It wasn't hard. Another insult came my way. "Faggot." Three very large football players, college guys with red, meaty faces and buzz haircuts, were staring me straight in the eye with bloodshot looks that wanted to kill. Having located the culprits, I attempted to ignore them. I figured, Why add fuel to the fire?

"Hey, faggot!" one of them called again, this time loud enough to cause others at nearby tables to put down their knives and forks and stare. "Who's the hooker? I never would've guessed you like girls."

Okay, that was going too far. Having pushed us beyond our substantial ability to tolerate rudeness, I needed every ounce of strength to restrain myself. Cher saw in my eyes that I was on the verge of exploding. She was equally nervous and uncomfortable but didn't want a scene. Figuring a barroom-type brawl was about to erupt, she decided to extinguish the fire—or at least try.

"Hey, look," she said to the three guys, having walked over to their table. "Please, cut it out. Please."

"Whatcha you gonna do to us, baby?" one sneered, while his buddies laughed.

"Please," insisted Cher. "Don't do this anymore because my husband has a lot of friends—"

"Yeah?" they interrupted. "He has friends?"

"And they can kill you," finished Cher.

Her advice sent them into hysterics. A real ugly scene was developing. I called Tony Riccio, one of the partners and a poker buddy of mine, over to the table and politely asked him to move the three assholes who were bothering us. He refused. I don't know why, but he did. That was fine with me. If he didn't want to help diffuse the situation, then I would handle it myself.

There were a couple of guys eating at a table in the back corner whom I knew. Casual acquaintances of mine, they often said they made their living in brass—knuckles, that is. After a brief discussion with them, I returned to my table, feeling satisfied that justice would be done. On my way back, I passed by the three jerks who were causing all the trouble and flashed them an overconfident smirk.

"That's it," one of them snapped, rising from his seat, and rising, and rising some more. Standing six feet, seven inches, he never stopped getting up. Or so it seemed. He was going to pulverize me. His friends were gloating. But what none of them knew was that my friends ate guys like them for breakfast. I looked toward the back of the restaurant and flashed a signal. My pals walked over and sat down at their table just as the waiter set their meals down.

"You're not really hungry," one of my friends said to the three helmet-heads.

"We aren't?" One of them looked up.

"No," he was told. "You aren't."

"Then what are we?"

I heard a thump on the table. It sounded like metal. I didn't bother to look.

"You're on your way home. That's what you are."

The message was received, if not loud then clear. Without hesitating, they walked out of the restaurant like shamed puppies, their heads bowed and tails between their legs. Unfortunately, we followed. Tony Riccio didn't like what he had seen and blamed us. I tried arguing, but to no avail.

"Sorry," he explained. "but you guys are always getting into trouble."

"But we didn't start it," I said.

"Doesn't matter," said Tony. "I don't want you and Cher coming back here anymore."

"I can't believe you're doing this to me." I shook my head.

Tony just shrugged.

Getting kicked out of the Americana and the London Hilton was one thing, but after what happened at Martoni's I was truly disappointed and hurt. The drive home was a depressing one. The confrontation had sapped her strength, and Cher went directly to bed. I sat in the kitchen and fumed. After a while, though, I decided being angry at such stupidity and prejudice was a waste of good time. Then an idea popped into my head and I hurried downstairs to the piano.

The next day, a crisp September afternoon, I was in the studio recording "Laugh at Me," the song I had written the previous evening. It was my retort—both sincere and sarcastic—to all the simpleminded goons who gawked at us. Cher loved the song when I played it for her the next morning. She also approved the idea of releasing it as a Sonny Bono solo, an idea that struck most people as odd.

But it seemed perfectly natural to us. Any other sensible group would have followed up a hit like "I Got You Babe" with a similar effort. We didn't, but only because "Laugh at Me" sounded better with me singing it alone. So we decided, "The hell with what we're supposed to do. Let's follow our instincts."

Fortunately, the rocket ride "Babe" had put us on was still streaking at supersonic speed. Whatever we touched was destined to succeed. In early fall 1965 I recorded "Laugh at Me." Three days later it was released; within five days, it reached the U.S. top ten and number nine in the United Kingdom. There were plenty of other things going on in the world more important than Sonny and Cher, but the frenzy that surrounded us made it seem otherwise.

The end of 1965 was a Sonny and Cher feeding frenzy. Everybody we had ever worked for capitalized on our success. On the heels of "Laugh at Me," Phil Spector released "Home of the Brave," a forgettable single by Bonnie and the Treasures. With Cher and me singing backup, it charted at seventy-seven. In October Reprise reissued "Baby Don't Go," and though that song had failed everywhere but L.A., it raced to eighth position in the United States and eleven in England. Atco even rereleased our debut single "Just You," which hit number twenty.

In mid-October we released our debut album, *Look at Us*. Right away it soared up the charts, peaking at number two domestically, number seven abroad. The success was blowing us away. With nothing to hold on to, we enjoyed the ride.

The success was everything Cher and I had ever dreamed of, and more. We had a slew of smash records, including a chart-topping single and a number-two album. We owned a house. Cher and I were world-famous. Yet the strange part about the whirlwind was that deep down I never trusted any of it. Whenever I thought of myself as a song-writer, producer, and singer, I compared myself to artists like Spector and Brian Wilson, people I considered true geniuses, and I got the willies.

Oh man, I wondered, am I in this league or what? The scary part was I knew the answer. I wasn't a writer, nor was I a singer or producer. I didn't even play an instrument, since five chords on the piano wasn't really playing. No, when push came to shove, I was faking it. I knew it.

I just wondered how long I could continue the charade.

"But we aren't fakes," I insisted, examining my long hair and buckskin vest. "This is really who we are."

I was sitting opposite a William Morris agent, who was trying to explain how Cher and I might want to consider altering our appearance.

"I'm talking longevity now," he said. "This long hair and stuff, it puts people off. It's a style. And styles change."

"Naw, you don't get it," I disagreed. "It's a do-your-own-thing kind of world, and this is our thing."

That discussion went back and forth for some time. The agent didn't get us. He didn't understand the culture. Cher and I weren't hippies; we weren't even close. We didn't do drugs, we didn't drink, we weren't protest singers. How-ever, we did identify with everything that the sixties youth culture represented. We supported peace and love and em-braced the idealism of the time. The culture preached a belief in humanity and the possibility of a more harmonious world. We were happy to spread the gospel that the times were a-changin'. The agent didn't understand.

But that didn't stop Hollywood's money men from mak-ing a beeline to our doorstep. In our favor, Cher and I weren't threatening. We were married. We were polite. We were also profitable. Once the big money was there, the sharks started circling as if we were chumming the waters. That's when I learned the lesson every performer learns: It's when those guys—the agents, the publicity guys, the managers, and advisors—start coming around that the trouble begins. They all start talking to you, telling you what they can do for you, and it's tough to resist.

Pretty soon, though, those guys who didn't want to know you when you were broke are calling the shots. The freedom and independence you enjoyed when struggling to make it disappear. Your identity goes the same way. Instead of the original goal of making music, the end becomes making money. It's a hard shot to call. The talk is sweet and enticing. But the minute these guys latch onto you, you are dead, gone, and likely to be forgotten.

Of course, when you are riding a bubble like Sonny and Cher were, there is no time to do much long-range thinking. The ever-increasing heights made us dizzy. At the start of 1965, we couldn't buy our way onto Shindig, the popular music-television show, but by midyear they were begging us to appear. Within months we went from sharing the marquee at the Hollywood Bowl with the Mamas and the Papas and Dean Martin, to selling out the Bowl by ourselves in less than twenty-four hours.

But fame was not measured just by what happened onstage. What went on offstage mattered as well. One weekend I got a long-distance phone call; the connection was poor and I had a difficult time making out what the caller was saying. His English accent was all I could hear. After asking the caller's name a half-dozen times, I was about to hang up when the connection suddenly cleared.

"It's Mick!" screamed the caller. "Mick Jagger!"

"Oh!" I laughed, embarrassed. "Sorry. I couldn't hear you."

"It's that rock'n roll, mate," he joked.

Mick and I knew each other from several years back. The Rolling Stones had recorded "Shut Up, Sit Down," a song I had written with Rowdy Jackson. They had always amused me. In the early days, Spector, Nitzsche, and I thought we were the revolutionaries; the Stones, we thought, were the grubbies, dirty-looking kids. But for all their posturing and pouting, they played hot, old-fashioned blues-based rock, the kind of music that I had loved since I was a teenager.

Mick's call had a purpose. The Stones were coming to Los Angeles and they wanted to crash at our house—at least Mick and Keith did. Five guys in our one bedroom wouldn't fit, so we somehow diverted them to a hotel. Never having met them, Cher and I didn't know what to expect. We figured something between haughty stars and dangerous animals. The next day Mick and Keith invited us to a concert that night in San Bernardino.

Cher and I rode out there on the group's bus. We weren't drinkers, but the Stones certainly were—Jack Daniel's preferred—and they wasted no time in transforming an otherwise boring two-hour ride to the desert into a boisterous party. Neither Cher nor I could imagine going onstage in the condition the Stones were in when they finally spilled out of the bus. However, they set us on our ear when they played their kicking-butt music like nobody's business.

It was the first time I had been to a concert where the crowd went berserk. Several days later I ran into Brian Wilson, the Beach Boys' mastermind, at Western Studios, where he recorded in the same compulsive style as Spector. Both men were in complete awe of each other. With uncharacteristic enthusiasm, I told Brian about the Rolling Stones concert I had seen.

"The kids were absolutely nuts," I said.

"Oh, they do that for us," he replied, unimpressed.

"But man, you should've seen the way the girls were acting up," I said. "Screaming, carrying on."

"That happens at our concerts," he said. "Dennis has to peel 'em off like fly paper."

A few more comments like that and I got the message. Brian was defensive. He didn't want to be upstaged by the Stones. Back then Brian considered himself the top dog, and, blue-collar craftsman that he was, he wasn't about to relinquish any part of what he considered his rightful throne to a bunch of scabby English boys. The Beach Boys enjoyed a certain amount of attention then, but I don't think Brian felt he got recognition for what he was capable of doing.

He and Spector were remarkably alike. Both were eccentric geniuses possessed by a compulsive, extremely competitive drive to be king. Neither ever rested, nor did they like to hear of successes by other people. Both destroyed themselves too. Paranoia bested Spector, while Brian succumbed to the drugs that people told him would take him to further heights. In 1966 word went around town that while Brian was recording "Fire," a song for an unreleased album called *Smile,* he insisted that all the musicians wear firemen's helmets. From then on, we knew we had lost him.

Shortly after our Rolling Stones rendezvous, Cher and I were asked to do what then was probably our biggest show. Ironically, it was before one of our smallest audiences.

"It's for these New York society folks," I explained to Cher, having just been informed of the gig myself by Charlie and Brian.

"I don't know." Cher wavered.

Her eyes told me everything I needed to know. Cher did not want to fly to New York.

"Not so fast," I said. "This is one we can't turn down, no matter what."

"Why?"

"Because it's for—are you ready for this?" I smiled.

"Tell me," said Cher, who had the patience of a child and hated being teased.

"Jackie Kennedy," I said.

"Jackie Kennedy?" sighed Cher, her eyes as wide as pool balls.

"Yup."

Cher was as incredulous as I was thrilled. Predictably, the more time she had to think about singing in front of the country's former first lady and her hoity-toity acquaintances, the more wigged out Cher became. She was so insecure that, given the chance, she would have refused. I understood.

Still not old enough to drink legally, Cher lacked the poise and confidence that she acquired years later. She was instinctually smart, though for the most part uneducated, having dropped out of high school. Her gaffes, when she made them, were doozies. For instance, when she was old enough to know better, but still a kid, Cher believed that Mount Rushmore's faces were carved by nature.

"You didn't really believe that, did you?" I asked. "I mean, it just so happened that all the faces of those presidents happened to appear in stone?"

"Yeah, I did," she said, sticking to her story. "The rain. Yeah, I thought the rain did it."

Another time when she was discussing airplane safety, Cher insisted that in the entire history of aviation only one helicopter had ever crashed. Cher wasn't the most worldly girl I'd ever met. Her only work experience had been behind the counter at See's Candy Store. Her imagination knew no bounds. When we played Las Vegas a couple years later, Cher was somehow convinced that billionaire Howard Hughes was going to call her. She talked of it constantly. It was her way of measuring her importance. If the most reclusive man she knew of summoned her, then she must be somebody. He never called.

It wasn't unusual for Cher to lapse into strange, mysterious personalities. She collected them as assiduously as the clothes in her closet. It was part of her unpredictable nature, the part of her that was impossible to figure out.

"What's with you?" I asked one morning as the Jackie Kennedy date drew near. "You're so quiet and elusive."

No response.

"Cher? Cher?" I said. "I'm talking to you. Please, come in, Cher."

"The movie we watched last night," she finally answered. "You know, the one with Gretta Garbo? I am that character she played."

What was there to say? I did what Garbo asked and left her alone.

When these moods struck, it was as if Cher disappeared into a black hole. She never talked about them, never tried to explain them. It was just understood that she reserved the right to have them. I realized that withdrawing was her method of surviving. She turned everything off. She put on blinders. Then she thought or did whatever she wanted without any outside interference.

Early in our relationship I didn't know what to make of these lapses into inner space. I didn't like it that Cher so matter-of-factly kept a part of herself separate and unreachable from me. But I not only learned to live with it, I think I came to understand it.

It was during those moments of deep, self-centered thought that Cher worked on creating the woman who emerged after our divorce: Cher the independent, who-gives-a-damn woman. I think that during those times she saw the things that she wanted for herself with extreme clarity, just as she'd once dreamed of being recognized and practiced signing autographs, and there was no question in her mind that these dreams would materialize one day.

The trip to New York was a brief one—the performance and then back to L.A. We flew first class, which was nice, but the prospect of meeting Jackie Kennedy was throwing us for a loop. We were excited about rubbing shoulders with real heavyweights. We'd come from modest, ordinary backgrounds. Now we were about to perform for the wife of the former president of the United States.

This whole affair gave me an eerie feeling. I kept thinking about the day John Kennedy was assassinated. Like everybody else, Cher and I had been shocked by the news of the president's death and had taken the loss personally. Like everybody else too we'd spent the entire day glued to the television, lying in bed and switching channels.

The night of our performance we were as curious as we were ready. A limo let us out in front of a stately apartment building on Fifth Avenue. A uniformed doorman stepped out of the locked front door, met us at the curb, and ushered us inside. Cher and I exchanged the same thought: money. Our hosts were holding the highly polished, double wood door open for us as we exited the elevator and entered their apartment.

The crowd was definitely something we'd never experienced. It was a new world and, though we didn't show it, we were intimidated. These people were all from old money, wealth that had been acquired over decades and centuries. We tried not to stare. The furniture was beautiful: the walls were filled with oil paintings by the masters, the kind we'd seen only in museums. There were numerous plaques and honors from institutions. The guests, in formals and tuxedos, reeked of status and money and a noble class that was completely foreign to our lives.

In retrospect, I can look back on this night as an example of why Cher and I took our first fall from the spotlight. We didn't walk into that Fifth Avenue apartment and tell ourselves, Wow, we've arrived. Our reaction was just the opposite. Inside, we had a feeling of not belonging. Instead of projecting confidence, we wondered how we were supposed to act. It was as if we were acting out parts that weren't scripted. I've learned that people act out parts only because they don't believe in themselves.

That was true of me. And I believe it was true of Cher too. We had a hard time accepting these situations because deep down we couldn't handle the fact that we'd also arrived. In other words, we suffered lots of self-doubt. Every step forward gave us reason to worry that we might slip backward. That was called pressure. Major-league pressure. Not only did I feel responsible for making hit records, I felt doubly responsible for not losing everything we'd gained.

We hadn't been in the apartment long before we were taken to meet Jackie. The guest of honor was holding court in one of the bedrooms. I held Cher's hand; it was cold, clammy, and shaking. Despite the cool facade I was trying to affect, I was equally awed and uncomfortable. But then we were being introduced to Jackie Kennedy, the most revered woman in America, and there was no time to think.

In a smart, tailored suit, she looked prettier to me than I remembered from pictures. I thought about telling her that but decided against it. Cher did say something about her outfit, but it did nothing to diminish the awkwardness of making conversation when there is really nothing to say.

"Your haircut is almost Shakespearean," Jackie said to me, a comment that seemed complimentary, but it later reminded me that Cher and I were just the players to her.

Cher and I had brought tiny Catholic medals for Jackie's children, Caroline and John, and we presented them to her. Everything was so formal, so strained, so impersonal. And then it was time to prepare for our set. Bidding Jackie a sweet good-bye, I am sure she was happy to get rid of us, since she had to have been as uncomfortable around us as we were with her.

We had hoped to make a remarkable impression that night, both socially and as performers. We had wanted acceptance from a crowd that looked on Cher and me as an amusing clown act. But it was no dice. Unfortunately, our sound system self-destructed and the hour-long set turned into one giant, embarrassing fiasco from which we were only too happy to escape.

At home, Cher and I had plenty of distractions to help us forget. My vice was cars and motorcycles. Cher's was clothing. The money brought by success allowed us to spend like two kids in a candy shop, but I enjoyed it only up to a point. My fatalistic bent kept me waiting for someone to wake me up from this dream.

And then it happened.

One day Cher came home from a day of shopping and deposited an armload of bags and boxes on the table. I watched the pile spill onto the floor and laughed. It made me happy to think that Cher had all this—the money, lifestyle, and fame. But then Cher took the wind right out of my sails. For no apparent reason, she plopped down on the sofa next to me, looking glum and full of discontent.

"What's wrong, baby?" I asked, unable to imagine what might be bothering her or why.

She took a deep breath.

"You know, Son," she sighed. "I can't wait until we're really big. You know?"

I didn't. Honestly, I didn't.

9

WHAT NOW, MY LOVE

Performers get to a point where they say, Oh, the charts aren't important. Don't believe 'em.

As 1965 wound to a close, the charts were the only way I was able to measure our success. In November "But, You're Mine," our much-anticipated follow-up to "I Got You Babe," rose to number fifteen; a Vault Records reissue of "The Letter," our cobwebbed Caesar and Cleo single, charted at seventy-five; my second solo record, "The Revolutionary Kind," inched its way to seventy; in March our cover of "What Now, My Love" climbed to sixteen, evidence of our commercial muscle. By summer 1966, Sonny and Cher were everywhere.

It was a heady, electrifying time. Hearts pumped, heads swelled, and we stepped with a lightness of being that was incredible. Everything Cher and I had worked for was paying off. The promises I had made to the scared, confused, skinny girl with stars in her eyes were being realized. The secret ambitions I'd harbored since boyhood were no longer punch lines to family jokes. Our dreams had come true. Our love had never been stronger or deeper. At home, Cher and I mewed songs of passion to each other. Onstage, our smiles overflowed with poetry. Our eyes locked and we shared the amazement and joy of standing on top of the world. We'd climbed Mt. Everest together and it was wonderful to breathe the rarefied air.

Then came the first hint of a downturn. In June our second LP, *The Wondrous World of Sonny and Cher,* finished up a disappointing thirty-four in the United States. Though it fared better in the United Kingdom, where it reached a respectable fifteen, I should've worried.

There were signs, numerous but subtle, that our market was going soft; I just failed to see them. A year later it was obvious what was happening. The music scene was changing rapidly. The Beatles, the Doors, the Stones, the Byrds, Donovan, and Dylan changed the game. They dressed rock and roll in psychedelic hues. Rock and roll became synonymous with drugs. Experimentation was the game of the day.

Cher and I had stated openly that we were not into the drug scene. As such, we were looked on as squares.

Yet I wanted to keep up; I tried. Everybody did. It reminds me of what happened to drag-racing cars. When I was a rebellious kid of seventeen the cars all had flat heads and pistons. The next year the engines changed to overhead valves and left me standing in the dust, saying, I'm outta here.

Same thing in music. The sound suddenly clicked into another gear. The sweet sound made by groups like Chad and Jeremy, Herman's Hermits, and even the Beatles in the early 1960s gave way to harder-edged music that was heavily influenced by drugs. Groups like the Kinks, the Rolling Stones, the Who, and the Byrds delivered a louder, more rebellious, and higher-voltage sound that was embraced by the kids who had once bought "I Got You Babe." Suddenly Sonny and Cher were no longer hip. We might have been young, but we didn't do drugs and we believed in working within the system, not throwing stones at it, and that put us on the outs. I tried chasing the newer sound for a while but never could get a handle on it. The LP *Inner Views* was my attempt at psychedelic music. Occasionally I'll hear some radio station playing "Pammy's on a Bummer," a moody, contrived song, and I'll ask, God, is that really me?

I started being plagued by second thoughts and doubts, even though the performing was still a thrill. I'd leave the stage buzzed, but as our fortunes began to change I sometimes found myself believing in Cher as an artist even more than in Sonny and Cher as a duo. From the day I started with Spector, I knew I was faking it and always anticipated the moment when my limited skills would be exposed. I rubbed shoulders with great musicians like Leon Russell and Jack Nitzsche and traded ideas with a genius like Spector. I was never anything less than honest when evaluating myself. I'd been around. I knew my weaknesses as well as I knew our strengths together. That's why I never doubted Cher. I might've doubted our staying power, but I never had anything but confidence in her talent. No one had to tell me Cher was hot. While my forte was writing, producing and plotting the behind-the-scenes action, Cher was pure magic in front of an audience. If it had been the other way around, I would've tried to make it on my own rather than hiding behind Sonny and Cher.

But that was the hand I was dealt, and I played it as best I could.

I never felt I had to compete with Cher, and I found it easy to write just for her. For example, I wrote "Bang Bang (My Baby Shot Me Down)" especially for Cher as a solo. It's a song she still performs in concert.

One night I was driving home after a particularly grueling day in which nothing went terribly wrong but little went as planned. The songs weren't charting, radio was lukewarm to Sonny and Cher, songwriting was painstaking, reviewers struck me as downright mean, and Cher and I had knocked heads over something or other. It just hadn't been a great day. Zipping down Sunset in my Astin Martin convertible, my mind as blank as my writing tablet, a string of words popped into my head: "Bang-bang, shot me down, bang-bang . . . oh, oh, oh."

The words were nonsensical, with no meaning whatsoever, but they did have a nice beat. I sang them to myself over and over, pulling into the driveway with one purpose in mind—getting to the piano, pronto. Since Cher was already sleeping, I had no distractions and began banging out the four or five chords I was able to play. After a while they began to take shape. More words came. By morning

I had reached a point where I could sing "Bang Bang" to Cher.

"I don't like it," she commented with an I'm-sorry shrug.

"Let me sing it for you again, OK?"

I auditioned the song four or five times for Cher, and each time she grimaced a little more. Finally she asked me to refrain from singing it at all.

"I really think it stinks, Son," she said. "I mean, you've done so much better."

"You aren't just saying that?" I said, half-joking.

I expected Cher to be honest, brutally so. She always said, "Sonny's songs sound like shit until they're unraveled." I couldn't play them, couldn't sing them, was barely able to write them. But once we got to the studio and I explained what I wanted to the musicians—who in these early days included Leon Russell on piano, Glen Campbell and Tommy Tedesco on guitar, and Hal Blaine on drums—my songs sounded as slick as anyone's.

"Bang Bang" was a good example. The song I played at home was a mere shell of what it sounded like after the tracks were laid. Then Cher cut the vocals. In April I took the song to KHJ radio station. They had broken all of our records, and I wanted them to give Cher's solo a send-off that would create some response. Previously, the station's program director, Ron Jacobs, had grabbed our songs like hotcakes. However, this time I had to twist his arm a little, but he eventually agreed to play it exclusively, and "Bang Bang" became Cher's first million-selling solo single, hitting number two in the United States and number three in England.

Despite the impressive numbers, "Bang Bang" didn't spring us from the doldrums the way "I Got You Babe" had catapulted us from obscurity. But the song convinced us—and others—that Sonny and Cher were still hot.

Unknown to Cher or me, Abe Lastfogel, the head of the William Morris Agency, and Colonel Tom Parker—Elvis Presley's manager—were discussing us one day. Colonel Parker, a man who didn't mince words when dispensing advice, saw a new way for the agency to make money off us.

"You've got another Elvis with those kids," he confided to Abe. "I know if I was you, my plan would be to make a cheap movie, put a lot of songs in it, and sell the damn album like it was cheap cologne. If you get it out fast, you'll have a hit and rake in the dough."

Soon after, the proposal was made to us and I took to it like a gambler to a slot machine. Making a movie was a definite step up. The Beatles had made a movie. Elvis flourished in pictures. I had written hit songs, million-selling LPs, and even though I continued to keep writing I wasn't breaking any new ground. The notion of making and starring in a movie made my enthusiasm soar. Secretly, I imagined pulling off a dual music and film career, like Sinatra and Dean Martin.

Cher's reaction to the movie was one of sheer boredom and disinterest. I was shocked. No one who knew her—which shows how little she allows anybody to really know her—could understand. Despite her refusal to attend the acting classes her mother forced on her, Cher had always had a special dream of being a movie star.

"I don't get it, Cher," I said one day as I was preparing to sign the contracts.

"It's not that I don't want to make the movie," she explained. "It's that I don't care either way."

That was in Cher's character. She didn't care either way. She was on a ride. But I was high on the prospect of making a movie, especially when I was given the authority to select the director. That chore consumed several weeks. I looked at reel after reel and talked to a slew of people. The job of selecting somebody was mystifying. Then somebody introduced me to a young filmmaker, Billy Friedkin.

Friedkin went on to great acclaim as one of Hollywood's more important directors by making such megahit pictures as *The Exorcist* and *The French Connection*. But in those days he was a highly touted maker of documentaries, known to everybody, including me, as Billy.

Billy was a character, a passionate man whom I likened to a lovable maniac. His artistic temperament was as broad and volatile as his imagination. He was charming, appealing, and—this is what initially drew my attention—he was talented. He also played poker—and still does—like a hired killer.

We became tight friends and dove into the film. After setting up an office at Paramount, we went about the business of finding a script, which meant interviewing dozens of writers. Nothing came of it. Then we received a long, unsolicited letter from a guy named Nicholas Hymes. Hymes, who knew somehow that we were calling the movie *Good Times*, outlined an entire story in his letter, and when Billy and I read what he had written, we thought, That's it, and hired him.

But when Billy and I read his draft, we knew we had made an error in judgment. The story line was okay, but Hymes wrote scenes that were so intense and surreal that they made no sense. For instance, a scene depicting a car being driven into a garage, which required writing no longer than this sentence, spanned pages, in which a car would drive into a living room and turn into a cigarette lighter, become a piece of furniture, transform into something else, and then suddenly turn back into the car again.

"What's this guy talking about?" I said to Billy after flinging a handful of pages to the floor. "Where is our movie going?"

"Jesus Christ," he shook his head, "I'll write it by my goddamn self."

So Billy tried writing a bit. Then we hired another guy, Tony Barrett, and as he delivered pages to us, Billy and I reworked them. As we were doing this, we hired a secretary to sit in my house and take our dictation, and she gave the transcribed work to another secretary, who typed everything up in the proper format. Working in the kitchen, she spent inordinately long hours over her typewriter, refusing to give us any pages until they were completed.

Initially we were impressed. Billy and I thought, Goddamn, we hired the world's most efficient, hard-working secretary. But after nothing came back from her for days, we checked up on her and discovered she was taking our script and rewriting the whole thing. We had give her ten pages to type and she was up to page sixty. "What the hell are you doing?" I said. "You're supposed to be typing the script, that's it. You're a secretary."

"But I'm also a writer," she told me.

"That's not what we hired you to do," I argued.

"I know," she said, packing up her things. "But I followed my instincts."

"Well, you can't write any better than you type," Billy chimed in.

The secretary wasn't about to be insulted. She looked right at me.

"Fine. Both of you, say what you want. But you," she said to me, "you can't sing. And your friend, Billy, I don't know what the hell he's done, but he's just an asshole."

With that, she walked out, her dignity intact. Friedkin and I were irate, but the scene was so unbelievable that we doubled over in laughter. What could we do but throw our hands into the air and laugh?

Given the way we were working, Billy and I hired a lot of secretaries, one of whom happened to be particularly good-looking. I preferred to work at night. Cher used to go to bed at ten o'clock. Working closely with someone, especially a female someone, you develop a rapport, which is what happened between me and this secretary. I gave a few flirtatious signals and found her receptive. One night the sparks flew and it happened. We made love in the office.

I thought Cher was asleep. She wasn't. In the midst of our lovemaking, Cher walked into the workroom. The air was immediately let out of that balloon. There's nothing like having your wife catch you with your pants down to ruin an illicit romance. Cher didn't scream; she just glared at me and walked out of the room. I got the cold shoulder treatment for the rest of the week, but that was it. Somewhere inside, Cher was resigned to the same double standard I was practicing. Men could fool around but women couldn't. Or perhaps she didn't care.

In any case, it just wasn't a big deal to her. She didn't feel threatened, and she probably felt relieved.

That was the only time Cher caught me.

Nowadays I'd never think of having an affair—even if I was guaranteed not to get caught. I've come to believe that cheating is a lie and an insult, but more important, it's a symptom of something wrong with the relationship. That was true of Cher and me, except we were too busy with our careers to notice.

Good Times, the story of a young singing duo in Hollywood who imagine themselves starring in movies, was Cher's and my Walter Mitty fantasy. It was up-to-the-minute art imitating life, though once we started shooting, we wondered if we were making art or digging our own graves.

Billy shot at his own pace. None of us showed much concern about budget. We figured when we finished was when we finished, as simple as that, and nobody would interfere. Wrong. When the expenses hit about $900,000, considerably over budget, Paramount pulled the plug. We had been warned but didn't pay any attention. Then the party ended. We were kicked off the studio lot. The movie was two-thirds done.

Billy and I were in a panic, while Cher, as she had been throughout the endeavor, was nonchalant. At the time Cher switched herself into automatic. Her attitude was, point me in the direction you want, tell me what to say, what to sing, and then I'm gone. And she was. Literally. If Cher wasn't required on the set or in the studio, she stayed away.

"What's she do with herself?" Friedkin asked.

"Man, take a look at her closet sometime and you'll see." I laughed.

That was the way it went. Shopping was Cher's thing, work was mine. We met in the middle, and that was Sonny and Cher. However, the relationship was still working. We admired the talents each of us brought to the relationship, relied on them, in fact, and allowed ourselves to mistake that admiration and reliance for love.

In the meantime, Billy went on a tear to finish the picture. Showing deft ingenuity and talent for finagling, he and his cinematographer, Bill Butler, drove all over town, stealing scenes here, scabbing something there, plucking film from someone else, acting in the streets. It was real jump-and-shoot stuff, and loads of pressured, ass-on-the-line fun, and the bottom line was, we got the job done.

Cher and I were in the midst of touring when *Good Times* was released in late summer. We met up with Billy in Chicago and arranged for a bus to take us to a theater where the movie was playing. That night Chicago was battened down by tornado warnings, which emptied the streets of traffic but added to the excitement. With great anticipation, we snuck into the back, anxious to witness the crowd's reaction to the film we had sweated and slaved over for months. If they liked it, we figured the movie might survive into Christmas and cash in on the holiday box-office bonanza.

But to our chagrin there was no crowd. After our eyes adjusted to the darkness, we saw that the theater wasn't full. Nor was it half full. Nor even a quarter full. About twenty-five people were scattered throughout the seats.

"What the hell is going on?" said Harvey Kresky, our agent. "Jesus, where is everybody?"

"It's a fluke," I said. "It's gotta be the weather. Just our luck a tornado rips through town."

Cher didn't say a word. She was baffled too, but whatever feelings she had she kept to herself.

"Let's try another place," I finally suggested.

We spent the rest of that night and the entire next day driving from theater to theater, covering the city, then hitting the suburbs, sneaking into the back after the picture had started. The results got worse and worse. Every time we got to a new theater, I would ask, "Harvey, are you coming in?" However, with each stop he got more and more depressed, since he was expecting a smash. Finally, at one theater, I asked if he was coming in and Harvey gave me an are-you-crazy look.

"What the fuck for?" he said. "What the fuck for?"

Easy for him to say. Cher and I still had to travel to Austin, Texas, where the movie's opening was tied into a citywide celebration and parade. We arrived and the mayor, in a big ceremony, proclaimed it *Good Times* Day. We rode in the parade, waved to the crowd, did radio, TV, and newspaper interviews, and finally went to the theater, where there were nine people in the crowd, including me and Cher and the mayor and his wife.

"It's a bomb," I told Billy over the phone. "No two ways about it, the picture is a stinker."

"We tried, man," he said. "Gave it our best. Nothing more you can do."

143

"Yeah," I sighed.

"You hurtin'?" he asked.

"No, no. I'm OK. Wounded a bit. But I'll be OK, doc. Just let me get back to the front line."

We laughed.

Cher and I learned quickly that the best antidote to failure is humor. If we could laugh at ourselves and our situation, we'd make it through the tough times. In the weeks following the *Good Times* debacle, we often recalled the image of Harvey Kresky going into one theater after another and getting gloomier and gloomier until he flat-out refused to go into the last theater.

In my heart, I never honestly believed the movie was going to be successful. I knew Sonny and Cher were already on the wane, and the movie's premise wasn't in sync with the times. But sometimes in life you put your train on the track and start rolling. By the time you realize that you're on the wrong track, you're too far to turn back, and it's easier to keep on going. *Good Times* was like that.

The experience hardened both me and Cher. It hardened us and it scared us. I found myself accusing Cher of not taking the movie as seriously as I did. I wanted a scapegoat. She refused to be one and disappeared within herself. Suddenly there was distance between us. I didn't know what she was thinking and it frustrated me. I got angry. I lashed out. I threw glasses and slammed doors. My short Italian fuse would ignite and I'd lose control.

Cher would absorb what I was doing, then let me have it. We did our share of fighting.

Panic hadn't yet crept into my mind, but I was feeling the pressure of maintaining the career that supported our marriage. I was among the more successful songwriters of the past few years, but writing had suddenly become difficult, a task rather than a creative endeavor. The effort was geared toward maintaining what we had achieved instead of forging new ground. I just wanted to keep the fire stoked. Whenever I began to write, I didn't think about poetry or musical hooks as much as *Oh man, I gotta write another hit song or we're cooked.*

The pressure could build only so much before something

gave. Fallout from the first explosion rained down on our managers, Charlie and Brian. I fired them. We'd been having differences for months, differences that were magnified by our slump. Whenever a group suddenly makes it to the big time and the money pours in, there is a honeymoon period during which everybody is ecstatic, from the stars themselves to their managers. They hug and kiss and don't think about the day when reality will set in, but it does, and then the truth, as unpleasant as it is, has to be faced. In other words, not everyone can be the star.

That's what happened between Sonny and Cher and Charlie and Brian. They dressed exactly like us, talked the same, visited the same restaurants, socialized in our circle. In essence, they became part of the act. Then they also began to perform, and Cher and I resented it. We were tripping over our shadows, supporting our competition. Finally, as the luster disappeared from our halo, we found it increasingly difficult to tolerate Charlie and Brian.

However, firing our managers was about as easy as getting rid of relatives. Everybody got pissed at everybody.

But Cher and I found solace and stability in the fatherly figure of Joe DeCarlo, with whom Charlie and Brian, ironically, had set us up. Joe was older and calmer than either of our old managers, an influence we found soothing, and he moved straight into the management role. His favorite line to us was, "Kids, don't worry. I'll take care of it." At the time, that was just what we needed to hear.

I didn't want to worry about Sonny and Cher any more than I had to, which was all the time. I plotted and planned and gritted my teeth, trying not to feel inadequate and looking for any crack in the wall that would let us back into the spotlight. Looking back, I'm thankful for the two things that kept me looking ahead—my tenacity and Cher's continued faith in my ability. One was no less important than the other. I needed to feel her confidence. As long as Cher believed in me, I could tell myself, Okay, I'll come up with something. I'm a creative person. I'll think of something.

Determined to stay busy and thereby increase the odds of our smoldering career catching fire again, Cher and I left for England in August to promote the overseas release of *Good Times*. We were also booked to several concerts, cashing in on our popularity there. "Bang Bang" was still high on the U.K. charts and Cher's latest single, "Sunny," a remake of the Bobby Hebb hit, was on its way to number thirty-two. After a few days in London I met with the local record distributor, who got all over me for a new Sonny and Cher record.

"If you don't have one, write one," he said. "I can sell it and make money for all of us."

I'd brought a tape of "Little Man," a new Sonny and Cher song, which I'd been working on at home but hadn't finished. I'd planned to complete it while in London, and now I had the proper motivation. While Cher visited London's department stores, I spent a couple of days in a studio and worked on the song. The final touches were added when I used the cap from a Coke bottle to pluck the strings on a grand piano, getting just the odd, Gypsy sound I'd spent days thinking about without knowing what the hell I wanted.

The record was released within three days of my telling the distributor that "Little Man" was finished, and it rocketed straight into the top ten. Back home, the song failed to crack the top twenty, but that was par for the course. Our expectations had long ago been tempered by the quixotic reality of show business. We hoped for more success than we got and tried not to let the disappointment interfere with our lives, though deep inside, both of us knew that our lives was inextricably tied to our careers.

At that time I sat around the house a lot. There were days when we literally had nothing to do. Cher shopped, did needlepoint, watched television, and visited with friends. I vamped. That's what I called stirring the waters—making phone calls, writing, trying to get work. Most days ended with Cher going to sleep before ten and me disappearing into the downstairs piano room where I did most of my writing.

In the quiet of the late night, I sat facing my piano with the knowledge that the right combination of chords, a catchy melody, and a little luck could change everything. The picture was bleak but not without possibility. I believed in Cher, and I liked to think that she believed in me.

That allowed me to sit in that tiny room, in perfect solitude, and wax philosophic.

That's exactly what I was doing one night toward the end of the year. I was in a glum mood and set about trying to play myself into a brighter disposition. As usual, I was just messing around, trying to arrange the five chords I could play into a pleasant, rocking order. Out of nowhere, I lit upon a chord change and began singing, "Life goes on/oh, life goes on . . ." The words reflected my state of mind.

A couple of hours passed and I kept working, though by then I found myself singing, "The beat goes on/the beat goes on." Another line popped into my head. "Drums keep pounding rhythm to the brain." Then I ad-libbed a cool fill: "La-da-de-da-de-de/la-da-de-da-de-da." By the time I crawled into bed, I knew I had a pretty good song, and when I woke up I was certain of it, because I couldn't get the damn hook out of my head.

As I wrote, I didn't realize that the song reflected my philosophy of life. But it did. In simple terms, it said everything I thought and felt. Failure was only the opportunity to do something else. Defeat was a part of every day. Life didn't end because people didn't go to see one particular movie or buy one particular record. My brain didn't shut off because one project failed. As long as I continued to draw breath, I knew that I'd come up with ideas for songs. I was a fighter. I might get knocked down, but I always got back up.

"Drums kept pounding rhythm to my brain," as my song, "The Beat Goes On" says.

That's remained true to this day.

But then I only thought about the fact that I had come up with a song that sounded better than any I had written in years. Anxious for some approval, I called Billy Friedkin early the next morning and over the phone played him an extremely rough tape of "The Beat Goes On." As a sounding board, Friedkin was 100 percent trustworthy. He had a good commercial sensibility, and his opinion, never wishy-washy, was delivered with the straightforward honesty an artist needs.

After the song finished, I took the receiver away from the tape recorder and asked what he thought.

"I love it," he said.

"The Beat Goes On" was released in February 1967. Though it was our strongest single since "I Got You Babe," people didn't exactly rush to buy it. However, radio jumped on the catchy song and it pedaled up the charts to sixth place, a feat that kept Sonny and Cher hot over the summer, despite the half-dozen lukewarm releases that followed, including "Plastic Man" and "It's the Little Things," songs whose titles reveal how out of kilter we were with the hip scene.

But Cher and I had each other, and through most of the summer we also had work, touring almost nonstop. When we sang "I Got You Babe" and "The Beat Goes On," we looked at each other and believed wholeheartedly in the words. They weren't just popular songs. To us, they were postcards from our hearts, the sound track to a personal love story that also captivated millions of people throughout the world.

Sonny and Cher might not have been the hottest ticket, but we had no reason to cry. In fact, I remember one plane ride where I actually caught Cher grinning, which was strange, considering that she hated to fly. Confounding matters even more was the weather—it was horrible. The ride was turbulent. Still, Cher was smiling. I gave her a curious look.

"I . . . I . . . I've got something to tell you," she said softly.

"It's OK, honey," I said, thinking maybe she had taken a tranquilizer and was feeling loopy. "Don't worry about the flight."

"No, no, it's not that," she said. "What I'm trying to say is—"

"Yeah?" I asked impatiently.

"I'm pregnant." She smiled, then broke into a nervous laugh.

"What?"

"I am." she nodded.

I grabbed her and squeezed, overwhelmed by happiness. Cher had been trying to get pregnant for months. Both of us were ecstatic. She had never looked or felt better. We traveled from city to city on a cloud. Several months passed as we anticipated the happy event. When the bulk of the tour ended in autumn, the future mom and dad sat at home and talked about raising a baby instead of our careers. The future seemed rosy.

Then one day Cher woke up with cramps. It was a hot Friday afternoon, and suddenly it got a lot hotter. Her pain was severe. Cher put on a brave face, but the discomfort was too much for her to hide. We were supposed to fly to Minneapolis that night and perform a concert the next evening, but it was obvious that wasn't going to happen. I told Joe DeCarlo to call the promoter and cancel the gig. Then Denis Pregnolato, our road manager and my confidant, and I drove Cher to the hospital.

"We can't cancel," Joe DeCarlo told me over the phone.

"What do you mean?" I exploded. "Cher's in the hospital. She's going to lose the baby. We can't do a show."

"The promoter says he'll sue," he retorted. "I don't know what else to say."

"Well, they can't expect Cher to perform," I said, incredulous.

"They don't," he said. "But you can do it alone. They'll go for that."

There are times when you feel like throwing in the towel and there are times when you literally can't afford to do that. As much as I didn't want to go to Minneapolis, I recognized that this was one of those times when I couldn't afford to handle the situation the way I wanted to. I was at the mercy of a man who wanted to make money and didn't give two cents for Cher's pain or the fact that we were losing a baby we wanted very badly.

As much as I didn't want to, late that night I boarded a plane with Denis and flew to Minneapolis, staring out the window the entire flight, into the black void as if it were a window to the unknown. I needed something or someone to tell me that everything was going to be okay. It wasn't. The next afternoon I went on a local radio station that was involved in co-promoting the concert and explained, quite emotionally, why Cher was unable to perform alongside me.

When I got off the air I was given news that made me feel even worse. Cher was okay, but she'd lost the baby.

That night I went onstage alone and performed an abbreviated show, one of the longest, hardest, and most emotional hours of my life. In my apology to the audience, I remember standing at the lip of the stage, trying to get the words out but finding it difficult to get beyond the pictures I had in my head of my frail wife alone in her hospital bed. My voice cracked and tears streamed down my face. There was no use trying to hide the pain. I just wanted to get through the show and return home.

I caught the last plane out that night and spent all day Sunday in the hospital with Cher. The next day I drove her home. I felt shitty for having left her.

"Let's not talk about it," she pleaded.

So we didn't.

The miscarriage was a tremendous blow to both of us, though. There was no denying that. It was hard to bounce back, because we never actually communicated to each other our tangled feelings about the loss. It was something that couples as close as we thought we were should've done. Each of us licked our wounds privately, a pattern that continued during the rest of our relationship. Instead of talking out our problems, we leaned on one another's shoulder. It was comforting enough just to know that we could depend on each other.

If that wasn't enough, which was sometimes the case when we resumed touring, then all we had to do was turn to our manager, Joe DeCarlo. Joe was always there, smiling his reassuring smile and saying, "Kids, don't worry. I'll take care of it."

Around Thanksgiving in 1967, Cher and I traveled to New York to promote the compilation album, *The Best of Sonny and Cher,* and we decided to stay over for the holiday. Ahmet Ertegun, the president of our record label, asked if we had any plans for Thanksgiving dinner. Since we didn't have family or feel especially close to anybody in town, I explained that we had planned to have a quiet dinner in our hotel room.

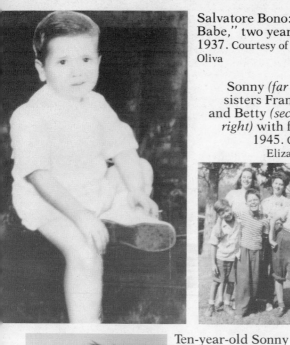

Salvatore Bono: "The Babe," two years old in 1937. Courtesy of Elizabeth Oliva

Sonny *(far left)* with sisters Fran *(behind)* and Betty *(second from right)* with friends in 1945. Courtesy of Elizabeth Oliva

Ten-year-old Sonny with a schoolboy grin. Courtesy of Elizabeth Oliva

A fifties wedding for Sonny and Donna Rankin in Hawthorne, California. Sonny was 19. Courtesy of Elizabeth Oliva

"I Got You Babe." Young and in love, Sonny and Cher
frolicking in the pool of their sixties San Fernando
Valley home. © Curt Gunther

Innocent, doe-eyed Cher and a young Sonny: A
moment of reflection on their way to the top of the
pop charts. © Curt Gunther

Relaxing in their bedroom: Cher dons flashy bell-
bottom Pucci-style pants; for Sonny, it's casual
trunks. © Curt Gunther

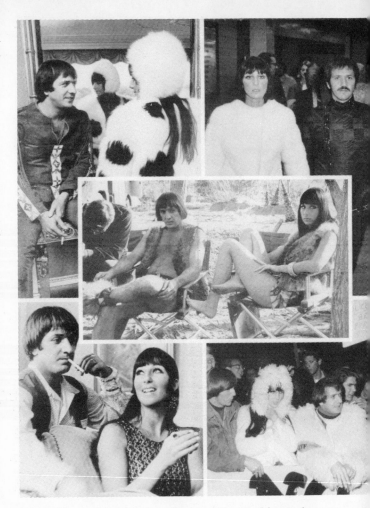

"Look at us!" From London to New York's Madison Square Garden, from the set of the movie *Good Times* to a Hollywood Sunset Strip protest, Sonny and Cher are decked out in some of the "grooviest threads" of the sixties. © Globe Photos; © Ron Galella, Ltd.; © Globe Photos; © AP/Wide World Photos; © AP/Wide World Photos

The many faces of "The Sonny and Cher Comedy Hour," masking their failing marriage. © Globe Photos

The day before Cher's twentieth birthday, Sonny surprised her with a 20-karat sapphire-and-diamond ring. Describing herself as turning "twenty-teen," Cher quipped, "That way I can stay a teenager for the rest of my life." That was 1966 . . . © AP/Wide World Photos

. . . In 1977, over a decade later, Sonny and Cher are
now divorced, glitzy, glamorous Vegas performers.
© AP/Wide World Photos

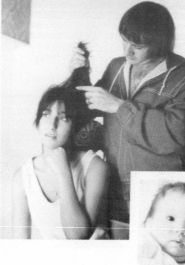

Sonny: Singer, composer, lover, and father. © Ron Galella, Ltd.; © Curt Gunther; © Curt Gunther; courtesy of Elizabeth Oliva

"You better sit down, kids": They played the happy family with daughter Chastity on their hit TV show but were already headed for splitsville. © Curt Gunther

1974: On a date to see
*The Rocky Horror
Picture Show,* Cher with
confidant and record
mogul David Geffen,
the man who helped
engineer the big split
and launched her solo
career. © Ron Galella, Ltd.

1977: A considerably
cooled Sonny and Cher
(now Mrs. Gregg
Allman) trying to revive
their careers by taking
their act on the road
again. © Ron Galella, Ltd.

Sonny and Chastity, nine, on the Greek island of Rhodes during a break from the film *Escape to Athena*. Sonny dons clown makeup, but he wasn't laughing when he discovered that his daughter couldn't read.
© AP/Wide World Photos

1976: Sonny and first daughter Christy (now in her thirties) share a rare moment of togetherness. "I mistakenly put my career ahead of everything," Sonny now admits, regretting his missed role as father.
© Ron Galella, Ltd.

1983: Sonny with Cher, third wife Susie Coelho, and Chastity at the opening of his restaurant, Bono's, in West Hollywood. © Ron Galella, Ltd.

On the rebound from his split with Cher, Sonny was consoled by a former cigarette girl from Pip's, Connie Foreman. To keep up appearances that Sonny and Cher were still together, Sonny, Cher, and Connie lived under one roof. © Ulvis Alberts, Globe Photos

Mayor Bono takes a break from his duties to cruise down the main drag in his town, Palm Springs.
© AP/Wide World Photos

Sonny (as Franklin) plants a bomb in Debbie Harry's (Velma) sky-high 'do as part of a devious plot that backfires in John Water's movie *Hairspray*. © New Line Cinema Corp. All Rights Reserved.

David Niven, Roger Moore, Telly Savalas, and Elliott Gould are a few who joined Sonny in the cast of *Escape to Athena*.
Courtesy of Sonny Bono

In 1987, millions of nostalgic, tearful fans watched a
reunited Sonny and Cher sing "I Got You Babe" for
the first time in ten years on "Late Night with David
Letterman." Sonny was so moved that he, too, had
tears in his eyes. © AP/Wide World Photos

Sonny, the politician, won a landslide victory for
mayor of Palm Springs *(middle)*. Sonny and wife
Mary with President and Mrs. Reagan *(above)* and
with President Bush *(below)*. Courtesy of the Ronald
Reagan Presidential Library; © Tony Costa; David Valdez: The
White House

Sonny, Mary, and son Chesare: A family, happy at last. © Sigrid Estrada *Inset:* Chastity hugs her baby brother Chesare. Courtesy of Sonny Bono

"Nonsense," said Ahmet, whose suave and friendly manner was impossible to refuse.

He not only invited us, but insisted that we join the Thanksgiving party he was attending. The party was a swanky society affair, reminding us of the Jackie Kennedy party where Cher and I had performed the previous year. But the magic of Ahmet, a cosmopolitan man who changes social gears like a chameleon changes colors, is that he fits into any social circle. We met him outside a charming New York brownstone on the East Side, and just by looking at the exterior Cher and I knew we were in over our heads.

"Don't be silly," Ahmet assured us. "You'll know a great many of the people."

For some reason Cher and I didn't believe him. We looked at each other knowingly and whispered, "Right."

Walking into the brownstone was like entering the Twilight Zone. The twenty or so guests all looked, sounded, and acted similar, but they were among the strangest crew Cher and I had encountered. All walks of life were represented, from aristocratic New Yorkers to high-society folks like *Vogue* editor Diana Vreeland to Andy Warhol and cronies Viva and Joel Schumacher, who was then a window dresser but is now a successful director.

"Are we in the right place?" Cher muttered under her breath.

"Better yet," I replied, "are we in the right time zone?"

The atmosphere was kinky, wild. There was a lot of cocaine snorting and drinking. The air was permeated with the acrid aroma of marijuana. Cher and I sat in the corner of a sofa like two aliens—and we looked stranger than anybody—not speaking to anyone. It was eerie, watching everybody get loaded and loony. Then the hosts unveiled a new painting, which actually wasn't a painting at all but a thin panel of colored water and oils whose design changed as it tilted back and forth.

Andy Warhol, who was pleasant to everyone but who had absolutely nothing to say, made a big deal explaining the piece, and everybody, from their stoned vapor cloud, cooed, "Unbelievable. Cosmic. Oh my God, this is making me freak out." Cher and I didn't have a chance.

Finally dinner was served. Our hosts summoned everyone to the elegantly set table. Crystal and china sparkled under a crystal chandelier. Salads and appetizers were served and, though people continued drinking and ingesting all types of drugs, they also scarfed down the meal. Then the turkey was brought out and set in the center of the table. Like any Thanksgiving gathering, everybody oohed and ahhed over the cooked bird.

Suddenly, the nicest-looking young woman there, a long-haired stunner who had been a mite wobbly on her feet for some time, slowly rose from her seat, catching everybody's attention. She smiled and appeared ready to say something. The room quieted. Then blooey! She vomited all over the turkey, covering it in the same green goop that Billy Friedkin would later use in *The Exorcist*. Except this stuff was real.

Reaction to this was mixed. While the sick girl ran off to the bathroom in tears, and her boyfriend followed, our hosts and their guests acted as if someone throwing up on the turkey was a perfectly normal happening.

"Oh, no problem," they all echoed one another. "It's OK. We'll fix it."

Hearing this, I turned to Cher and said, "I don't think it's OK, do you?"

"No." She winced.

That settled it. Politely but quickly, we made our get-away, as did Ahmet. Ironically, Cher and I ended up having Thanksgiving dinner in our hotel room as originally planned—though we found it hard to swallow much food.

The mileage I got from that story was better than a Japanese import's. I was still talking about it as the new year rolled around and my regular poker game resumed. Cher shopped for clothes to escape the pressure of our uncertain career. I liked holing up in a smoke-filled room and playing cards with the fellas, a gang that included several agents, Joe DeCarlo, Billy Friedkin, and his director pal Francis Ford Coppola.

Somehow, one of those jokers got Cher and me invited to a trumped-up affair at Tony Curtis's house. It was a half-hour drive from our place in Encino to Tony's fifty-four-room mansion in Holmby Hills, an ultraexclusive residential area in the slopes above Beverly Hills. We drew our breaths as we passed through the main gate and confronted the biggest house we had ever seen.

More palace than home, the regal setting was populated that night by Hollywood's hip royalty, including the then bright, enfant terrible director Roman Polanski and his beautiful starlet wife Sharon Tate. I hit it off with Tony, who is as bright as his smile, from the start. From the moment we arrived, he showered Cher and me with the kind of attention that made us wonder what in the heck was up with this guy.

"My dear kids, how nice to see you," he greeted us. "So glad to have you for dinner. Wonderful, wonderful. I have heard so much about you."

He didn't stop. What I discovered later is that Tony is not merely a great actor, he is also a hustler, a salesman's salesman. He must have had me pegged for a sucker before we even arrived. During dinner, he leans close to me and tells me about another house that he owns. I don't think I showed much interest; after all, Cher and I were content with our house in the Valley.

But then Tony started describing this house, which was not simply a house but another mansion. Thirty-four rooms. Spectacular acreage. Views. It wasn't just the house, though, he explained. It was also what the house symbolized. A home was like a trophy that represented your life. Those with the biggest homes were life's biggest winners. He used himself as an example, rattling off the movies he had starred in, the famous names he had worked with. Then he flashed a smile.

"And you, Sonny." He grinned. "Don't you want people to see you as a winner?"

The following day Cher and I went to look at the house. Tony personally showed us around, taking us into every one of the thirty-four rooms. He walked us through the grounds, pointing out various fruit trees, flowers, and other exotica. He stood by the swimming pool like a used-car salesman and described the pleasures we would have swimming on hot summer days. He asked us to imagine kids splashing in the water.

That did it.

"How much do you want for it?" I asked him in the driveway.

"I think you'd be stealing it at two hundred forty grand," he said.

I looked at Tony, looked at Cher, looked at Tony, looked at my feet, looked back at Tony again and finally said, "OK, done." We shook hands and suddenly Cher and I were the owners of our own Bel Air mansion. We moved in several weeks later. Cher was in heaven. She had been waiting all her life to live in a mansion, and now she'd arrived. I loved the house too, but I knew what it cost to maintain such a lavish life-style and it made me more nervous than a squirrel in hunting season.

"It's kinda scary, having a house this big," I said to Cher the night we moved in.

"Oh, don't worry." She laughed. "There are locks on all the doors."

I gave her a look.

"Just kidding, Son," she said. "What's the problem?"

"Oh, nothing, no problem, Cher," I sighed. "I mean, we just used all our money to buy this place. Now I'm wondering how we're going to pay the rest of our bills."

"You'll think of something," she said. "I'm sure you will."

10

BANG BANG, I HIT
THE GROUND

Q: How dry did the well get?

A: 1968 opened and disappeared with only one new Sonny and Cher release, "Good Combination," and that was in January. It never made it past number fifty-six. It was as good an indication as any of how the rest of the year would shape up.

Cher and I wore great clothes, knew all the right people, and resided in a mansion with a Bel Air address, but we barely scraped by on meager royalties and a handful of legitimate concerts. Many a day and night passed when all we did was putter around our thirty-four-room dwelling, a shrine to our previous accomplishments and the chain that reminded us of how costly it was to maintain such a position and life-style. Dire straits forced us into doing things we thought beneath us, like commercials. We even sang at a wealthy businessman's backyard party, where we were treated more like a sideshow attraction than artists.

But the phone never rang. We had to take what was offered and accept the fact that time had passed us by. Sonny and Cher were passé. It was an excruciatingly painful realization, one I never accepted no matter how hard and how many times I was slapped in the face. I might go down, but I never stayed on the mat for the count.

Still, life was hard. When you hit bottom, things go bad in every direction. It makes you believe in karma. The plummet is even worse when you know that everyone in the world knows that you were once on top but aren't any longer. Some of my happiest days were when I didn't have two nickels to rub together. However, it's impossible to accept poverty after having been spoiled by the wild applause and seemingly endless river of money that comes with stardom.

I've never used drugs, but I'm certain that fame is more addictive.

I knew that our fall from grace was hard on Cher, but as selfish as it sounds, it was even more difficult on me, because I knew that our relationship depended on our being successful. Although it was unspoken, both of us understood that there was an unwritten clause to the contract that kept us together. It superseded everything we said about loving each other, needing each other, being unable to live without each other. If I couldn't deliver professionally, it wasn't going to happen on a personal level.

I knew that. I feared that. I trembled at the harshness of that reality.

Cher had her goals. Though unstated, they were quite obvious. She was determined to be the brightest, biggest star in the galaxy. I knew that no one, including me, was going to stand in her way once she set her mind on something. In fact, my biggest concern was that she'd see me as standing in her way and discard me like so much unwanted baggage.

Not that Cher complained. She didn't. She simply disappeared inside herself and became an expressionless, nearly inanimate shadow of the spark plug who could light up a stage and energize a crowd of thirty thousand. She saw only the downside of life and affected a mood of perpetual boredom and melancholy as she waited, with me, for something to happen.

It didn't. And the more nothing happened, the more I felt pressured to come up with something.

I played in a weekly poker game that included my movie pals Friedkin and Coppola, and while they had only their cards to grumble about, I often complained about feeling creatively bankrupt. I was encumbered by a sense of desperation. I didn't know what to write. I didn't know how to write. The confidence that had sprung me and Cher from the crowd of also-rans who populated Hollywood had been replaced by paralyzing self-doubts and worries—professionally and personally.

I remember telling Cher over and over, "Don't worry, hon. We'll pull out of this."

She raised her eyebrows, looking up from her needlepoint, and offered an unconvincing smile. "I know."

But I knew I wasn't trying to convince Cher as much as I was trying to convince myself that we'd rise. Unfortunately, there didn't seem to be any light at the end of the tunnel.

I was bored with music. Or so I told myself. And the more I hung out with Friedkin and Coppola, the more I envied their careers, until I found myself wanting to be in the movie business. I told myself that I'd done the music trip. I needed new challenges. New frontiers.

"Then do it," Friedkin said during a card game. "Get into movies."

"How?" I stammered.

"Get a pen and a pile of paper and write a damn movie," he said.

I thought about it for a while, and it didn't seem like such a bad idea.

I liked the challenge writing a whole script presented. I remember sitting at the kitchen table one night. Cher was already in bed. A hefty stack of white paper sat in front of me, waiting to be filled. Suddenly I was gripped by a feeling of opportunity. I felt duty bound to seize the chance. It was as if I were standing atop a mountain of fresh, untrammeled powder, the first one to ski down the mountain slope.

I envisioned the movie from beginning to end and I gave it the title *Chastity*. It was the story of Cher, a philosophic, loving interpretation of this enigmatic, multitalented woman who had taken hold of my heart and filled me with a drive and passion that I thought were known only by great poets and heroes of timeless epics.

With nothing else on my agenda, I started to write. Scenes were followed by dialogue. I wrote feverishly, all day and well into the night. One morning Cher picked up a few pages and started reading. The next day she asked for more. She loved what I was writing. Knowing that I do my best, most inspired work when someone gets enthusiastic about what I'm doing, I was fueled by Cher's compliments and ground out the screenplay.

When it was finished I began showing it to a few friends and got the type of encouraging reception I wanted. Cher, as I saw her, was like the masks representing comedy and tragedy, an unsolvable paradox that fascinated and perplexed me. The script in which I tried to capture her was glaringly overwritten, but it was a time when artists in every medium wanted to make a statement, and I was no different. I wanted to be profound and pushed every scene to the edge, and then some.

I threw everything I knew about Cher into the script—love, romance, rock and roll, spirituality, and lesbianism. The story wasn't merely a quest for identity but a search for the meaning of life.

I showed the finished script to Friedkin. He liked it. He understood everything I was trying to convey—the drama, dynamics of character, and the mystery of life. Unfortunately, he wasn't available to direct, which should've given me reason to pause and consider what I was getting into. But I was thinking full steam ahead. My sights were already set on the finished product grabbing movie audiences by their collars and rattling their hearts and minds.

In retrospect it was pure craziness to believe for one second that I had created a masterpiece, especially in the aftermath of *Good Times,* but no one appeared with a contrary opinion. My passion was unbridled. I had a script that I felt passionate about, and in Cher I had an actress who I absolutely knew to possess that special quality that set her apart from every other actress. She only needed the right vehicle, which I figured was *Chastity*.

There were just a few problems that needed solving. Like we didn't have a studio interested in making the film. We didn't have a director. And more important than either of those two minor dilemmas, we didn't have any money to make the damn picture. Without a studio, we needed investors and we didn't have one.

"Screw it," I told Denis Pregnolato one evening. "Screw the whole damn system. I'm gonna make this movie anyway."

Denis didn't offer any resistance. He shrugged and began to think. He was a great planner, and I knew he'd stand behind me and make my schemes work.

"How much are you going to need?" he asked.

"I figure a hundred fifty thousand dollars," I said. "Maybe two hundred thousand."

"Sonny, be realistic," he said. "Nobody makes movies for that little."

"We'll see," I said defiantly.

In Hollywood, it's unheard of for anyone to finance their own movie. It runs counter to every rule in the book—a book that I had obviously not bothered to read. You just don't use your own money. That's the reason for studios and investors. As I discovered, though, shooting a movie without financing or a distribution deal or any other backing is tantamount to committing a slow and painful suicide, a process that began when I started dumping every penny Cher and I had into the film.

We did scramble to raise money from outside sources. Ahmet Ertegun, bless his heart, floated us some cash. We managed to persuade a few investors to give us money too. We even traveled to New York to schmooze with people we heard were good sources, but the only thing that trip produced was an interesting encounter with surrealist artist Salvador Dalí.

In New York, Cher and I checked into the St. Regis, where we hooked up with Billy Friedkin and Francis Ford Coppola. Dalí resided at the hotel then. He spotted Cher and me walking down the hall, and from the way we looked, he must have assumed we were kinky. He invited us up to his penthouse for dinner. Cher and I thought this was quite a coup.

A couple of hours later, Cher and I and a few others went up to Dalí's room. It was like walking into a Helmut Newton photograph. Women in see-through blouses, their breasts very much in evidence, lounged on sofas. Gay men rubbed their boyfriends' legs and shoulders. Every kind of sexual preference was represented in a bold, uninhibited manner.

"We're in kinkville, right?" I whispered to Coppola.

He shrugged and stared at Dalí, who, with his out-stretched mustache and odd clothing, looked as surreal as the paintings that filled his walls. Dalí talked a mile a minute. It required great effort to understand what he was saying, but once I realized that he had no idea what he was talking about, that it was simply gibberish, I enjoyed the conversation. The big amusement was a battery-operated toy fish whose tail flapped back and forth.

"This is what nuns in Spain use to masturbate," Dalí kept repeating.

Of course, we had been invited for dinner, but after an hour or so, nobody was mentioning anything about dinner. I did not even see a table. None of us did. Another hour passed, and the time we spent grew more and more awkward as it became quite evident none of us were players. Dalí was obviously into sexual escapades of some sort and we were not his type.

"Fine, fine," he suddenly announced over the din, "let's all go to dinner. My friends, we are all hungry. We eat."

Everybody reconnoitered in the restaurant next door to the hotel, where two large tables were reserved. Dalí's kinkos grouped themselves at one table, Cher and I and other friends at the other. Dalí sat down with us. He watched as we studied the menu, smiled, and then said, "Will you excuse me for a moment, please?" No problem. It gave us time to gossip about the evening. But that was the last we saw of Dalí. He sat down with his friends and did not say a word to us the rest of the night.

"So, Sonny, I guess you're not going to ask Dalí to invest in the movie, eh?" laughed Coppola.

"Ah, I think he'd have to pay me." I laughed. "Jesus Christ, what'd we get ourselves into? Anybody know?"

The same could have—and should have—been said about the movie. What had we gotten ourselves into? The fund-raising nearly wiped me out. Then, just when we were to the point where we could begin shooting, Joe DeCarlo, our manager, came to me with a proposition.

"I think I've got something worked out that'll put us over the top," he said.

"Okay, what's it going to cost?" I replied.

"Ready for this?" he asked.

I nodded.

"Your furniture."

"Our what?" I exclaimed.

"Your furniture," he repeated. "You pawn your furniture to this guy I know. He gives you ten grand."

"Deal," I said, not even bothering to think.

After hiring a director, Alessio de Paola, and casting the parts, we packed up our crew and traipsed off to Scottsdale, Arizona. Shooting was long, tough, laborious work, work made more difficult by the unyielding desert sun and our inability to afford the luxuries that cool hot tempers.

New problems unfolded every day. Equipment broke. The weather was bad. Somebody got sick. The script needed changing. Someone's air-conditioning broke, tempers flared, fights broke out. All that and more. We weren't too far into the process when my gut began to tell me, Oh-oh, this isn't the movie I envisioned when I was writing the script. When you've got something special, you know it. Inside, you know. And inside, I knew that my movie wasn't special.

But we were pros. We dealt with the problems the best way we knew how. We consulted a Gypsy psychic. Everything else had failed, so why not? She was an older, flamboyant woman whose skin had been ravaged by too much sun. Her mind was also suspect. But who knew? Everybody went to her, hoping that she would tell us that the movie was going to be a hit, that our fairy tale would have a happy ending. We used the information she supplied as if she were Hollywood's top script doctor.

"Something very good happen to you," she told me one day. "It happen on this movie."

"We're gonna have a hit?" I asked.

"No, I not say that," she answered. "I say something good is going to happen."

"If not a hit, then what?"

"You come back another day." She smiled. "We'll discuss then."

Sure enough something happened, but it wasn't good. When I wrote *Chastity*, I put in some pretty steamy sex scenes, including ones that I drew from Cher's past. The scenes, by design, tested the sexual mores of the period. People who read the script worried that they were pornographic. I argued that they were true. I wasn't that strongwilled on the set, though. When shooting the love scenes between Cher and her leading man, Stephen Whittaker, I backed off considerably from what I'd put on paper. I realized the difference between writing those scenes at my desk and watching my wife act them out with a good-looking guy.

It was still plenty hot, though. And every once in a while I found myself wondering if anything was going on between Cher and Steve. I would catch them looking at each other. Sharing a joke I was not privy to. Or exchanging a pat on the back. Something told me there was an intimacy between them. Nah, no way, I would think. But the mere thought that there was some hanky-panky going on scared the hell out of me.

Not that I had been faithful to Cher. Some months earlier I had a brief fling with a secretary. Unfortunately, my rationale will sound like a cop-out, and it was. But I had been raised by people who accepted a double standard for men and women. I bought into the idea. Back then, I thought, Oh, this stuff isn't serious. It's just playing around.

But, God forbid somebody else was attracted to my wife!

Either I failed to notice that Cher and Steve were playing out their romance for real or I did not want to see it, but everybody else knew. The set was full of talk. Finally, Cher's double pulled me aside one day and said, "Don't you know what's going on?"

"What?" I asked.

"Cher and Steve," she said. "You've got to put a stop to this."

Having put off the confrontation for as long as possible, I told Cher that we had to talk, and later that night we did. Neither of us had ever been more uncomfortable around each other. I never asked Cher to confess anything, nor did she. The looks we exchanged were hard and deep. We knew what was at stake.

I didn't really fear that Cher had a thing for her co-star as much as I feared what her drifting meant. She was losing faith in me, the faith that had buoyed me for so many years and inspired me throughout Sonny and Cher. I knew that if she lost her faith in me, I would lose her.

I was determined not to let her go. The standard cuckolded husband's line, How could you do this to me? didn't even enter my weary brain. Rather than confront Cher and back her into a corner, I simply laid the facts on the table. I loved her and hoped to have a family with her someday. But more than that, she and I had more than a hundred thousand dollars invested in this film, our entire savings, everything that we had to show for our career as Sonny and Cher, including our furniture, and we needed to stay together through this thing. We needed to help each other.

Cher was a woman of few words. She sat without emotion as I spoke. When I finished, she didn't have much of anything to say. I walked out of the room wondering if my impassioned plea had gotten through to her. Apparently it did. The flirting stopped. Cher and Stephen backed off, and things between Cher and me went back to normal as we chugged laboriously toward the end of the movie.

On the verge of wrapping the picture, the Gypsy lady's eerie prophecy came true. We'd been trying but had had no success getting Cher pregnant. One night we made love and woke up the next morning feeling as if an outside source had delivered the magic necessary to work the miracle. We just knew Cher had conceived. We were overjoyed when the results were confirmed. It was like finishing one production and starting another.

Ironically, as the movie ended, I was the one, not Cher, who succumbed to morning sickness. I was exhausted. Making the movie had been an ordeal, emotionally and physically, which had depleted my body of every ounce of strength, including the reserves. Cher saw I was sick and summoned a doctor. Lying in bed, sallow and pale, I told him that I could not move. He ordered me to stay in bed for twenty-four hours, then gave me a shot that knocked me out for most of that time.

It was the first time since Cher and I had been together that I literally gave up. I put myself in somebody else's hands. I just could not go on. Woozy and dazed, I repeated to myself, "Thank God this is over. I just want to go home."

We'd been home several months. An afternoon sun was streaming across the table. Cher and I were sitting next to each other. I put my hand on her firm, round stomach. She smiled.

"We ought to go legit," I said. "I mean, we are going to be parents."

"What d'ya mean, legit?" she asked.

"Let's get married."

"Married?" she grinned. "To you?"

"Would you?"

It had been our secret for close to five years now that Cher and I were not really married. Nobody had ever bothered to investigate our Mexico elopement story, but we began to worry that someone would discover the truth. Both of us had the feeling that Cher was not going to have a miscarriage this time. We were going to be mother and father. We were not hippies. Basically, we were straight arrows. The right thing to do, it seemed, was to get married.

We did marry, but not until Chastity was nearly a toddler.

We let our attorney research how we might be able to go through with a legal ceremony without an army of press descending upon us like a plague of locusts. Several days later a plan was hatched and a few days after that a minister showed up at our house. Our attorney was there, my friend Denis Pregnolato, and that was it. We stood in the middle of our den, I kissed the bride, somebody poured a drink and yelled, "Salud," and within three minutes we were legally husband and wife. There was no glamour, nothing that resembled the feelings that had brought us together and made us a team. Nothing as emotional as standing onstage, looking into each other's eyes, singing the words "I got you babe" and knowing that was the absolute truth.

But if the sparks didn't fly like they had years earlier,

Cher and I were still a team, devoted to and dependent on each other, and now legally wed. Even if it wasn't emotional, the piece of paper was significant.

However, it wasn't as significant as the fact that costs on the movie, including postproduction, had soared upwards of three hundred fifty thousand dollars. Needing every cent we could lay our hands on, Cher and I hit the road. We did fourteen concerts. With the movie resting heavily on my shoulders and occupying all my thoughts, the tour was a pain in the ass. We flew into a town, checked into a hotel, did the show, went back to the hotel, rose in the morning, and followed the same routine as before, only in a different city. The show was the same. The audience appeared the same. It was mind numbing. The only familiar sights we had were each other's loving eyes and soothing smiles, and thank God for that.

"You're incredible, Son," Cher said on the plane returning from the tour. "I hate this crap and you're still going."

"Going crazy," I said. "Right now, I've got so many things going that I can hardly keep my head straight."

I was trying anything to make money. I felt as if I was in the middle of a battlefield. I was fighting my ass off. It was like playing five chess games at once. I knew if I stopped, we were fucked.

But that was the only way. We didn't have money, we didn't have furniture, and it wasn't clear how long we'd have a roof over our heads. I wanted the movie out. I wanted to reverse the flow of money from out to in. But the director was painstakingly slow in cutting *Chastity*. I badgered him constantly: Hurry up and finish. Our last bit of hope rested in that film. He didn't understand that as well as I would've liked, and my impatience took over. I couldn't wait. I fired him and Denis and I began helping the editor cut the movie ourselves.

Not only was I desperate, I had nothing else to do, so I went to the cutting room every day and stared into the editing machine, growing more and more anxious. Truthfully, the movie stank. And before we could make a penny back, we first had to sell the movie to a distributor. However, the last thing I wanted anybody to discover was the truth—not just that Cher and I were broke, but that our movie was a dog. In Hollywood image counts for everything, and I'd be damned if I was going to be perceived as desperate as I really was.

I hatched a plan. For five thousand dollars I bought an old Rolls-Royce, an immense, black gas guzzler, and hired a chauffeur. If we went to the studio we made sure everybody knew that we were arriving in a chauffeur-driven Rolls. Most days, though, we were borrowing money from the chauffeur to buy our lunches. A few years earlier we'd had an entourage. Now it was me, Cher, the editor, and our chauffeur. All I wanted to do was sell the movie before anyone discovered the truth.

When the movie was finally cut, the film editor placed the reels into ten shiny silver cans. I sat in a chair in the editing room and stared at those cans. Ten cans. My entire life was inside those cans. I reflected on the significance of that. It was pure madness.

But not as maddening as trying to sell those ten cans of film to distributors. Day after day, Denis and I lugged those extremely heavy cans from the back seat of my Rolls-Royce into one studio after another, from one distributor to another, without getting a single expression of interest. Not even a nibble. But did I worry? Ha! I used to look at my reflection in those cans and think, Oh man, what the hell did I do? I should be locked up.

Then it got worse. Denis and I made a last-ditch trip to New York, where we tried to interest several East Coast distributors. Cher and I always stayed uptown in the pricey Hampshire House or St. Regis hotels, but Denis and I could only afford a low-rent hotel in the garment district. Returning to my room after a dinner in which Denis and I could only commiserate on how awful life was, I discovered that my room had been ransacked, my valuable Patek Phillippe watch stolen and all the money in my wallet taken.

"Let's get the hell out of here," I said to Denis.

"We're leaving tomorrow," he said. "Try to get some sleep."

"Let's leave tonight," I insisted. "I'll sleep on the plane while I rest my head on those damned cans of film."

After all my moves had been played, after we were completely tapped out, after I had called in every favor owed me and drained myself of last resorts, I called the head of the William Morris Agency, Abe Lastfogel. We were close. He had always acted like a father figure to Cher and me. I told him that I needed a high-level meeting, a sit-down with the most powerful of the agency's power brokers.

A meeting was arranged at the Hillcrest Country Club, the agency's unofficial recreation center, where the power brokers played poker and golf and kibbitzed. I felt that I understood how agents thought—at least at Abe's level. They tolerated slumps. They sympathized. Every so often, though, they expected you to hit one out of the park. If you failed, they did not pay too much attention to the game.

Arriving at the meeting two minutes late, I flew past our managers, Joe DeCarlo and Harvey Kresky, both of whom I had already given up on. Fortunately, Abe and his brethren were also late; they filed in a few minutes later. Another thing about agents. The more powerful they are, the shorter they tend to be. At least that is how it used to be. Abe, a king among mortals throughout Hollywood, was barely five feet tall. The others all had an inch or two on him. Seated in the middle of the long conference table, Abe was flanked on either side by five little guys wearing suits and holding foot-long cigars.

Greetings were made. I piled the ten cans of film on the table. I did not want anybody to miss them. Then it was time for me to speak my piece. I did not hold anything back.

"OK, here it is, plain and ugly," I said. "I'm on my ass. I'm on my ass like I've never been on my ass. I've got a movie here. I've tried to sell it. I have taken it to every distributor and studio in town. Nothing. Now I need you guys to come through for me. I've come through for you. I've made you a lot of money. Now it's your turn. Sell this damn movie and get me off the hook. Because if you don't, I'm under. I'm gone. The water's up to my nose.

"I made the movie myself. Put my own money in it. My house, my furniture, my life. It's a good movie. And if we get it out, we'll be OK. But I need you guys to move on this thing. I had three hundred thousand dollars cash. And it's gone. It's all in these ten cans of film.

167

"There. I've said what I had to say. I'm finished. Thank you."

I sat down, figuring that I had made an impassioned speech that could have gotten a smile from Scrooge. I had talked to these guys in a language they understood—cash. I waited for a response. And waited. There was only silence. The agents looked at each other. Then Abe looked up and down the lineup. Finally his eyes met mine. He cleared his throat.

"Well, my son," he said.

I thought, My son, he called me my son. I am still in there good with the big guy.

"Well, my son," he said. "The situation looks bleak."

With that, Abe Lastfogel rose from the table and walked out of the room. Wordlessly, as if on cue, the other agents followed him out, a parade of short men. I was left sitting at the table with my two managers, Joe and Harvey. They had let me do all the talking, now I wanted them to say something, but they didn't.

I finally broke the quiet. "Well, what does that mean, the situation looks bleak?"

"I think it means that we're in big trouble," answered Joe. "I think it means that you're not going to get any help and, well, you've had it."

The three of us sat at the table in silence for several more minutes. We were in utter shock. After a while, it made no sense to sit there anymore; we got into our cars and drove home.

I didn't know how aware Cher was of our financial difficulties. I did my best to mask the total disaster it was, and Cher was not interested in the business aspect of our lives. But by late fall she was pregnant, and the last thing I wanted was for her to get upset and risk another miscarriage.

The baby was everything to us. It represented our love. It symbolized our hope. It was the future.

Cher was convinced she was having a boy. I didn't care. I just looked at Cher, her belly swollen with another life, a miracle, and I marveled. We used to lie in bed and gush over how happy we were. I wonder if we were conning ourselves. If we were, we were doing one hell of a job. One night in mid-November I couldn't sleep. Cher was sleeping soundly next to me. I flipped on the night-light and opened the diary she had given me on my thirty-third birthday:

November 15, 1968: I'm so lucky God gave me my wife. I love her more than anything in this world, and I will do everything in my power to make the world know that she's a great lady. I'm more proud of her than I could ever put into words. Our baby will be lucky. He or she will be surrounded by love.

My whole identity was geared toward helping Cher realize her goals. What about mine? My goal was to give her everything she dreamed about and wanted. I didn't see it then, but there was no balance to our relationship. The responsibility was lopsided. It wasn't healthy.

There was no time to analyze, though. Life was a constant scramble to keep our heads above water. After one visit to the obstetrician I made some excuse about wanting to ask the doctor another question and left Cher talking to the nurse in the waiting room. We were barely making our bill payments, and I worried about making them in the future. As the due date got closer, I did not want hassles about money. It was a difficult subject to bring up, and I hemmed and hawed, making both me and the doctor uncomfortable.

Finally I removed my watch, a diamond-studded beauty I had bought in England, and handed it to him with an oblique, embarrassing, "Here." He looked at it, probably saw that it was the real thing, and tried to give it back.

"No, keep it," I said. "If the heat ever gets worse . . ."

"OK," he said, "but—"

"No, it's yours," I said, and left.

Our situation was funny in a sad way. We lived in an enormous mansion that had no furniture. We were famous but had no money. One night George Schlatter, the producer of "Laugh-In," drove me home after a dinner party. He knew we were struggling. He booked us on "Laugh-In" together and separately, maximizing our exposure. Pulling up outside the huge gates of our huge home, I asked him to stop. I was embarrassed to drive up the driveway.

He understood.

"It's tough," I said.

"Look," he said sympathetically, "just get it back together. You have something good. Make it work again."

Easier said than done. Fortunately, we were distracted by the 1968 presidential campaign. Cher was largely apathetic when it came to politics, but I wasn't. I got heavily caught up in the Democratic contest. I identified strongly with the youth movement, the antiwar sentiment, and civil rights, and believed wholeheartedly in the ability of ordinary people to make changes. I campaigned heavily for Bobby Kennedy, though he was assassinated (while we were filming *Chastity*) before I could ever meet him personally. I then supported Vice President Hubert Humphrey.

By late fall I was traveling with Humphrey on the campaign trail, enjoying the access I had to one of the country's most powerful men, but feeling disillusioned by all the hyperbole and hypocrisy I witnessed. In my diary I wrote:

October 23, 1968: We've been barnstorming all day. Am giving the vice president moral support in each city. It's very hectic. I hope it's worth it. Right now I can't tell. Maybe I'll know more tomorrow. Right now it seems like I'm the only one who really knows what the problem is.

I hope I can make him move if he does get to be president. That's just something that we'll have to wait and see.

The more I see of politics, the less I like it. It seems like a lesser stage of show business and very phony. It's like who can out-talk who.

I hope Humphrey wins. He's the best of the three candidates. One thing I don't understand, though. If these men each run a confused campaign, which they are, how can they run a country? I hope there's an answer I don't know about. The more I see of the world, the more I think it's jive.

That diary became a great escape for me, a private place of great solace where I was free to dream and romanticize and wonder about the cards life had dealt me and not have to worry about wearing a poker face. But it was an even greater source of entertainment for Cher. I used to write in bed while she snoozed beside me, and then leave the notebook in the bathroom for Cher to read.

Cher loved to read my diary, and occasionally she jotted down thoughts of her own. In late November 1968 she came out of the bathroom laughing about how hard it was to sit on the toilet and write in the diary with her pregnant stomach sticking out so far.

"What'd you write?" I asked.

"You'll see," she said. "Read it yourself."

Later that night I went into the bathroom and opened the diary. My book had turned into our book. Cher was thrilled about writing in it, and I was ecstatic about what she'd written. She was as happy and as in love as I was. She said that she'd never known such happiness in her life.

The best was being pregnant. She was so hopeful, busting out with joy. Her first thoughts every morning concerned the baby. She spent hours daydreaming of how much we were going to love the child. Girl or boy, she didn't care.

She called me a great husband. She couldn't wait to become a mother.

"That's nice, what you wrote," I said. "I got teary-eyed."

"I mean it, too," said Cher. "Every day I thank God for making me so happy. In my whole life I never thought there was happiness like we have. Can you believe we're going to have a baby, Son?"

"No, Cher. I can't. I can't, really."

"I daydream about how we're going to love the baby," she said.

"I love you, Cher," I said. "I can't even express how much my heart beats for you."

"I know. I know that if we didn't have any money, we would still be happy," she said. "How do I know? Because we love, like, and trust each other like we do no one else. I can't wait to see this baby. Our baby. The baby made by me and you."

171

*   *   *

As soon as Cher started labor we piled into the chauffeur-driven Rolls, which we'd put up for sale, and sped to the hospital. I shot home movies of Cher being admitted to Cedars Sinai. She was in labor four or five hours. During that time my concern was for Cher, but I realized I was going through some subtle changes myself. I had tremendous guilt about the kind of dad I'd been to Christy. I'd done a poor job. I was determined not to make that same mistake with this child.

Our precious new daughter was born on March 4, 1969 and we named her Chastity Sun. Chastity, because she was conceived while we shot the like-titled movie; and Sun because she brought light to our lives.

"A little voice tells me this is a new beginning for us," I whispered to a dozing Cher.

She opened one eye and smiled.

"I love you, Son," she said. "I love our daughter too."

March 28, 1969: It's up to me to build a whole new thing for us, and that's a big job. Cher gets scared unless she understands my thinking completely, but I know what she must become and I know how to get her there. She doesn't understand where my head is at, so she worries needlessly. I understand that she was constantly disappointed most of her youth. Consequently, it's hard for her to understand that I'm not the person who brought her up.

I saw myself as someone who delivered what was promised. I was a winner.

Cher had said that she'd love me even if we didn't have any money. I'd believed her when she said it.

Still, we were in a major jam. Every day's agenda was the same—survival.

May 11, 1969: I guess I could rave about how lucky I am, but I'm almost afraid to. My wife is fine and back to her beautiful self, and my daughter, like her mother, is also beautiful. So as far as the homefront goes, I guess it couldn't be better. Thank God.

Since the last time I wrote in the book, we've been to England, New York, and Muscle Shoals, Alabama. We performed on Tom Jones's show in London. We spent a week talking about a Broadway show in New York, and Cher recorded an album in Alabama. It's a great album. I think it's the best she's ever done.

When we got home I wrote three songs. It's the first time I've felt like writing in over two years. It feels good.

As far as the movie is concerned, we finally got a deal. With American International Pictures—for $250,000. It should be released on June the 24th. We probably won't know what the reaction is until July. If it happens, I'll start another one right away. I'm convinced Cher will be one of the best actresses of our day, and I hope I'm the one who proves it.

Cher's solo LP, *3614 Jackson Highway,* only added insult to injury. Ahmet still believed in us, but his right-hand man, producer Jerry Wexler, wanted to record Cher without me. He wanted to produce too. Not only did I lose my role as producer, my credibility went out the window too. I would've been dealing with a major identity crisis, but the LP stiffed, and we were all down the tubes.

Cher and I put our house on the market. It also failed to sell. The realtor told us that people were not interested in large homes. We should have known. Our records did not sell; I wonder what made us believe that our personal property would fare any better. Then the Internal Revenue Service hit us with a whopping two hundred thousand–dollar bill for back taxes. "What's next?" I used to mutter. "What's next?"

I was certain our lives were being tested by a power greater than any known to mortal man. Everything hinged on the movie.

The pressure caused Cher to go through some weird times. Perhaps she was suffering from postpartum depression. She began to feel that Chastity didn't love her enough. She cried if the baby didn't smile at her. Cher's childhood had made her insecure, and so she believed she was an inadequate mother. It was difficult to figure out who needed

173

the most pampering, Cher or Chastity. I was afraid Cher would abandon Chastity—not physically but emotionally. I feared that she would convince herself that Chas didn't love her and then not want to be a mother anymore.

"You're close to the most perfect mother I've ever seen," I told her. "The world wouldn't be so screwed up if more mothers were like you."

"But Son," she whined, "I just don't feel the part. I don't feel like the baby is loving me. I can't explain it. I just don't feel it."

"Cher, Chas isn't even one," I said. "She loves you. I see so much of you in her. More than people know. More than you know. I guarantee you, though, that one day the whole world will know what a wonderful woman you are. I'm so proud to call myself your husband."

However, I wasn't too proud of my limited talent as a movie maker. Both Cher and I were extremely sick with viral infections when *Chastity* finally opened in Idaho and Oklahoma. Contrary to predictions, it enjoyed bonanza box office during its first week. Then the picture died. The distributor attempted to revive interest by printing new posters that showed Cher's head atop the body of another, extremely buxom, woman. It didn't help. At that point, none of us knew what the hell to do. If there was a next move to make, it was beyond me.

Joe DeCarlo then suggested that we try playing night-clubs. Cher and I hesitated. We weren't nightclub performers. We thought of ourselves as rock and rollers. We sang in concert halls. We didn't have a slick act. We didn't think of ourselves as a younger Steve and Eydie. Unfortunately, the nightclubs were the only venue open to us. The hotels were cheap. The hours were grueling. But our situation depressed us. We were scared shitless, and we needed the money.

"It's a big change for us," I noted in my diary, an entry dated July 4. "I hope we accomplish what we're trying to do, and that's to finally convince people that we're entertainers."

We debuted at the Flamingo Hotel in Las Vegas, doing two shows a night as the opening act for Pat Boone. We were booked for four weeks. On the first night Cher decided that she absolutely hated the idea of performing in nightclubs. In a nightclub, the audience was right there in her face, which scared the hell out of her. She was overcome by terrifying stage fright and insisted there was no way she could go through with it.

"Don't look at them," I told her. "If you don't like seeing the audience, don't look at them. Look at me."

"That'll make me even sicker." She grinned.

"Way to go." I laughed. "Let's use that joke tonight."

I thought we blew Pat Boone off the stage, that's how well we went over with the audience, but still, every night was a struggle to drag Cher past her fear and onto the stage. At the start of the second week she got sick. Then I got sick. We returned to Los Angeles, spent the week recuperating, and returned to Vegas, where we finished out the engagement to outstanding reviews. Although Cher hated it, and continued to get sick every time we hit Vegas, I enjoyed the work and looked forward to more.

Reading between the lines of my diary, I can see the chauvinistic limitations I had at the time, as well as my fear of losing Cher.

July 27, 1969: We have a lot of offers and will be working most of the year. If God stays with us, if all else goes according to plans, we should be in very good shape by the end of the year.

This is the first time we've ever had to grind since we started happening. But in a way, it's good. It brings you back to reality. It has given me new values. I grow each day. Cher has done so well here. It's still a struggle but she's getting better and better. I expected that. I don't know if she'll ever be fully confident onstage, but her magic grows.

She fights me a lot of times, but I never let her get too far out of line. I can't and she knows it. And she knows that I know it. But she sure can be hell when she wants to be.

Cher was tired and frustrated and took it out on me. She hated the travel and she hated not being a star. The more

I pushed her, the more she resisted and the more we disagreed and fought. But she knew that we'd played out all of our options and had to create new ones. There was no choice.

Signed to the Fairmont Hotel circuit, Cher and I turned into professional vagabonds. We bounced up and down the U.S. and Canada like Ping-Pong balls, traveling from San Francisco to New Orleans, Dallas to Pittsburgh, Toronto to Windsor. We took Chastity and her nanny, which was a great joy, but the routine of being on the road was as foreign to us as the tux I wore and the evening gown that Cher slipped into every night. Every show was a battle, every ending a triumph. We hung on to each other, clinging with all our might through the eye contact we shared onstage.

Out of that nervousness and misery, we gradually developed a humorous and fairly sophisticated repartee, which later turned into our stock-in-trade when the "Sonny and Cher Comedy Hour" made us the bickering Romeo and Juliet of prime-time television. However, it began with our simply talking to each other, pretending that we weren't standing on a stage in front of people. We kept the jokes that worked and pretty soon we had a comedy routine to punctuate our musical act.

"I just started doing a spot in the show by myself," I said. "People talk and write about us a lot. Usually I don't mention this kind of thing onstage, but somebody got me upset enough to talk about it."

"What?" asked Cher.

"Somebody put out a really lousy rumor about me," I said. "They said I sing like a frog. So what I'm going to do is sing one song by myself and then that way at least everyone will know the truth. You don't mind, do you, sweetheart?"

"Croak your heart out, froggie," she quipped. "Croak it to me."

"I think I know where the rumor came from," I said. "Now I'm going to—" Cher interrupted me. "What's the matter with you?"

"I think I got a wart," she said. "You must be a horny toad. An Italian horny toad."

"Okay, I'm going to zip along," I said, casting a wary look at Cher. "But keep a light on her. I don't trust her when she gets in one of these moods. I got a hunch I'm getting screwed, you know?"

"I got a hunch you're not," she snapped. "In fact, I'd be willing to lay odds on it."

The laughs were loud, but they died as soon as we left the stage and collapsed in our hotel room. We were under tremendous strain and stress, trying to revive our career, feeling unrelieved guilt for placing our jobs before our darling little daughter, living odd hours and always having to pack and unpack and catch airplanes. In airports we used to run into acquaintances like Glen Campbell, our former guitarist, who was then enjoying major stardom, and Dick Clark, who had once showered us with compliments on "American Bandstand," but it was clear that we were no longer peers. They were on top and Cher and I were struggling to keep afloat.

If I thought that we had hit bottom in that fallow period before I wrote *Chastity,* I soon learned that the pit we'd fallen into went down even further. Cher and I were working, but there was nothing to convince us that we still weren't continuing to sink.

I worried constantly about Cher's tolerance. I knew that she'd reach her limit and then no more. That would be it. I looked over my shoulder constantly, but I saw nothing. Probably because she showed nothing.

In September she left me a short message in my diary, professing her love and admitting that she was very unfeeling and unsympathetic. She knew I was trying.

I believed her. I wanted to, at any rate.

"I don't know where we're going," I told Cher after one show. It was close to 3 A.M. and she was exhausted and close to sleep. I was searching for an explanation as to why we were in formal attire at an hour when most people were sleeping in their toasty beds. "You just have to hang on, ride with me."

"I'm here, Son," she yawned.

"We're survivors," I said. "I don't know where we're going. But I do know that we just have to keep moving. That's the secret. Keep moving."

October 9, 1969: We have one more show to do, then we go home. It's been a lot of fun in Windsor. But Cher said something to me today that made me stop and think. She said, "You don't have all the answers."

She's right. The trick is to have the right answers at the right time. Anyway, I go home with much thinking to do.

Working steadily the rest of the year, Cher and I continued traveling a bumpy road personally. By January 1970, we were struggling to find the chemistry offstage that we shared so easily on it. I agonized at night, wondering if the criticism Cher inflicted on me might not have a kernel of truth. Was I too bossy? Was I nothing but a dreamer? Did I really live in a fantasy land?

I knew each argument we had added weight to the precarious balancing act that kept our relationship together. I found myself lying in bed and returning to a particularly steamy love scene Cher and Steve Whittaker shared during the filming of *Chastity*. I scolded myself. Why didn't I get it on film? It was the only one that worked. It was the moment I realized Cher's heart was straying from me. It caused tremors of fear to palpitate through my heart.

March 4, 1970: Today was my daughter's first birthday. Chastity didn't quite know what was going on with the party, but she was all for it.

Cher worries that the baby doesn't love her enough. But soon she will see that her mom is the world's most beautiful woman. It won't be long. Every child should have a mother who is as wonderful as Cher.

Cher, please forgive me for the past few months, for hurting you so. To say that I'm sorry sounds thin. For some reason, we sometimes hurt the thing we love most. This is a terrible sin, but that's why I'm so blessed. Because you have so much in your heart, you forgive me like a saint.

I demand so much. I'm a fool. You give more than any man could ask for. Be happy, my love. We are Romeo and Juliet in this century.

Despite constant fighting over our demanding schedule, Cher and I worked our asses off that summer. It probably cost me my relationship with Cher, but all I saw was the chance to get a leg up on things and stabilize our debts, and I went for it full throttle. We guested on several television specials that showed our act off quite nicely. Our repartee was sharp, resulting from as much offstage practice as onstage. In July we guested on a summer special costarring Michelle Lee, James Farentino, Ken and Jackie Berry and Dick Van Dyke. Our manager began to receive inquiries from producers.

Nothing materialized, though, and by August we were hard on the road again, clubbing it two times nightly. We were up and down on planes. Packing and unpacking. Walking through smelly hotel kitchens late at night. Not communicating well and missing Chas. Cher and I differed on exactly where our career was heading. She thought we were on a treadmill going nowhere fast. I figured the break we needed was just around the corner; all we had to do was work hard and keep our eyes open. The difference in our opinions represented the schism in our relationship. There was no easy solution.

Then we bottomed out, if not professionally then personally. We were in New Orleans, booked into the Blue Room. After opening, Cher and I returned to our room in silence. We had been feuding for several days. Because we were each other's best friends, it was hard on us. She went to sleep. I cracked open Mario Puzo's novel, *The Godfather*, and did not set it down till morning. It was the first book I had ever read in one sitting.

The following days were no better—only I did not have a novel to distract me. Without my life's companion, I opened my diary and wrote:

August 26, 1970: Well, we're back in New Orleans. Working in a nightclub. Business is better than last year. People are talking to us about our own TV show. But so far it's just talk. We shall see.

Cher lies beside me fast asleep. She's a good wife and a true mother. The baby gets cuter every day. I must admit the kid has it made.

I must've been deluding myself. A performer has to be part con artist, and I was trying to do a number on myself. Why? Survival.

September 8, 1970: We are still in New Orleans. Today was our day off, but we worked on a local TV show for crippled children. We were successful in our job, but it was not a good day for Cher and me. As usual, she thinks I'm wrong, and vice versa.

I don't know if it's good to write when you hurt. But when you have no one to talk to, I guess you must. We are playing a waiting game. Right or wrong, I must command respect. My main fault is I always let it falter, and then things require so much more to get back to normal.

I feel alone, which means if I'm forced to, I'll live alone. I feel like a razor and I could slash anyone to pieces. My wife doesn't believe in me anymore. She argues that I'm pushing too hard. She has challenged me. That's a mistake. I'm too set in my ways. I have chosen to live in this pig sty of a world in my own style.

I'm determined. There is only one place for me—on top. Half of my energy is wasted convincing Cher to try as hard as I do. If only I knew what needed to be done. Faith!

I am sick of Cher's doubts, and I swear by God I will no longer tolerate them. I intend to make my mark on this earth. If you read this, Cher, this is the last time I will tolerate your stupid adolescent ways. I'm sick of being misunderstood.

I was stymied by our situation, humiliated and tortured by my wife, and ultimately confused by life. I didn't understand why Cher refused to see things the way I did. Offstage, we barely spoke. The silence was as deafening as the music we pumped out to large concert halls. She resented the hell out of me for shattering her dreams. She made me the bad guy and saw herself as the victim. As we entered our second week in New Orleans, the pressure grew to an intolerable level.

The problem didn't have to be articulated. I saw it every night we stepped onstage in the nightclub. We were dressed up. I put on a tux. Cher wore a gorgeous gown. We rode in an elevator, stood in the kitchen of the club, and popped out onstage. We were hit by the bright lights. We were thinking glamour, excitement. But then we'd look out and see the audience—twelve people.

If you see that scene in a movie, it's a pretty sad picture. When you watch your audience shrink from tens of thousands to something like a dozen, it makes you feel miserable. The visuals are obvious. You don't concern yourself with doing a good show as much as with thinking, Can I get out of this situation? Cher and I knew we were in trouble. Just being onstage was enough. We didn't need words to describe it.

Cher let me know that I was blowing it. At the time her admiration for me was zip. That devastated me. I knew that if I lost her admiration, I'd also lose the marriage.

The air was heavy all the time. Our enthusiasm for life was too low to pick up. Both of us were worrying about the same thing—survival. There was just one important difference in the way we addressed our concerns. I thought about the survival of Sonny and Cher. Cher just thought about Cher.

I'd made mistakes. I'd admitted them. I was also insecure and afraid. But I wasn't a quitter. I wanted Cher to realize that. I wanted to make her understand that I was only trying to act the way I thought a man was supposed to.

It was time to talk. It was time to say, Okay, I know what you're thinking. Let's talk.

With the air-conditioner in our hotel suite humming on high, I sat Cher down on the sofa. Although Cher's face was as impassive as always, I looked into her eyes and saw the turbid emotions that ate at both of us. I knew she wasn't going to say anything; I had to take the initiative.

"We can't go on like this, baby," I said.

Nothing came from her. A tilt of her head, perhaps, a subtle acknowledgment.

"Look, if there's a move to make, make it. I expect you to. No hard feelings. You know?"

"I don't know, Son," she said. "I don't know what to do. I only know that I can't go on like this. We're nowhere. No different than a year or two ago. I hate the fighting. I hate what we're doing to each other."

"I hate it too," I said. "I can't take the put-downs anymore."

"Yeah," she sighed. "I just don't know what to do. I wish I did."

"Listen, Cher," I said. "We've never been anything but straight with each other. Good and bad, we've always been honest and nothing but."

"So?"

"So what I want is three years. Give me three years to pull it off. Three more years. I know I can pull it off. After that, if nothing happens, then—"

"Don't say it," she said.

"Three years then?" I smiled.

"Okay."

Later that night I went out with several of the guys in the band, and Cher picked up my diary, which had turned into a conduit for our feelings. We communicated more openly in writing than we did face to face. In the morning I opened the diary, discovering Cher's entry. It was dated September 11, and it was uncharacteristically apologetic.

Cher had missed me. More than that, I think she felt sorry for me. She hadn't known the extent of my anguish.

"We need to talk," I said after finishing Cher's entry and finding her in bed, waiting for my reaction with big, questioning eyes.

"Oh, Son," she sighed. "Do you remember long ago? We'd first met, and I told you about when I was young and had to go to school with rubber bands over the toes of my soles so my shoes wouldn't flap while I walked. I hurt so much then and I can feel the hurt now. I really need you now more than ever. I am still your baby and the things you say about me are true."

"I need you to believe in me, Cher," I said pleadingly. "I can't make it without you. You're everything to me. My stability. My generator. I need you to stand beside me."

"Son, don't doubt me. Please don't doubt me," Cher implored. "You're a great man. I'm not sure that I'm a great woman. You're a great husband. I'm just a good wife. All things are relative. I am you. That's scary to me. Even if you left me, you couldn't rid your body of me. Oh God, I can't believe I'm saying this out loud."

"I'm sorry about the Prince and I couldn't help it," Chip explained. "You're a great man. I'm not angry that I'm a great painter. You're a great husband. I'm also a good wife. All I've ever wanted is for you. I just wanted to marry you. If you'll let me. You couldn't tell your mother or me at all that I cared before I'm seven, his son said.

PART IV

BANG BANG, MY BABY SHOT ME DOWN

11

SHE DIDN'T EVEN SAY GOOD-BYE SHE DIDN'T TAKE THE TIME TO LIE

I can't figure it out," I said to Cher.

We were snuggled up in first class on a plane heading for New York. We had just finished a several-week run at the Sahara, in Las Vegas. Both of us were exhausted, talking only because we had not yet fallen asleep.

"What?" she said, looking at me with only one eye, and even that was half-open.

"We're having fun in the show. The audience loves it, they're responding real good. What do we have to do to get the big commercial break? To be accepted by the networks?"

Cher was slow to respond. When I looked over at her, I saw she was asleep. I wished I was too, but my mind was working overtime. Something was happening to the bigger acts who played in Vegas that had not happened before. They were popping. An example was Tom Jones. From his sellout successes at the Flamingo he became a star and got his own TV show.

Cher and I were drawing in Vegas. We had shared the Sahara bill with comedian David Brenner and Frankie Avalon, and I figured that we were the draw. I was constantly evaluating our position, examining the crowds, considering how the hotels received us—a true benchmark of your worth—and, strange as it seemed, I concluded that Cher and I were rising. Without so much as a hit record, we were generating heat.

Early that fall Cher and I flew to New York on a promotional trip and checked in to the Waldorf-Astoria. We had not been to Manhattan for six months, since playing the Waldorf, and that gig had been a near disaster. Prior to that show, my back went out. We were desperate and needed every dollar we made, but I woke up with a pinched sciatica. I couldn't move without excruciating pain. It was so bad, Cher and our road manager, Denis Pregnolato, had to turn me sideways in bed so that I could pee into the wastepaper basket.

A doctor gave me a shot of Demerol to get me onstage that night, but the following morning the pain was even more debilitating than before. Several years earlier we had met Steve Lawrence and Eydie Gormé on a Kraft Music Special and they had told us about a doctor, an ear, nose, and throat man, who also cured backs. I was skeptical, but Steve insisted that the guy was magic. Eydie had gone to him on a stretcher and walked out a new woman.

"What does he do?" I asked.

"He sticks swabs up your nose," said Steve, "and a little while later, everything's okay."

Cher, who had once visited him for a sore throat, remembered his name. We called and explained the problem. An hour later, he was beside my bed, dipping these long swabs of cotton into a bottle and then sticking them up my nose. Way up. Was I this much of an idiot? What the hell kind of treatment was this? Twenty minutes later, he pulled the sticks out and said, "Okay, get up and walk to me."

"Come on," I said. "I can't move."

"Get up and walk," he insisted.

Fine. I would try. I swung my feet around, expecting pain. Nothing. I stood, expecting to crumble. But I stayed on my feet. I took one step, then two, and then I walked straight across the room as if I had never been laid up. I bent down, up, and spun around.

"Goddamn, it worked!"

"That's the fun of being in the miracle business," the doc said.

Now Cher and I were back in New York. My sciatica was fine. But there was still the possibility that another miracle might be performed. We were told that Fred Silverman, the genius programmer at CBS Television, had seen our show and was talking about a television show. Something was brewing.

About a week later, Silverman arranged for us to serve as guest hosts on "The Merv Griffin Show," which CBS was then broadcasting opposite Johnny Carson's "Tonight Show." With our act as tight as ever, Cher and I went over big. Silverman sent us a congratulatory letter, saying that he had become a fan and expected great things from us. I expected great things from us too, so I was not about to get too excited.

Quite unexpectedly, though, the pot started to boil. Johnny Musso, an old buddy of mine from my promo days, signed Cher to a record deal on Kapp Records. Considering our recent track record, he was taking a risk. I asked him why. He said he believed in us. When I asked why again, he said that he just did. But there was a catch to his deal—he didn't want me to produce. He wanted to use Snuffy Garrett.

Fine. That was okay with me. I was bored by the studio and Snuff was a friend who dated back to Liberty Records.

Overlapping this was another fortunate deal. Fred Silverman arranged for Cher and me to star on our own summer replacement series on CBS. The deal was for seven variety shows. The hour-long shows were formulated around our nightclub act, which was by then razor sharp. If the ratings were good, we were assured, something permanent might develop.

Well, the ratings were good. And in September Cher's song "Gypsies, Tramps, and Thieves" was released. Seven weeks later it was number one. We were out on the road playing county fairgrounds when the electricity began buzzing. I noted the gate at each show, so I knew the crowd size we ordinarily pulled.

At one midwestern gig, held at a quarter-horse racetrack—an enormous stadium—something odd occurred. Cher and I had been resting in our trailer when I decided to check the crowd. I stepped outside and my head whirled. The stadium was practically full and people were still streaming in. I told Cher to poke her head out the door.

"Jesus, will you look at the crowd," I said. "Someone big is playing here. Who the hell is on the bill with us?"

"I don't know," said Cher. "Ask the promoter."

I walked around. Finally, I found the promoter, who was in a delightful mood, thinking about all the money he was making.

"Who do you have booked here?" I asked. "The crowd's enormous."

"Just you guys," he said, looking surprised. "You're the only ones booked."

I was surprised but immensely pleased. I realized what was happening to us. After the performance, Cher and I were returning to our motel when a little kid ran alongside us, pointing and screaming, "There they are, Mommy! Sonny and Cher! From TV!"

I gave Cher's hand a tight, affectionate, happy squeeze. I got a glimmer of a smile in return.

Back in our room Cher fell asleep, while I sat up in bed, analyzing our climb back to notoriety. We were on our way back toward the top of Everest. We were out of breath, aching, battered, and bruised. But we were going to reach the summit—again.

I couldn't sleep that night; I was too excited. I had begged Cher for three years. And now, less than twelve months later, I was on the phone to everyone I knew, asking, "Can this be? Is it happening again?"

I wanted to ask Cher. I wanted to celebrate with her. I wanted to make love to her. But she was sleeping.

The heat surrounding Sonny and Cher was rising as 1971 wound to a close, but before anything too great happened to us, I decided to take care of an unpopular piece of business. I fired our manager, Joe DeCarlo. Our old managers, Charlie and Brian, had each been getting 10 percent. When they were let go, Joe took both their shares, giving himself 20 percent of what for a long time really amounted to nothing. Now that the television series was about to put us back in the big money, I didn't think that Joe deserved a free ride. Denis Pregnolato, our road manager, was doing all the work, and Joe was pocketing a disproportionate amount of the profits. So I performed the deed that no one else had the guts to do.

It seemed as if everything was falling into place. In December the *Sonny and Cher Live* album went to thirty-five on the charts. A new Sonny and Cher single, "All I Ever Need Is You," blasted up to seventh place. Best of all, "The Sonny and Cher Comedy Hour" got a green light from CBS and became a weekly prime-time series.

We were playing Vegas, closing out the year with a nice paycheck. Our shows were sold out before we even got to town. It was undeniably exciting. It was a time of celebration. At least it should've been. Sonny and Cher were on the marquee in enormous letters outside the hotel. Traffic up and down the strip was blocked nightly by people going to our show. And we knew that once the TV show hit, it would only get bigger. But you wouldn't have known any of it by looking at Cher. Before one performance, Cher and I were getting dressed in the bathroom when I tried to drum up some enthusiasm in Cher.

"What's wrong?" I finally said.

She looked at me. "You know, I was just thinking, I wish we were really big, like Dylan or the Rolling Stones."

"But we're as big as anybody," I said. "How can you not recognize that? You can't get into this place. Can't buy a seat for less than $500. What do you mean, big?"

"I mean, I want to be big, really big," she said. "You either understand or you don't."

Well, I did not understand. What I thought I understood was that I was on the receiving end of a complete shellacking of everything we had ever accomplished. Totally invalidated. Cher had told me to deliver, and I had delivered. Now, suddenly, when we were standing on top of the mountain, nothing Cher and I had, not our career, not our mansion, not our fame was satisfying. And that hurt. That hurt because I felt as if I had pulled something special off—for her and for me.

It was only later that I began to understand what Cher was saying. She was tired of Sonny and Cher. She did not simply detest the work, the travel, the monotony, and the audience; she resented me. She hated sharing the spotlight. She really wanted to be bigger than Dylan and Jagger. Only she wanted that fame and attention and adulation all for herself.

She had her reality. I had mine. That was the problem. We had drifted apart. Yet we still connected, still intertwined, still drew life from the same umbilical chord, and to think of severing ties was downright suicidal.

The new year began and virtually overnight, Cher and I had gone from has-beens to hot stuff. Suddenly we had steady, glamorous work, fat paychecks, a platform to work from, visibility beyond our wildest imagination, fame . . . everything! We committed ourselves to making the show work, even reinvesting most of our salary in the show. The weekly budget was thirty-five thousand dollars—peanuts in prime-time land.

We recognized the golden opportunity. In many ways we were not the same people we had been when Sonny and Cher hit in 1965. For one thing I had had my nose done a couple years earlier, asking the doctor to take it from immense down to simply large. Cher had had her nose done and had gone to New York to have her breasts reshaped and firmed up, a painful experience when she returned home with infected scars. In our personal lives, we were trying to be parents. We owned up to a certain responsibility. And emotionally, well, our relationship was in a strange, undefinable netherworld, stuck between husband and wife, best friends, mom and dad, partners, and complete and utter strangers.

However, the show was a blast to do. Even on our bad days we had fun. Cher had always dreamed of wearing glamorous gowns designed by Bob Mackie, who dressed Diana Ross, Carol Burnett, and Dionne Warwick. So we hired him. Our writers were top-notch and included Steve Martin and Bob Einstein. Cher, who was able to deal with her stage fright by working to the camera instead of the audience, enjoyed hiding behind the various characters she played in skits.

Everything Cher and I had been doing for years gelled. The show worked. It was hip and kooky, but the best and most memorable part was the opening dialogue between Cher and me:

"Thank you, I really appreciate it," I remembering saying during one show, bowing to the cheering audience and then glancing, grudgingly, at Cher. "Cher deserves a little hand too."

"What about his suit?" she asked, motioning to the lime-green suit I was wearing. "What are you, the jolly green midget?"

"You're starting tonight, huh, Cher?" I nodded.

"No," Cher said coyly.

"You look good," I said. "You look good, precious. Your hair looks so nice. You really . . . Fair Cher. Fair, fair Cher." Then I recited a short poem. "Fair Cher/with the raven hair/for sure you're a winner/but when you stand next to me . . . you look like a beginner."

The audience cracked up.

"Thank you very much." I bowed and turned to Cher. "What an ovation, huh? Do you know why they applauded like that?"

"I think your microphone went dead," she said with impeccable timing.

"She's just kidding," I said. "You folks know what a great talent I am. And in appreciation of your good taste, I've got some great plans for you. What do you think of this—a music school?"

"Fantastic," said Cher. "You should enroll immediately."

"Come on, Cher," I said. "I didn't get to go to any kind of show-business school, and because of that I made a lot of mistakes."

"Yeah, like singing." She laughed.

"You made a lot of mistakes too," I replied.

"Only one," she deadpanned. "A short one."

Joking aside, Cher and I appeared to have put our mistakes behind us—at least that's how success made it appear to me. Cher was impossible to read. But on a superficial level I had no qualms that we were as strong and as happy as ever, and with Chas, we formed a cozy little family unit in our thirty-four-room mansion.

Eight weeks into the season, a visitor appeared on our doorstep. Tony Curtis. He was, as ever, the master salesman, his smile broad and bright. He wanted to congratulate us on the incredible good fortune we were enjoying, and, it turned out, he also wanted to take a bit of the fortune for himself.

"My dear kids," he said upon entering. "I have the perfect home for you.

"We aren't looking to move," I said.

"You're stars," he said. "You should reside in heaven."

Cher and I accompanied Tony to his house, the breathtaking Holmby Hills mansion where we had eaten dinner several years earlier. Cher was smitten with the house; she had been since our first visit. To her, the mansion was the pinnacle of her Cinderella fantasy. I understood. For me, the house was a trophy similar to the cars I collected. We strolled the grounds, looked around, dreamed, and gazed.

Cher and I decided Tony was right. We liked heaven, and before leaving we gave the shrewd, persuasive actor seven hundred fifty thousand dollars of our money in exchange for title to the fifty-four-room, thirty-thousand-square-foot residence. In retrospect, the purchase turned out to be a grave mistake. The house gave off bad vibrations. The owners before Tony had been divorced. Before them, the owner had drowned in the indoor pool. And before that gruesome event, one of the owners had been shot. Beyond all that, though, the mansion was just too damn big for a tiny family like ours. I saw the place as a monument to our status, but in reality the house was large and cold and good only for hiding out and hiding troubles.

Cher furnished it in three days. I don't think anyone ever sat in the living room.

A hectic calendar was partly to blame. Cher and I were kept quite busy by the show and whenever there was a break in the schedule I booked us on out-of-town concerts. That's where the big money was. We were pulling in fifty to sixty thousand dollars on a good night. Working steadily, we banked in the neighborhood of four million dollars that year—a lot of money in those days.

But I knew we had to capitalize on our comeback. This time I didn't trust success. Cher and I had lived through the ups and downs of show business, and I knew which one I preferred. I also saw the opportunity to build up a savings for the day when we would not have to work so hard. Cher only thought about the present, though. Her complaints were like a broken record. She hated the grind. She hated performing. I don't think we ever played Las Vegas without her getting sick and using that as an excuse to cut our run short.

Las Vegas was a strange place for us. We were huge. We broke house records. I loved the atmosphere, the dark artificiality of it. It was a Disneyland for adults. I don't think Cher liked anything about it except that Howard Hughes lived there, and she felt that somehow they were connected in spirit. I realized that, like Hughes, Cher was reclusive. She hid out in our hotel room, ordering room service, watching television, waiting for Hughes to call, and refusing to go outside until we had to perform. He never did call her.

Cher's mystery man Howard Hughes might've been the richest man in Las Vegas, but I was much more interested in meeting the man who owned the town, and there was no question about who that was. His name was Elvis Presley. I'd never seen Elvis, but like everyone else was fascinated by the power he exercised over an audience. We'd played Vegas at the same time. Cher and I thought we were doing well packing three hundred seats every night at the Flamingo, but down the Strip Elvis was pulling in two thousand people a show at the Hilton. That was unheard of.

"Cher," I asked one night, "you want to fly into Vegas and see Elvis?"

As expected, she said no. She hated going to Vegas when we were getting paid for being there, and not even Elvis could get Cher to Vegas if she didn't have to be there. But my pal Denis had no bigger hero than Elvis. He couldn't wait.

We flew into town the following night and caught Elvis's late show. He knew we were in the audience and before the performance one of his guys came to our table and invited me and Denis backstage after the show. Great.

Then the show started and I was blown away. I'd seen a lot of performers. I'd been around a lot of really top talent. But I'd never seen anyone like Elvis.

He was both the worst and the best of showmen. The show actually was quite mediocre. His performance was by the numbers. But Elvis had charisma like nobody's business. He possessed a powerful magnetic charm, a force that mesmerized and hypnotized the crowd. I'd never seen anything like it. When he moved, he lumbered across the stage with considerable effort, by that time a gross, overweight shadow of the hip-swinging, roguish lover boy who had sung rock and roll and rhythm and blues in a way that made him a one-man revolution. But people went berserk with the smallest twitch of his lip. If he winked, people screamed. If he smiled, women fainted.

It was obvious he didn't give a shit. I imagined that like Cher, this living legend would've preferred to stand in his dressing room in his glittery outfit and trade handshakes for money rather than go out onstage. He read the lyrics to several songs from a sheet of paper. During one song, he even stopped in the middle, turned his back on the crowd, and chewed out his guitarist. When the lights flicked on and off accidentally, he made faces at his lighting technician. But after the last number, the crowd stood and cheered until Elvis reluctantly sang another song.

Afterward, Denis and I went backstage, where we found Elvis in his dressing room, seated on a sofa between several Las Vegas lovelies. His lighting man was in the process of apologizing, though it didn't seem that Elvis was listening to him as much as he was to the whispers of his girlfriends. I worried about what to say to him. Small talk is no simple task at any level, and complimenting a legend is even more difficult. However, Elvis gave us a warm greeting, a friendly hello. Right away he began talking about how much he liked Cher's and my version of "What Now, My Love." He told how he had sent his henchmen scurrying all over Memphis late one night in search of a copy so he could listen to it before recording the song himself.

"How's the Colonel?" I asked, referring to his longtime manager, Colonel Tom Parker.

Elvis seemed uncomfortable with the question.

"I don't see much of the Colonel," he said. "My daddy takes care of most things."

Then Elvis asked what I thought of the show.

"Gee, it was great," I said. "I mean, I can't believe you can do whatever you want—read your lyrics, chew out your guitarist, whatever."

Elvis looked at me as if I were stupid or had said the wrong thing. I worried. Then he chuckled.

"Well, goddammit, Sonny," he said. "I am the fucking King."

Now Cher and I even traveled on our own private plane. We literally should have been flying on top of the world. Crazed mobs surrounded us at airports, clamored to see our shows, afforded us the luxury of buying every comfort ever price-tagged in a store. We had everything that either of us wanted or dreamed of having, everything that Cher had given me three years to manufacture. Except for one important thing—companionship.

Whenever I looked at Cher on the plane or in our dressing room, she was always absorbed in needlepoint. She was bored. Disinterested.

The romance that worked so well on television was, in fact, exactly what we'd sold to television, and exactly what television had sold to advertisers—a commodity. Offstage we weren't living the life of husband and wife as much as we were living out the expectations of Sonny and Cher. That was a reality too painful, even impossible, for either of us to admit. Rather than face facts, we struggled to ignore them.

But even that eventually became too big a task.

November 4, 1972: The whole world has changed since the last time I wrote—God, a year or so ago. Cher and I are now the stars of our own TV show. We have a million-dollar house, and I guess you could call us rich. We have a lot of money in the bank. Now for the bad news.

Everything exploded between Cher and myself. Neither one of us could define our relationship and I suspect it will be a while before I can.

Chas is three and a half now, and she's fantastic. She doesn't know Mom and Dad are on the ropes. I'm sure everything is relative. For the past five years, I've been worried about our career and I never worried about us.

On the way home from taping "The Sonny and Cher Comedy Hour," I was struck by how humorless real life had become. A road engagement was upcoming. I was running through the schedule with Cher. Suddenly she informed me that she did not want to go. There was a signed contract, I explained. Whether she liked it or not, we were committed. She did not like it.

"What do you want to do, then?" I demanded.

"I don't know," she said.

"You want to give it all up? Sit home? Shop till we run out of money?"

"No."

"Then what?" I fumed.

"I don't know. Something. I'm just confused."

"Confused?"

"OK, miserable."

November 11, 1972: I guess I should write something just for the hell of it so I'll have something to read later. Cher wants to run like a racehorse, but she can't find a track. I used to be the jockey, but she quite nicely shoved the saddle up my ass. Sonny and Cher, those little devils, are still on television. The hearts America loves. We are trying to preserve that so we won't wind up where we started—on our asses. Stay tuned. It gets more exciting by the second.

There had been worse days in my life. Once when I had been married to Donna, I was fired from my job for moonlighting. Christmas was approaching. We had no money. Just piles of bills and obligations. Somehow I got a job singing in a nightclub. On our meager budget, I figured that

I needed the job for four weeks, at least. If I held out for the month of December, we would be able to meet our bills.

I did not make it. I was fired after only two weeks. The manager told me I was a lousy singer. Tell me something new, I thought. My car died on the freeway going home. It was the middle of the night, extremely cold, and so foggy I was unable to see more than six feet in front of me. It was the night before Christmas Eve and nobody stopped to help me. It took until dawn, but I pushed that damn car all the way home.

Yeah, I had known worse times. But big deal.

On paper, Cher and I could not have been doing better. She had closed out 1971 with a top-ten hit, "All I Ever Need Is You." In April 1972 "A Cowboy's Work Is Never Done" also went top ten, and the album *All I Ever Need Is You* peaked at fourteen. Another single, "When You Say Love," adapted from the Budweiser commercial, climbed up to thirty-two. And our television show was among the highest-rated programs on the air.

November 15, 1972: I don't know the answer to so many things I thought I did. Most of all my wife. We're in Las Vegas. People love us. But they don't know the truth. Neither do I.

It was a Saturday night. The room was packed. Cher and I were breaking attendence records, while ignoring our personal difficulties, which didn't seem anything more than usual. Between shows Cher, Denis, our guitarist, Bill Hamm, and I went over to the Hilton lounge where we caught Tina Turner in action. Then we went back to the Flamingo, did our late show, and received three standing ovations. Afterward I kidded with comedian David Brenner, our opening act, about all the dough we were making for doing what we loved to do. Show business didn't get any better.

I met Cher outside the dressing room. Together we took the private elevator upstairs to our opulent suite. Both of us were exhausted. The conversation we traded in the elevator was strained, but we still managed shallow chitchat that was typical of the truce we called when we were on the road and forced to share close quarters. We walked down the hall and opened the door. Cher dropped her bag on the chair and I tossed my jacket on the sofa. I saw the bed and imagined how wonderful it was going to feel to cover myself up and shut my eyes. But as I unbuckled my belt, Cher shot me a pained look that was completely foreign to the repertoire I knew so well from ten years of being with her.

Something was wrong. Drastically wrong. It jarred me wide awake.

"I want you to leave the room," she said.

"Why?" I asked, caught off-guard.

"Because Bill Hamm is coming up," she said.

I was curious. Real curious. Bill Hamm, a likable kid in his early twenties, was our guitarist. He was writing lots of songs then. I figured he wanted to play some for Cher. Or that they were working on songs together and Cher was too inhibited to work with me in the room.

"Yeah, what's he want?" I asked innocently.

"I want to sleep with him," she said.

Her face hardened. She was braced for my reaction.

A voice in my head screamed, "What!"

My body froze.

I went into shock. Cher might as well have put a gun to my head and shot me.

"What?" I stammered.

"I'm in love with Bill Hamm," said Cher.

Cher's revelation came from so far out in left field that I did not know how to respond.

"Cher, are you crazy?" I screamed, reacting instinctively. "Do you know where we're at now?"

"He's coming up, Son," she said. "And I want you to leave."

"You can't do this, Cher. We'll talk about it. Let's talk, OK?"

I had never suspected that there was anything going on between them. The news caught me flatfooted.

"Listen, don't do it, Cher. Just don't. Think about what you're saying."

"I've thought about it," she said. "I'm going to. He's going to be here any second."

Quickly I raced through every possible avenue of recourse. What was I supposed to do? Hit the guy? Kill him? Quietly relinquish my wife? Roll over and play dead? Acquiesce to her whim without a sour word? What?

Then Bill walked in the room. He had a dumb look plastered on his face. Clearly, he was oblivious to the scene Cher and I were playing out.

"Hi, how ya doin'?" He smiled.

But then Bill picked up the vibes right away and his smile vanished. Suddenly the three of us were caught in a weird, twisted triangle. We stood there facing each other. No one knew what to say. We were awkward, tense, speechless. The lid was off. Cher had made the first move, and she had done it with fearless nerve.

She'd been successful too. I was absolutely frozen; I didn't know what to do other than look at them in utter disbelief. My eyes moved back and forth from Cher to Bill like a pendulum. I wanted desperately to make sense out of the situation that made no sense at all. There was a row of whiskey bottles lined up on the bar. For a moment I considered clobbering Bill over the head, then breaking another over Cher's, perhaps destroying the entire suite.

"Son?" she said.

With a final look at Cher, I turned and walked out of the room. No yelling. No slamming the door. I was a zombie who'd been defeated.

I went downstairs to the casino and began playing blackjack when Bill's girlfriend tapped me on the shoulder.

"Have you seen Bill?" she asked.

"You haven't heard?" I said.

"Heard what?"

In a matter-of-fact voice, as cool and restrained as I could manage, I explained the situation. The sentences still came gushing out in a spill of raw, injured emotion. I told her that he was with Cher; that they were upstairs in our bedroom; that I had been asked to leave; that Cher had declared her love for Bill; that Cher had told me she wanted to sleep with him. That I wanted to kill them.

Her only response was to repeat, "What?"

Finally, I said, "Let's go up to your room," and she did not hesitate. We slept together that night, trying to secure retribution through our own lovemaking, though in truth we bumped at each other with the enthusiasm of two people who had just been mugged. Early the next morning Bill returned to his room. His girlfriend and I were still together when he knocked on the door. I answered.

"Oh hi, Bill," I said, ready for a fight of some sort. He was upset, but he brushed by me as if I were not there. I grabbed my things. "See ya later," I called.

Cher was lying in bed, wrapped in blankets, when I returned to our room. It was about 5 A.M. Her eyes were open. Without saying anything, I took off my wedding ring, set it on the night table, and lay down across the end of the bed. I wanted to fall asleep, wake up with the light, and realize that everything that had occurred was an unpleasant dream. Cher turned over, and both of us dropped off into restless, disorienting sleep.

I heard her stirring several hours later and sat up. She was looking at me.

"It's not too late to change things," I said.

"We can't," she said; then, after a long pause, she asked, "What did you do last night?"

"I screwed Bill's girlfriend."

"That's funny." She laughed. "Bill and I didn't even go to bed together."

I wanted to wring Cher's neck, but I settled on talking to her. We talked the entire day. About everything—our career, our relationship. We reminisced about how we'd met, our early days together, and we discussed how much we had loved each other and how that love was gone. We talked about Chas and what we'd each be losing if we split. Cher was very calm and casual, almost as if she'd played this scene out in her head countless times until she had everything down pat.

I, on the other hand, was a wreck. I knew that this was my last stand with her, my last hope for saving whatever there was left to save, and my only option was to talk. I tried talking sense into her. I attempted to talk her out of calling it quits. I knew she didn't love Bill Hamm, as she claimed. I knew he was a pawn in the game she played in her mind. He was an excuse. She had claimed that she wanted to sleep with him and then hadn't. He was the straw that she could use to break my back. He was her way out of Sonny and Cher.

In the context of what was happening I suppose I was making sense, but I'm sure that I was also stark raving mad. The words spilled out of me like oil out of a broken main. I was desperate to find that one thing I could say that would make everything better again, but I couldn't find it. In that kind of situation, your mind is splintered. You say one thing, think another, and listen to this inner dialogue you can't make out. It's the closest I've come to real craziness.

No matter what I said to Cher, she insisted on her love for Bill.

The hours slipped away. As showtime approached, I was in a daze. There was no way I could go onstage without resolving this mess. Finally I asked Cher to call him up to the room. We ended up meeting downstairs in the dressing room.

"Look, guys," I said, "this isn't going to work. Let's back out now and salvage something."

"No, no," said Cher. "You're wrong, Son."

"We're in love, man," Bill chimed in. "There's no rationale. I'm sorry, man. It happened. We just fell in love."

The discussion went nowhere fast. It was a futile waste of breath. Then Bill left, and Cher and I returned to our room.

In the meantime Denis, our manager, was frantically trying to locate us. We were not answering our phone or the messages slipped under our door. At four that afternoon, I finally paged Denis and said, "We have a problem. We can't go on." Demanding some kind of explanation, he asked us to meet in his room, and I told him about the soap opera that had developed since the end of the previous night's show. Denis listened in horror and shock. Then he exploded in anger. He immediately canceled the two shows Cher and I were supposed to do later that night. Then he went to look for Bill. He wanted to kill him.

The funny part of this incident was that he forgot to tell David Brenner that the show was no go. At eight o'clock David was standing backstage like always, in his tux, waiting for his cue from the band. After ten minutes, he realized the band had not played his usual cue and thought, It's too quiet. He peeked out from the curtain and discovered there was no audience. He ran to Denis.

"What the hell is going on?" Brenner asked.

"That's exactly what we're all trying to figure out," Denis replied.

Denis became the intermediary. Later that night he calmed down enough to forget about decapitating Bill and spoke to Cher. She wanted to get out of town, and he agreed that it was probably a good idea to leave. He wanted to get both of us out of the battlefield before news of what had happened leaked to the press and got back to the brass at CBS. Cher wanted to go to San Francisco with Bill. That was fine. Denis made the arrangements and got her and Bill on the first plane. He also hired a private detective in San Francisco to follow Cher, thinking it best that he keep tabs on her. As luck had it, though, the detective lost Cher's car before it left the airport.

In the meantime, he booked me, Chastity, and the nanny on the next plane to Los Angeles. I can hardly remember leaving Las Vegas. I didn't take any luggage. I didn't speak to anyone. I was too numb to function normally. At home, I went directly to bed, where I remained, more or less, completely and hopelessly depressed, for the next two weeks. My weight dropped to one hundred thirty pounds. My health deteriorated. The life and spirit that had kept me going drained right out of me. I was beaten.

I didn't know it, but Cher called Denis at 5 A.M. the day after she landed in San Francisco. She wanted to come back home, but she feared my reaction. Denis said, "Don't worry. Just come home." We still had one more show to tape, the Christmas show. Cher arrived the next afternoon. By then Denis had let the show's producers know what was going on. It was kept as hush-hush as a government secret. No one was talking. No one knew what to say, including me and Cher.

I saw her that night as I was dragging my spindly body into the bathroom. I acknowledged her presence in our bedroom, which I'd taken over, with an angry glance. She said, "Hi." I nodded and groaned, "Hello." We were zombies, strangers, enemies. Fortunately, we had fifty-four rooms and there was plenty of space where we could shut ourselves off from each other and revel in the pain of our crumbled relationship.

At the end of November, I went away by myself for two weeks, traveling to France, England, Nassau, and Miami. I was desperately trying to get my head together, to think clearly and size up our situation. Most days I was depressed, mirroring Cher's usual mood. My mind vacillated between thoughts of death and thoughts of love for Chastity.

December 9, 1972: We finished our Christmas show tonight. When it's put together I'm sure it will look very warm and loving, but I've never felt colder and more hateful. Cher and I can only talk to each other at certain times. What can I say? Nothing. Is it over? I don't know. I keep asking myself questions for which I don't have any answers. All I can do is hope for the best and then work at it.

A few days later Cher and I talked for an hour, maybe more. Actually, I did most of the talking. In a familiar repetition of discussions we'd had before, I told Cher that she had to realize that we were involved in a business, a highly profitable business, and though the marriage was gone and the love lost, it was silly to give up the tremendous sums of money we were making. I'd come to terms with the reality of our situation. I accepted it, and I wanted her to know where I was coming from. I was OK with her pursuing whatever personal life she wanted. I'd do the same. But Sonny and Cher were names too valuable to simply walk away from.

She agreed.

I called Denis the next day. He and his wife were about to leave on a Christmas vacation. I told him that I had some news for him. Good news, for a change. He was all ears.

"We're going to try to patch things up," I said. "Cher and I decided to make a go of it."

There was a long pause.

"You're full of shit," he finally said.

Then it was my turn to pause.

"You're probably right," I said. "Goddammit."

December 26, 1972: Cher and I came from no kind of family life. Cher used to worry about that. I would tell her not to worry. We would build our own. I always believed that, and so far, after ten years, we have put things together, built things from nothing.

Now again I have no family. I have one in name only for our public. We are famous. I guess I wouldn't trade those ten years for anything. They were the best in my life—that's something. The Cher I have been writing about these past few years is gone. She is a changed person.

Our relationship is no longer adequate. She wishes to venture out now without me, and she did. It's no longer our house. It's half mine and half Cher's. The same with our money, daughter, and everything else.

That's the way we live now. No plans, no future. To stay healthy long enough so we may separate without it being a disaster and ruining everything we've built. I don't know if that's possible, but at this moment that's what we are attempting.

To say we misunderstood each other after ten years of being together sounds stupid, but I guess I'm stupid. That's what happened. I thought I was teaching. She thought I was intimidating. She wants freedom, which I have taken from her, and now she shall have it.

Which way does Sonny Bono go now? I was committed so deeply to one stage in life that now I'm in a complete dilemma.

I wonder how all this came about. No. I don't. An incident happened. I don't think I should write it down.

I'm not sure why. Okay, screw it. Cher slept with Bill Hamm. She told me she loved another man. My lady has changed completely. In fact, she's not mine anymore. Nothing is for sure. But nothing has any real meaning, and I'm looking for a reason.

Maybe I'll become a stronger person. Maybe. I don't know.

12

YOU BETTER SIT DOWN,
KIDS

August 21, 1973: I see by reading what I wrote last
that I was pretty scared. Well, again my whole world
has changed. Nothing really new, though. The last time
I wrote I wanted Cher to come back to me. That's no
longer my desire. The best I can do is be Cher's friend.
I cut the cord.

It's funny. It's so hard to free yourself when you
have loved someone so hard and so long. But when
you do it's like a thousand pounds off your shoulders.
Someday I must write a blow-by-blow of the last ten
years. I must say, my life has been anything but dull.

I have a lover now, Connie. She's been a part of my
life for several months. Don't ask me where everything
is going. I don't know.

Cher and I still have a TV show, and the public still
thinks we are married. We are both very involved in
our careers.

At home? Connie and I live together as husband and
wife. We live in the same house with Cher and the
baby. Cher has her boyfriend. That's another story I'll
have to explain. My public wife is Cher. We do that
to maintain all the things we want right now. That's
the way it has to be.

But this is going to be some year. This is going to be the year of change. I'm working hard in my head and I feel extremely enterprising. So I must say I feel good. For the last eight months I've felt stagnant. Now I feel the opposite.

Like many times before. I was down . . . but not out for the count.

I was haunted by the days I'd spent immediately following Cher's departure with Bill Hamm. Like a recurring hallucination. I couldn't shake the picture I had of myself walking into our cold, empty mansion and doing nothing but lying on the floor with my head on a pillow and staring into the roaring fireplace. I saw my life in flames.

Even more devastating than the pain I felt from the breakup of our marriage was seeing that Cher did not seem especially disturbed by it—from what I could see, anyway. Was she that callous? Weeks had passed before I regained the strength and the desire to climb out of bed, and even then I still walked around in a semicomatose stupor. Cher, though, kept going as if on autopilot. Her face was a mask that refused to admit any hurt or pain.

Strangely, we remained more than civil and were even friendly to each other during working hours. It was a big put-on that should've won us an acting award long before Cher did *Moonstruck*. At home, though, the truth came out. Suddenly our years together evaporated as we became two strangers living separate lives. Our once-homey mansion was engulfed by an arctic chill. Despite the luxury of fifty-four rooms, we desperately needed more space.

Cher felt that way, anyhow. Soon after returning from San Francisco, she rented a hideaway of her own on the beach in Malibu, a place where she and Bill could be alone together. I never gave Cher a word of grief about her fling with Bill, just as she had never harangued me for my affairs. I didn't get angry because I didn't believe that there was anything meaningful between them. He was her pawn, no different, I believe, than recent boyfriends like Rob Camilletti or Richie Sambora. She wore Bill Hamm like an ornament on her arm.

Once married life was over between us, I never had a problem with Cher seeing other men. We were adults; she was entitled. I understood Cher's thinking. She had won her freedom and wanted to exercise it.

Cher was likewise relieved when I rebounded into an affair of my own. She was still with Bill then, and at the time I was operating under the guise of a bon vivant, flying to Europe, hanging out at clubs, partying like a kid dodging curfew, and hitting on chicks right and left—anything to act as if I was unaffected by the deal with Cher. When I told her I was traveling to France, her response was, "Wow, Son, you've really got guts."

Of course, Paris was a mistake. When I landed there, I was down and out. Instantly, I knew I had made an error in judgment. Paris oozed romance. Every corner I looked around I saw lovers strolling, laughing, kissing. It was torture. I felt anything but amorous. I was alone and miserable. Nobody I met spoke English. Even the television shows were beyond my comprehension. I returned home after spending just enough time to make it seem as if I enjoyed myself.

Then one night I went to Pips, a glitzy nightclub in Beverly Hills, which served as a hangout for celebrities and backgammon bums. I was not there ten minutes before I was talking to the sexy cigarette girl, Connie Foreman. She had beautiful hair, a sympathetic ear, and a tender smile. We began dating the following night, and before long Connie moved into my half of the mansion.

Only the public and our daughter, not yet four years old, were unaware of the truth. Chas was too young to understand what was going on with her mom and dad, but things at home were still pretty confusing. Cher shuttled back and forth between our house and the beach like a commuter service. Within several months she broke up with Bill and quickly involved herself with keyboard player David Paich, who later earned fame in the band Toto. When that ended she latched onto Elton John's lyricist, Bernie Taupin.

Initially I heard constant rumors that Cher wanted to get back together. People close to us would try to console me by saying, "Don't worry. It's just a fling," or "She's a kid who has to go through this phase. It's just a phase, Sonny." Numerous friends counseled me, "You guys still love each other. It's only a matter of time before she comes back." And I believed that. I wanted to believe it, anyway. Occasionally, the messages people delivered were quite specific. "Cher wants to get along with you," they said. "She's miserable. She's anxious to do such-and-such a date." We were performing a concert in Hawaii when our secretary told me flat out that Cher wanted to reconcile.

The rumors tore at me. I was expending so much effort to remain friendly. Cher and I both let our lawyers do the fighting, which allowed us to remain on pretty good terms, even though a lot of that was an act. I was determined to hang on in some way, though. I didn't have any problem letting go of Cher. That was done. But I didn't know how I was going to survive without Sonny and Cher.

Finally I had had enough of the rumors. One day my hopes were up, the next they were dashed. I couldn't take it anymore and sought Cher out on the set.

"Is it true, what Paulette said about you wanting to get back together?" I asked, my self-esteem on my sleeve.

"No," Cher said succinctly. "That's not true."

After that I did not pay the whispers any attention. I knew Cher and I were history.

The show still went on, though. Personally, Cher and I may have hit bottom, but professionally we were still flying. Midway through our second season, our contract still had three more years. Cher and I had been through everything imaginable. Divorce was just another hurdle. As long as the ratings remained high, I thought Cher and I would do the show.

I was wrong.

At a hazy point during Cher's flings with Paich and Taupin, I was the recipient of a lesson in cutthroat gamesmanship. First, understand that Cher and I spoke daily, on the set and off. The tone was always cordial and friendly— testimony, I believed, to the mutual respect we maintained for one another as well as the time we had shared in the trenches. Suddenly, though, Cher's attitude underwent an abrupt, one-hundred-eighty-degree change.

She turned into a real ice maiden. The transformation was inexplicable as well as sudden, a shock to the show's entire crew. Overnight and without warning, Cher became testier on the set, less of a team player, less of a collaborator. She turned insular and became less approachable. Whenever something was asked of her, she labored over making a decision until the last possible minute, always giving the same excuse for taking so long: "I have to talk to David."

From then on she never did a thing without mentioning this guy David. It was always David, David, David. Cher was like a broken record.

I thought she was talking about David Paich. But I soon learned the truth. The David Cher was constantly referring to was not our keyboardist. No, David Paich was already history. Unknown to me, lurking in the weeds, there was another David—David Geffen.

Up until that time I was still directing the flow of Sonny and Cher, but Geffen's presence brought another, extremely powerful force onto the scene. Today Geffen, the founder of Geffen Records, is one of the most powerful, respected, wealthy, and also feared men in Hollywood. After our initial meeting, I wrote him off as a little wimpy guy, and I never thought he had the stuff that has allowed him to accomplish all that he has in his life.

It was one of my great misjudgments. Before long I knew exactly the kind of guy David Geffen was—a brilliant, calculating, extremely shrewd man, who would do whatever he had to do, no matter the cost—moneywise or human—to achieve his goal. Geffen was exactly the kind of man Cher was attracted to—a powerful guy who took charge of her life and made things happen. To me, he was a ruthless cutthroat.

He took over the role I had always played, which made it inevitable that Geffen and I would butt heads.

With Cher's personality change on the set, I instinctively sensed that there was another game plan at work, a game that did not include me, and I attempted to resist. I believed in myself so much that I thought I could handle anything involving Sonny and Cher. I had built us from ground up into a show-biz institution—twice. Now an interloper was trying to wrest it away from me, like a common thief. I dug my heels in.

Whether or not we were a couple, Cher and I had as tight a bond as anybody. The proof was on the stage. I knew the only way somebody could ever overtake Sonny and Cher was if Cher decided to shoot Sonny in the back. That was the only way—and, not surprisingly, that is what happened.

Target practice began when the sales pitch Cher bought from Geffen began filtering into our work: that she was the real star of Sonny and Cher, that she ought to get rid of the stiff—me—record by herself, position herself to segue into the movies, and so on. The eventual prize was wealth and superstardom, exactly what Cher and I had been working for. The difference was that she would not have to share.

Nobody has ever admitted—or ever will admit—to this, but I've always felt that Geffen's first move in breaking up Sonny and Cher was to arrange a television deal with CBS for Cher's own series. The flip side of that plan was played out in my dressing room after a taping, one of the show's last episodes. In a scene that smelled like it was choreographed by Geffen, Cher told me that she no longer wanted to do the Sonny and Cher show.

"What?" My jaw dropped.

"I already gave notice to CBS," she said.

The punch came out of nowhere. My legs backpedaled and my mind spun as I tried to stay on my feet.

"We've got contracts," I stumbled. "I mean, you can't. We are signed to record deals, nightclubs."

"I'm not backing out," she said. "I've already given notice to everybody—the record companies, the clubs."

"You did?" I asked. "I don't know what to say."

"I gotta go," said Cher, who then turned and whisked herself out the door, leaving me doubled over and dazed.

But I was not about to go down easily. I chased after Cher and cornered her in the hallway as she was about to exit. Cher hated confrontations, I knew, and I fastened my eyes on hers like two rivets waiting to be soldered. My plan was to talk sense into her, and in the minute or so that I had before a crowd developed, I gave it my best shot. When the barrage was over, Cher looked at me as if I had made some good points.

"Well, I want you and David to get in a room and talk," she said. "Whoever wins, wins."

"No," I said. "No way. I'm not going to do that."

"Well," Cher sighed, then walked out the back door, got into her car, and drove home.

I got the message. I was not just losing the game. The game was over.

The last bit of taping was rough. Cher was strategizing for the survival of her own career and I was strategizing for mine. The tension that permeated every minute came out in strange ways. In one skit Cher played Mother Nature and stood atop a mountain. I was a seeker of truth, struggling to climb the peak. During rehearsal I inched my way to the top and delivered my line: "Mother Nature, what is the secret of life?"

Without missing a beat Cher snapped, "Go fuck yourself," and then batted her eyes toward the camera.

I bit my tongue. Nobody laughed. The wisecrack had too much sting.

"Can we try it again?" the director asked.

"Not without lawyers," I muttered.

Again, nobody laughed. The truth was just not humorous.

It was January 1974. Cher and I both knew the jig was up. For more than a year we had been pretending, going to great lengths to preserve something that existed only in people's imaginations, record stores' oldies bins, and my deluded perception of the future—smiling at each other backstage before slamming our dressing-room doors, checking into the same two-bedroom hotel suite on the road to give the impression that our marriage was still intact.

There was more acting off the stage than on it, and I was among the most devout and determined of the great pretenders. But I was frightened. Sonny and Cher was what I knew. It worked. It paid handsomely. I was not about to be the one who ended it.

But then Cher refused to work anymore.

That was the next phase of a plan to take Sonny out of

Sonny and Cher. Sonny and Cher, through our corporation, Cher Enterprises, had a number of contractual commitments—such as MCA and Caesar's—all of which were tied to multimillion-dollar annuities spread over ten and fifteen years. But if Sonny could not deliver Cher, then the contracts would be breached, Geffen could then negotiate new ones, and those new contracts would involve only Cher.

His strategy was simple, but its implementation was anything but that.

The week of the final episode of "The Sonny and Cher Comedy Hour," I filed for legal separation from Cher. I'd absorbed enough. I wanted it over.

Immediately after the Friday night taping, Cher and I flew in separate jets to Houston for our final concert together. Two shows were scheduled for that Saturday, one in the afternoon and one in the evening. They were sandwiched in between a ripsnortin', Texas-style rodeo. Cher and I arrived at the Astrodome in separate cars, accompanied by our separate entourages, who walked ahead of us and made certain that our dressing rooms were very separate.

The only thing we managed to do in tandem that day was to appear onstage, no small feat itself. But we were getting one hundred fifty thousand dollars for the day, which was also no small feat. People will do extremely strange things for great sums of money.

That final show was about as strange as it gets, too. It was surreal. Bizarre. Excruciatingly painful. We were the biggest, hottest act in the country. We were playing the largest indoor venue in America. But we could barely manage a civil hello, let alone look at each other when we got onstage; we managed to avoid it.

A portable stage was set up in the middle of the infield, where the rodeo competition had been held. The odor of cow and horse dung wafted up. The whole place smelled like shit. It was an appropriate metaphor for what Cher and I had become, the whole dismal, depressing, distressing situation.

The shortest live performance of our career seemed to drag on forever. During her costume changes Cher dashed into her little changing stall beside the stage and ranted to anyone who was nearby, "I can't wait till this fucking show is over. Goddammit, how much longer? I hate this. I hate it." I was equally disturbed, but not quite as angry as Cher. For me, the last show was quite emotional. The crowd and their adoration were testimony to everything that Cher and I had built. And now it was over. When we walked off the stage, I was completely drained.

After the last note had been sounded, Cher dashed offstage and disappeared into her waiting car without saying a single word. Not even a sentimental look back. Of course, that would have been out of character. Not for me, though. I took my time. Strolling through the backstage area, knocking shoulders and shaking hands with stagehands, roadies, and technicians who had worked with us for years, I fought back tears. The mood was humbling, nostalgia-filled, and, more than anything else, sad. I felt as if I had broken up with my high-school sweetheart in front of the entire student body.

I dropped wearily into the backseat of the car that was taking me back to the hotel. I just wanted to get back home and rest. One of my buddies offered an encouraging word, like, "Well, at least it's over. You made it. Now the worst is behind you." There was some truth to that. But I was beaten and bloodied, a guy who had survived the wreck but sustained numerous injuries.

As the car sped along the highway, I thought, Yeah, I made it. But I also wondered, Am I gonna live?

With Geffen pulling Cher's strings, orchestrating Sonny and Cher's demise like a ruthless takeover artist, I knew our separation would soon escalate into an ugly battle. It was just a matter of time. That issue was settled on February 20, a couple of weeks after our Astrodome good-bye, when Cher officially filed for divorce.

Her reason was not irreconcilable differences. Nor was it any of the other myriad nebulous choices one checks when dissolving a marriage. No, Cher took a more aggressive tack. Adopting her characteristic role of the victim, she charged me with involuntary servitude. When the news reached me I recoiled in shock. Cher's charge was a callously legal way of saying that she had been my slave. Not my wife, my lover, my best friend, my inspiration, or the mother of our child, but my slave!

My blood boiled. I knew what the ploy was. It was impossible to sit through weeks of discussions with our separate teams of lawyers, and not know what Cher and Geffen were attempting to do. Cher and I were employed by Cher Enterprises. Cher and I were fifty-fifty partners. That is not only how the corporation was set up, that is the law of community property in California.

But they wanted to make me out the bad guy, a horrible, even criminal, slavemaster who was trying to control this woman's life for my selfish benefit. And it worked—to a degree. The public believed it. They had no way of knowing the accusation was untrue or that the divorce was all tied to money. But, when Cher wanted out of her contractual obligations, when she wanted to split Cher Enterprises fifty-fifty, I said no.

Why? I had worked eleven years alongside Cher to build Sonny and Cher into a major act. We still had contracts for millions of dollars with record companies and nightclubs. I had structured the deals so that money would continue to come in for years down the road—annuities. What her side wanted was for me to take my half and walk away. Meanwhile, Cher would gracefully step into the broken deals and the cash would continue to flow.

The evidence was obvious. CBS had already announced that "The Sonny and Cher Comedy Hour" would, the following season, be restructured and called "The Cher Comedy Hour."

I believed then, and I believe now, that when you spend eleven years building a company there is a residual factor involved, and I felt entitled to some of those residuals. Consequently, I countersued Cher for fourteen million dollars and then dropped a thirteen million–dollar suit on Geffen.

They retaliated. One night I returned from the studio and found all the locks at home changed. I could not get in. Instigated by Geffen, Cher, some detectives, and our old manager Joe DeCarlo took over our mansion. It was out of character for Cher. I suspected someone was behind her.

I called home and spoke to Chastity. She said, "Dad! Dad! They're taking over the house!"

July 14, 1974: I'm not writing in this diary very much. Maybe when my life gets settled again I'll write more often. When I predicted a year of change, I couldn't have been more on. Things sure have changed.

Cher and I are now legal enemies. We are divorcing and suing over the rights. Our TV show is gone, our career as Sonny and Cher is over. We do not perform together right now. We don't perform apart, either.

Up to this point, Cher and I have had only skirmishes, and it has taken a long time to get to this point. I have no good feelings left for Cher. There is no place for her in my personal life. If I have good fortune, I can do it all in one battle. That's what I'll have to try to do.

You think a lot before a fight. Unfortunately, a fight is the last and lowest form of communication.

At first my natural instinct was to resist. There were too many things in my head that needed changing. But as things became real, I had to become real too. There's no predicting the outcome. We shall have to wait and see.

Cher, a master of multiple personalities but definitely not a fighter, let Geffen do her sparring. Not long after we returned from Houston, she and Geffen moved in together, renting director Blake Edward's Beverly Hills house. Word then began circulating that Geffen had fallen madly in love with Cher. I never bought that. As is common in Hollywood, theirs was more a relationship of convenience and display than fireworks and passion.

Still, they lived as a couple, and the most unfortunate and nasty part about it was that Cher, in true passive-aggressive form, forced me to deal with Geffen in order to spend time with Chastity. I still cannot figure out why she positioned herself in the background and made Chas a pawn in the struggle between me and Geffen, except, I suppose, that she simply did not want to deal with the nuisance of making decisions with me.

So I wound up negotiating with Geffen over when I could and could not see my daughter. The situation was humiliating and upsetting, and it foreshadowed the embittered custody battle for Chastity that Cher and I waged later on. One holiday weekend I took Chas to Palm Springs. I was supposed to have her back home by 6 P.M. on Sunday. For whatever reason, it was impossible to get her back on time. I called Cher to tell her.

"Son, I don't want to discuss it," she said. "Since you set it up with David, let me put him on the phone."

Geffen then got on the phone and chewed me out as if he had legal authority, which he did not. When he finished, I calmly told him that I was the father and that Chas would be home when I could get her there. End of discussion.

I wracked my brain trying to figure out why Cher had turned authority of Chastity over to Geffen but was confounded by Cher's black hole of a personality. As well as I knew her, there was just no reading Cher. One minute she might be on top of a situation, the next she might be crying for help. She could be a subservient geisha girl or a killer. She had the potential for being as ruthless as she was mystical and far out.

There was no secret code to break in reading Cher. If she was a mystery to those who knew her, she was an even bigger puzzle to herself, I think. One day I called to speak with her about Chastity. Chas had told me she was feeling neglected by Cher. Somehow Cher had become a sort of surrogate mom to actress Tatum O'Neal. I remember picking Chastity up at school and driving her to Cher's set and hearing how unhappy Cher was making her.

"Please, Dad," she pleaded. "Please don't bring me there. I don't want to go."

"What's the problem?" I asked. "She's your mom."

"No she's not," said the five-year-old. "She is more a mom to Tatum than she is to me."

I took Chas to my place and called Cher. She answered the phone, which was a small miracle since she rarely answered her own phone. I detailed the situation Chastity had laid out. Cher expressed surprise and claimed she had had no idea. She wanted to know how I knew, since I spent less time with our daughter than she supposedly did.

"I know because she told me, Cher," I said. "Do you talk to her?"

There was a pause. Then:

"Hold on," she said. "I want David to get on the line."

That, of course, infuriated me, but there was clearly a right and a wrong here, and I was the one with good footing. So I waited. Cher put me on hold. Her minute turned into five minutes, and then five became ten. As I was about to hang up and try again, I heard a click. Then voices. Cher was crying.

"David, you've got to help me," she wept.

Apparently, they had forgotten about me or they thought that I was waiting on another line. I placed my hand over the mouthpiece and listened as Geffen tried to placate Cher's runaway emotions with soothing words.

"I just want to be a good person," she said tearfully.

"But you are, Cher," he said. "You are a good person. You have to think positively."

"No, you don't understand," Cher responded. "I just want to be good. I want people to love me for who I am."

As I listened, it took a huge amount of restraint for me not to butt in and scream, "Oh bullshit, Cher. I've heard that excuse countless times." See, I knew Cher's M.O. Feeling guilty about Chastity, she donned her victim's mask and sought the love that she should have been giving our child. In the midst of Cher's pleading, the phone went silent. Then there were several clicks, after which I heard only Geffen's voice.

"Sonny?" he said.

"Yeah."

"Cher asked me to tell you not to worry about Chastity," he said. "Everything's OK, and she'll get back to you."

No matter how much pain there is when a marriage ends, if children are involved, they sustain far more serious injuries than either of the adults. Chastity was just a little kid then, a blond ragamuffin who stood knee-high to her dad. Her dimpled smile was the key to the world; her sixth birthday was her biggest concern. I saw this precious little girl as a fountain of inspiration, a source of unconditional love, and it broke my heart every day to think of her being yanked back and forth like the flag in the middle of a tug-of-war.

Cher and I never had a problem dealing with Chastity except when Geffen was around. Handcuffed in terms of options, I was forced into a diplomat's juggling act until a judge ruled on the divorce. In the meantime, Chastity was only one of the problems plaguing me—a major one, but still just one of a long list that began with the question Who am I?

Without missing a beat, Cher hung her past life in the closet like an old dress she was ashamed of and immediately went to work on her own variety series. It was an instant smash. Cher herself soared to spectacular heights, rocketing up into the galaxy of superstardom. She was featured on the covers of *Newsweek* and *People* magazines. The basic story line had her slipping out from the tentacles of the Svengalilike creature who controlled her every move, and emerging as a symbol of the emancipated, independent, and powerful woman. Women embraced her as a role model, and suddenly everything that I knew Cher was capable of began happening.

I had no problem with Cher's success. My attitude was always More power to her. What I took exception to—and still do today—was that Cher marketed herself from a victim's point of view. That was a lie. Cher was never a victim. But her accusations have continued, and the net effect is that it cast me as the bad guy, the evildoer from whom she had to escape.

It proved almost too much to live down. I had created the act, written the songs, produced them, provided the vision, choreographed everything . . . and what happened? Cher walked off with the franchise.

Sonny and Cher was something I had loved doing, and I was reluctant to give it up—even after it was long over. Why? My whole sense of identity, every nugget of self-worth and professional validity I possessed, had been tied up, packaged, and sold as the short, mustachioed, Italian half of Sonny and Cher. I did not want to let that go.

Slowly, though, it was obvious that I had to do something. People told me so: my manager; my agent; friends.

Nobody is forgotten as quickly as yesterday's star. After endless discussions, I heard myself repeating the words that were spoken to me in various meetings: Sonny and Cher was just a good ensemble show. If we put together a good crew, bring together the same elements, it will work. Look at Cher. There is absolutely no reason on earth why Sonny Bono cannot have a hit TV show too.

Like a battered football player, I listened to endless pep talks from my circle of advisors. I repeated those words to myself. I allowed myself to believe that I could stay in the game. In early summer the concept was pitched to ABC. Networks love nothing better than to imitate the competition's hits. Consequently, ABC bit. And why not, we thought. If CBS was having success with the Cher variety hour, what could be better than a variety show starring Sonny?

ABC provided a golden opportunity, though the chance to prove myself on my own show did nothing to clear my disillusioned head. It was pretty clear I was fighting an uphill battle.

August 14, 1974: Still in limbo, but at least things have a direction. I start to work in a week and a half.

What does it all mean? It's a good question. I'm tired. I've been knocked down more times than I can count. I have always gotten up, though. I don't know how to lay down. Maybe that is good.

I finally got to a position where people believed I could do what I said I could do. Now I must be judged all over again. Everything I am, do, or say will be judged all over again. Nothing about the past matters anymore. With the help of God, I can make it all work again.

There's only one thing in life that I am absolutely sure of, and that is my role as a father. I didn't do my best with Christy. But I'm determined not to make the same mistakes twice. My little Chastity is everything to me.

13

I'M TOO BIG TO CRY

January 19, 1975: My show went off the air in thirteen weeks. It didn't work for a lot of reasons, but it was the only game in town. So I played it. As I look at the words I wrote previously, I can see I was in a completely different place than I am now. Before, I had Cher and she and Chas were my life. But this time I was alone, and it was a bitch.

Cher now has a show on the air. It did very well last year. This will be her second season.

I have no set direction in my head at all, yet I am trying hard to find one. I'm back in my own house now and it's beautiful. This house is the only real home I have ever known. I love this house and I know it's my friend. I wish I could say things were great now, but they aren't.

However, some things are sure a lot better than last year, and I'm happy for that. Connie's not with me anymore. We haven't been together since before Christmas.

I guess if I ever wanted to do myself in, it was the last holiday season. Everything went wrong that could possibly go wrong. My show was canceled. Compared to Cher, the public considered me a low-down pimp. The house was a colossal mess—lumber, paint, dirt, and sawdust everywhere. The only thing in it was a bed and a TV. I hated everything, but there was no place to go.

I was trying to get Con off my back. The only thing she did well was fight. Connie and I should never have done more than dated. But I was on such a huge rebound that I jumped right back in.

I'm really pissed off at myself for getting into that. Things were bad and I only made them worse. I wasted a year and a half. That was stupid. Real stupid.

Anyway, by the time Christmas came around I was living alone. I didn't know anyone and didn't want to know anyone. You might call that being depressed. I'd call it something worse. When Chas came over there was no place in the house to go, so there was nothing for her to do. Poor thing. The holiday was a big mess. Next Christmas will be different, I promise.

Christmas Eve I was supposed to take Con out to a party at Cher's. What a strange relationship Cher and I have. We fight each other and we're still friends. Has it always been like this? I don't know.

Anyway, she and Geffen were having a Christmas bash, and they invited me. Ho, ho, ho! Fine, I accepted. However, Con and I got into a big fight and I called her up and said forget it. That one is over.

But I went to the party anyway and met a woman whom I ended up taking to a dinner and a movie.

Indeed, you have to figure that a guy who was in the throes of divorce, who had just busted up with a woman he became involved with on the rebound, would want either nothing to do with the opposite sex or a fantasy come true. At first my preference was for the former. I wanted to dig a hole in the ground and hide. But instead, I ended up on a date with Raquel Welch.

Honest to God. Both Raquel and I were guests at Cher's Christmas Eve party. Neither of us had dates. A mutual acquaintance introduced us, and we found a common ground to talk about: the holiday blues. Both of us had been reluctant to venture out of our houses, but with nothing better to do we had gone, despite our inclination to grovel and feel sorry for ourselves. Over hors d'oeuvres, Raquel and I shared small talk and laughs.

"What the hell," I blurted, letting my impulse catch up to my imagination. "You don't have anything to do tonight and neither do I. What do you say we go have dinner and take in a flick?"

She smiled. "I'd love to."

Raquel and I left the party, enjoyed a nice Italian dinner at a quiet restaurant, and then bought tickets to *Towering Inferno*. Her image aside, Raquel was an intelligent, articulate, sophisticated, and witty lady; a wonderful date, especially on Christmas Eve. The only problem was that her image was difficult to brush aside. Throughout the evening I kept looking over at her and thinking, My God, that's Raquel Welch.

My inner dialogue was one-sided: Sonny, you're a guy, and that's Raquel Welch. You're Italian, and that's Raquel Welch beside you. You're gonna be divorced in a few weeks, and that's Raquel Welch you're sitting next to. There are hundreds of millions of guys who would kill to take Raquel Welch out, and who is the lucky dude? Sonny Bono. Think about it, man. That's Raquel Welch whispering in your ear. Listen up. Are those the magic words she's cooing?

Sure enough, Raquel was whispering in my ear.

"Do you think this movie is as bad as I do?" she said.

"Kind of," I agreed. "You want to leave?"

We left the theater, climbed into my car, and turned on to the empty streets of Westwood, the neon signs of the movie-theater marquees casting a faintly festive glow on the pavement. Briefly, I let my imagination go. It was fantasy time, time to be wild, frivolous, and daring. For God's sake, it was Christmas Eve, and I had obviously been a good boy. Why else would Santa have put Raquel Welch in the passenger seat of my car?

But Raquel's yawn snapped me out of my hormonal reverie. She was tired. Apologizing for being a party pooper, she explained that her two children would be getting up early the next morning to open their presents. I understood. On the way to her west-side home, I touched on some of the angst and guilt I was suffering by not getting to see Chastity when she opened her gifts. Raquel, who was also divorced, commiserated with me about the difficulty kids have when their parents split.

In the end, we had an unexpectedly pleasant time with each other: two single parents on the night before Christmas.

"It's not easy," I sighed, walking Raquel up to her front door.

"Thanks for a swell evening," she said, pecking me on the cheek. "Merry Christmas."

"You too." I smiled.

Spending Christmas Day alone was depressing, but not as depressing as the remnants of my career. After the cancellation of "The Sonny Comedy Revue," I was desperate to get something going. I let my PR man, Jay Bernstein, a fast-talking sharpie who proved much more successful launching Farrah Fawcett's career than mine, talk me into getting a nightclub act going. It wasn't so much an act as it was taking the failed "Sonny Comedy Revue" on the road.

I agreed only after hours and hours of brainstorming that produced nothing more than headaches. I wanted David Brenner to open for me, but when he wasn't available we signed comic Richard Lewis, who was just starting out. We broke the act at a club in Oshkosh, Wisconsin. Every night sold out. We packed the crowds in for two weeks and thought we had a hit on our hands. We went around celebrating, slapping each other on the back. Of course, we neglected to admit to ourselves that the club was the size of a large dining-room table. Why spoil a good party?

Our next stop was the Playboy Club in Lake Geneva, Wisconsin, and I could not wait to get there. The stage was much larger, the size of the audience was tenfold, the lighting was professional, the money was bigger, the entire package was exactly what my bruised ego craved. But the moment the curtain rose, reality hit us like a ton of bricks. The same thing happened at Harrah's, in Lake Tahoe, where Tim Conway opened for me. We pulled a meager one hundred to two hundred people a night, and the rooms held five times that. From the stage, it looked as if we were playing to ten people, and they didn't like the show.

Tim had his act timed to the minute—a half hour with laughs, twenty-two minutes without. I purposely did not get dressed until he reached the twenty-two-minute mark. More often than not, he wrenched open my dressing room door, found me naked, and screamed, "Jesus, don't change. It'll be the best joke of the night." He also used to leave me notes like, "Dear Sonny, sorry I can't make it tonight. I got run over by a tractor and my legs are mangled. I will try to make it tomorrow."

It was gallows humor on- and offstage. We finished the run in Lake Tahoe feeling like two worn-out gladiators. Later I learned that Tim is funnier off camera than he is on. Back home, we hung out together for a while, and I appreciated his sensitivity. He understood what I was going through and used to say, "You're a talented guy, Sonny. It's a shame you're in a box like this."

More than once I wondered if I would ever climb out of that box.

"Son, you gotta come down to Palm Springs," said Jay, my PR man turned social organizer. "Right now."

I had debated whether or not to pick up the phone, and when I heard Jay's upbeat voice on the other line, I rued the decision. My mood was foul. By spring 1975, my life had become a graduate-level course in how to have an identity crisis. In fact, I was going for my Ph.D.

What act I had was down the drain and whenever my name was mentioned in the paper, it was apt to be a target for Cher's slings and arrows. She described me as a brutal dictator. Sure, I had a dominating personality, but brutal and dictator were complete exaggerations. She recounted fights and painted me as mean. Aside from ordinary spousal blowups, the worst battle we ever had was also our funniest. We had gone to see a movie, *The Dirty Dozen,* and on the way home we started discussing which of our friends had a killer instinct.

"You're even like that," I said. "You have a killer instinct."

"No, I don't," she argued.

One thing led to another and our friendly debate developed into a loud shouting match. Frustrated, I commanded Cher to stop the car and let me out. Cher pulled over, let me out, and sped home, leaving me to walk ten miles home. Later, Denis Pregnolato picked me up. My blockheaded determination to walk home was the extent of the irate machismo she found necessary to criticize.

Likewise, Cher has always described herself during our final years together as a near-suicidal, ninety-one-pound hostage, and painted me as an uncaring slavedriver. If Cher was ninety-one pounds and near-suicidal I never knew it and she failed to communicate her dire condition. If I was a slavedriver, Cher never complained about it. But the fact of the matter was that Sonny and Cher was a team effort. Lots of people had input into Sonny and Cher—not the least of them Cher.

I knew why she said such lies. For as long as I've known her, Cher has played the part of a victim. She's played it to the hilt. As such, she's needed a villain, and who better or more convenient to cast in the role than me? I had no means of defending myself. She was famous and beloved. I was a nobody or a has-been. No one wanted to hear my side of the story.

I found it too easy to feel sorry for myself. With our divorce negotiations dragging on and my ego shot full of holes, I was a mess of self-pity, bitterness, jealousy, and all those ugly, petty emotions. When Jay called, pressing me to drop everything (which, I admit, did not amount to anything) and meet him in Palm Springs, having fun was not foremost in my mind. Of course, that is what pals are supposed to do.

"Sorry, I'm not in the mood," I said.

"How can you not be in the mood?" he asked. "I'm down here with two beautiful women. Two beautiful, young women."

"Sorry, Jay," I replied.

"Can you hear me, Son?" he asked. "Is the connection going bad? I said, 'We've got dinner reservations for seven-thirty.' Talk to you later."

Click. He hung up. It was early afternoon. I thought,

What the hell? I showered, got some clothes together, and caught the shuttle to Palm Springs. At the time, I had bought a hideaway in the desert, a little home where I could disappear and cool out. Jay brought the girls over at seven and we sat and talked over a drink. The girls, Liz Treadwell and Susie Coelho, were as pretty and pleasant as Jay had promised.

Dinner was at seven-thirty. We joined a group of people at the restaurant and settled in at one end of the table. Until that point it was not clear how Jay and I and the girls were supposed to pair up, but by the time our meals were served Susie and I started clicking. We stayed out till two, then our foursome went to my house for a bit. I drove Susie home as the sun inched over the mountains. Here was this great-looking girl with a terrific laugh who made me forget my troubles. Undoubtedly I wanted to see her again, which I did that afternoon. Later we exchanged our L.A. phone numbers and began dating regularly.

Without thinking about what was happening, I found myself in pursuit of this great-looking model. Was I ready for a relationship? No. But I was desperate for something positive in my life. I didn't want to be alone anymore. I wanted to be loved. I needed to feel the affection of another person. I began to feel that with Susie.

In the meantime, Cher had become involved in a peculiar relationship with rocker Gregg Allman. From what I heard, their love affair had all the ups and downs of an elevator ride, red-hot one minute and nonexistent the next. The public saw it as a strange mix, but to anyone who knew Cher it made perfect sense. Nothing attracted Cher like a mean, tough, and potentially dangerous rock and roller. She was turned on by the excitement of a life-style lived on the edge.

Gregg lived on the edge. The gifted blues man was an acknowledged druggie, a coked-out southern cracker, who was known to be one of rock's most volatile personalities. He'd been married twice. His previous girlfriend, actor James Arness's daughter, Jenny, had committed suicide. He appeared bent on self-destruction.

So what was Cher doing with him? She was straight, not a drinker, and as antidrug as I was. Yet whenever she mentioned his name, it was always a soft, understanding "Gregory." She never called him Gregg. On the surface, Cher looked as if she had truly fallen in love and was trying to save her rebellious southern beau from the demons that drove him to the hard stuff.

I thought there was something else on her mind, though. In Gregg, Cher found a man similar to her own father, an ex-drug addict whom she had let die without saying good-bye to him. Although Cher's dad had cleaned his life up by then, she never forgave him for deserting her in childhood. It's the reason she couldn't bring herself to answer his numerous pleas during his final days. By rescuing Gregg she could absolve the guilt she felt about letting her father die unforgiven by her.

In any event, the relationship appeared to make Cher happy and it also pushed my chief nemesis, David Geffen, out of the picture. As a result, Cher and I began speaking to each other again. Our occasional phone conversations turned into regular chats. I gave her the rundown on Susie and she let me in on her life with Gregg.

They puzzled me. Although Cher and I had been in the midst of a messy divorce, I'd gotten a phone call from her while weekending in Palm Springs with Chastity. Cher had told me that she liked Gregg more than she'd ever liked a guy. It was a lot bigger than a normal deal. Hearing that, I had advised her to go ahead and marry the guy.

I flattered myself by thinking that Cher still depended on me in some way, if only for advice on her personal life. But I thought of myself as solid. I continued to believe that Cher trusted my abilities. It felt good that I was still influencing Cher's life.

It was then that I decided enough was enough. I called my lawyer. The divorce was ruining my health. I wanted an end to the armies of litigators who had been pounding me. I needed peace of mind and to get on with my life. Sonny and Cher was a thing of the past, and if I was going to have a life, I had to begin concentrating on the future.

I was not able to do that with the divorce still dragging on. The endless negotiations, allegations, rumors and insinuations, the bickering over our career, and the squabbling over money that existed only on paper were the biggest drain of energy I'd ever experienced.

So I made the decision. It was time to settle.

Ours was a unique divorce in that we were dissolving not only our relationship but also a multimillion-dollar corporation. As far as I was concerned, Cher and I were equal partners in bed as well as in the boardroom. I resented that she was able to go on with her career, capitalizing on our past success and continuing to make millions while I was slogging my way across dime-sized stages for gas money.

I figured I had contributed at least 50 percent to Cher's career, and I reasoned that I was at least 50 percent responsible for her stardom.

Arguing the point was futile, though. The only sensible way to settle was to deal with the facts and divide our possessions. Cher wanted the big fifty-four-room mansion on Carolwood, and she got it. I retained ownership of our thirty-two-room mansion on St. Cloud, the first home we had bought from Tony Curtis, which we had leased until I moved in with Connie the summer before. Cher got permission to void all existing Sonny and Cher contracts and work on her own. She received 50 percent of all publishing royalties from the songs I wrote, checks she still cashes. As for my claims, the judge ordered Cher to pay me seven hundred fifty thousand dollars—a sum she could either pay out of her pocket or work off by performing with me for a limited run as Sonny and Cher.

Cher chose to work it off. The concerts would be scheduled at some later, mutually convenient date.

That was it. The end.

The divorce was finalized on June 26.

Four days later Cher married Gregg Allman.

Nine days later she again filed for divorce.

"When am I going to grow up?" Cher cried to me on the phone one day as her marriage to Gregg, already a public joke, was quickly becoming a tragedy.

"Do you love him?" I asked.

"Yes," she stammered. "But—"

"But what, Cher?"

"But . . . but we don't get along," she sobbed. "He might as well have come from Mars."

I asked if he had hurt her physically. Cher said he hadn't. But he criticized her for working too hard. She was, he maintained, no fun to be around because she was never there. What did he expect?

"He just hangs around the house all day," Cher said, "doing God only knows what."

They were two odd ducks. Once Cher and Gregg came over to my Bel Air house. She liked the privacy of my pool area, something her house didn't have. I was shocked when they stripped right out of their clothes and dove into the swimming pool nude. Cher had become very liberal—her clothes would fly off. But part of her was still the same. She was still gullible and naive. Cher had heard of a guy who had sawed apart and then ground up a car and eaten it. And she believed it!

"That's impossible," claimed Gregg. "You can't eat a car."

"That's what I heard," argued Cher.

"I don't care," he said.

"I don't care that you don't care," replied Cher. "I heard this guy ate a car."

They never did resolve that issue. But Cher's private life was more than I could keep up with. I was busy taking my act from one smoky nightclub to another. I learned more about her from *People* magazine than I did from talking to her on the phone. By late fall Cher's personal trauma had carried over into her television life and her show took a dive in ratings.

I did not wish failure on anybody, and certainly I would never wish it on Cher. I chalked up the show's ebb in popularity to the viewers' changing tastes and bad karma.

I had my own problems. Thanksgiving was approaching and I was playing a crackerbox Denver nightclub. Susie was back in L.A. It was a pretty depressing time for me, using past accomplishments to provide for the future. I did not want to think that my best days were behind me.

It was after the show and I was in my hotel when the phone rang. I figured it was Suze.

"Son?"

"Cher?"

"Yeah, how're you doing?" she asked.

"Not bad," I lied.

"Listen, how'd you like to do our old act again, you know, the Sonny and Cher show."

I was as stunned as I had ever been. If I had put a quarter in my bed's Magic Fingers, it would have pitched me across the room. I wondered if I had heard right. Speechless, I pulled the receiver from my ear and stared at it for the longest time, till I heard Cher ask, "Sonny? Sonny?"

There'd been some talk about us getting back together, but I was resigned to it being just that, talk. The deal seemed an impossible one to put together. There was just too much history and too much rancor to overcome.

Apparently, though, Denis and Cher had talked and cut through all the nonsense that had hung up our managers, agents, and lawyers.

I pinched myself and then held the receiver back to my ear but was still unable to speak.

It was a moment before my mind began to work again. Cher's proposal hit home and suddenly the excitement of the big time began to build in me again. I would be returning to nationwide, prime-time television. That was the kind of exposure I needed. More important, I hadn't been able to make it solo, and now neither could Cher. What'd that say about me? It validated all my claims. I'd finally get the recognition for my contribution to Sonny and Cher.

After several minutes of silence, I said, "Well, let me think about it."

"Okay," Cher said icily. "Call me."

For a guy who had been accused of having a macho ego, Cher's offer should have been a problem. It wasn't. I was trying to play it cool. I had an ego, but it wasn't too macho to miss a great opportunity. Besides, I had nothing against Cher. Our postmarriage relationship reminded me of a movie scene where two spies, one American and the other Soviet, sat on a park bench together. If they had to, they would shoot each other. Otherwise, they generally liked each other and enjoyed sharing a drink even though a war was being fought.

Before agreeing to do the show, I had to convince Susie that I was not going to fall back in love with Cher. She saw the threat and freaked out. But we'd barely had time to discuss the problem, which wasn't really a problem, before news of the reunion leaked to the press. CBS called a hastily arranged press conference the first week in December, which brought a swarm of reporters and photographers to Television City.

Cher and I stood in front of the questioners and their whirring cameras and proved that, even though divorced, we still had our impeccable timing.

"After being together for eleven years, you suddenly realize how difficult it is to do your own show," I fessed up.

"I know," quipped Cher. "I saw yours."

Ba-boom.

Taping started in February. Cher, who had found out she was pregnant soon after our press conference, and I got along surprisingly well. In fact, she probably enjoyed working with me more than before, since we did not have to deal with being married. She had her life and I had mine, and that took the stress off our working relationship. Also, I was a sympathetic ear for all of her problems with Gregg.

Despite the fun we were having with "The Sonny and Cher Show," the ratings were not the gangbuster results the network was hoping for. The show consistently hovered in the mid twenties, which was neither bad nor good. I chalked up the middling numbers to viewer backlash. Doing a show married was one thing, but to stand in front of an audience and joke about being divorced was not the classiest thing in the world.

The ratings reflected that. Our second season didn't play as expected. As the ratings fell, "The Sonny and Cher Show" fell into the willy-nilly hands of the network brain trust. They switched us from one time slot to another like a pawn in a chess game. The show was finally put on Friday nights, which had been a death trap even in our heyday. Finally, after a few episodes, "The Sonny and Cher Show" was given the ax. It didn't come as a surprise, but it was disappointing since Cher and I had both wanted to continue the show.

But that freed us up to do a series of concerts. Cher was supposed to use the gate receipts from those shows to pay me seven hundred thousand dollars, the sum she still owed from our divorce settlement. Every night sold out, and I was in heaven. The jeers and insults yelled by drunken hecklers in tiny clubs were like a bad dream compared to the electricity of a huge arena. Neither of us argued over which songs to sing, and we delivered the jokes with the same old snap. But we weren't out long before Cher's hatred for the road was revived.

It was like déjà vu. Cher was bored; she got sick; she missed Elija Blue, her baby boy; she became insular and depressed. According to our divorce settlement, we were supposed to work a certain number of shows. But Cher's abhorrence of travel finally proved too much. After the halfway mark, she called off the rest of the tour and paid the remaining money out of her own pocket.

And that was it for the professional life of Sonny and Cher, except for its afterlife in record stores.

As for Cher and I, we returned home like two war buddies, closer than we had been in years. All in all, it was a good time.

Following this frenetic and unexpected year-and-a-half-long ego-boosting career resuscitation, I ran headfirst into a dilemma like an insurmountable brick wall: What next? What the hell was I going to do with myself?

Well, the one thing I vowed not to do was to go back to the nightclub circuit.

But that still left me with options—everything from song-and scriptwriting to lounging by the pool, playing tennis, getting fat, and even acting. Sensing myself overqualified in some areas, underqualified in others, and plain not interested in or ill-suited to most, I chose acting. I was a fly-by-the-seat-of-my-pants kind of guy, and what was acting besides faking it?

Although financially sound, I looked on acting as a way of keeping my name in the public mind. When all was said and settled, my ego proved a beast beyond taming. It was not out of control, but it growled for food every so often. I sold NBC a series idea, "Murder in Music City." The pilot was shot and then got the ax. I acted in a miniseries, "Top of the Hill." I was game for anything, comedy or drama.

At the same time, I was bugged by a nagging sense of self-doubt. Something told me that I was just spinning my wheels. Get real, I told myself: How many times do you have to appear on "The Love Boat" before you realize that your career has turned into the Voyage of the Damned?

I rationalized my tenure on shows like "Fantasy Island" as a fun-in-the-sun time while I waited for something to click in, waited for something to magically drop into my lap and fill the void left by Sonny and Cher. It had always happened before. I would get a vision, a creative notion, a melody, and then I would pursue it. But nothing was happening.

That included my relationship with Susie, which was motoring along under its own power. Oddly, years earlier Cher had been the one to tell me that I should ask Susie to move in with me. Given her track record, personal advice from Cher should have been taken at the recipient's own risk. I was lukewarm on the idea, and I should have followed my gut instinct. But I was lonely and wanted to be with someone and Susie was a nice, good-looking girl with show-business aspirations.

In retrospect, neither of us was together for the right reasons. She wanted to act and be a part of the business, and I was her entrée. Unfortunately, I was the wrong guy. I was sinking deeper and deeper into a rut. If you want to use someone as a springboard, they had better be hot. I was ice-cold. Nonetheless, without ever analyzing why, we stayed together and hoped something would happen to one of us.

However, by the start of 1978 it was Cher who seemed to be making all the news, but not all of it was good. Her solo LP, *Cherish*, was a flop, and a joint album with Gregg, titled *Allman and a Woman*, also failed. When Cher, who hated sharing the spotlight, failed to put her name in that album's title, I figured something was wrong. In January my suspicion was confirmed when Cher once again filed for divorce from Gregg. It was the third time one of them had filed during their three-and-a-half-year union.

Around that time, Cher and I became neighbors again. She sold our old fifty-four-room mansion and moved into another oversized, Moorish mansion. I had also sold my house and bought a large home on a hill. Coincidentally, the two homes were within a baseball toss of each other on Benedict Canyon Drive. Despite Susie's earlier jealousy, she and Cher ended up getting along pretty well, which was fortunate, since Cher preferred to lie in the sun by our pool rather than hers.

And she liked to sunbathe in the nude.

Seeing Cher on the chaise longue in the altogether was no big deal. The nudity didn't bother me, and the sexual attraction was long over. But Cher's body did surprise me—particularly the two tattoos on her butt.

"I see you've started collecting art," I hinted.

"Oh, those," she said, patting her rump and laughing. "I just got 'em. They're nothing."

Calling her butterfly tattoos nothing was like ignoring a sandstorm in the Mojave. That was exactly the effect Cher wanted to create. She liked to do things for the shock they created. She still does. She'll create some controversy and then tell her critics to stick it. It was a trick she learned from me and I had learned it from Phil Spector.

But every time I thought I had Cher—or at least a part of her—figured out, I found another contradiction. One minute she was lying naked in my backyard, the next she was more difficult on the phone than the president. One afternoon when I went to pick up Chastity for the weekend, I asked her how Cher was doing, and Chas rolled her eyes in a way that answered the question for me.

"You're never going to believe this one," she said.

"What?" I asked.

"She was hiding in the closet," said Chas.

"Why?" I said.

"She says she wants to disappear and she's afraid you'll see her," said Chastity, her brown eyes as wide as gumballs.

"Is she like that often?" I asked.

Chas shrugged.

"She's just weird sometimes, Dad."

I understood.

But my biggest concern was the effect Cher's weird behavior was having on Chastity. I never doubted that Cher loved Chastity, but there were times when I thought Cher needed to devote more time to parenting than to her career. And I was guilty of the same thing. Like many divorced fathers, though, I was handicapped by the reality of joint custody. In practice, joint custody translates to two weeks and holidays—unless Mom is traveling somewhere more exotic than Dad.

The time I spent with Chas was sporadic. Cher didn't play the bad guy, but whatever she decided about Chas was the way it was.

I tried to give Chas quality time, though. Following Cher's divorce from Gregg, I landed a part in *Escape to Athena,* a war movie starring Roger Moore, David Niven, and Telly Savalas. Susie and I were going to live in a hotel on the island of Rhodes in the Aegean and I thought it would be a great experience for Chas.

I didn't realize how good an experience it was going to be for me too.

I enrolled Chas, then about ten years old, in the fifth grade at an English-speaking school. A few days passed before the teacher told me there was a problem. Chastity had trouble concentrating. She wasn't able to do her homework. I was confused. Chas was a bright kid—incredibly mature in ways that I'd never dreamed of as a child. My first reaction was to find fault with the teacher. But that was just a defense mechanism because I didn't want to admit my failure as a parent.

Yet I couldn't help but hear what the teacher said. Chas could hardly read or write. She was in fifth grade, but her basic educational skills were several grades behind. How could we have let that happen? So every night Chas and I sat down to do her homework, and at first I wanted to blame Cher. She had yanked Chas from one location to another, so she'd never spent significant time in any one school. But the truth was, we were both responsible, and I blamed both of us. Cher and I had both been selfish "career" people and had been so preoccupied with satisfying our egos that we didn't ever realize the effect it was having on our daughter. This was also true in my relationship with my first daughter, Christy, which I deeply regret.

From those two weeks in Greece I discovered how easy it is for parents to tell themselves how much they love their child. It's just as easy to tell but more important to *show* your child the same thing. I'd never failed to tell Chas that I loved her. I'd vowed not to make the same mistake that my father had made with me. Instead, I'd made other mistakes. My daughter couldn't read.

I had to ask myself how much I loved her if I had let that happen.

Chas, I knew, could learn to read, but I wondered if I had what it took to learn to become a better parent.

At home, Chas started to buckle down in school and I studied my priorities.

Both of us vowed to improve our grades.

PART V

THE BEAT
GOES ON

14

WHY CAN'T I STAND UP AND TELL MYSELF IT'S WRONG

I stood in front of everyone, listening on automatic pilot. I'd heard the words before.

"Family and friends . . ." The Rev. Gregg Anderson smiled as he looked out toward the one hundred guests who were seated in the nondenominational chapel, "we are gathered here tonight, on this happy occasion, to witness the love and, not incidentally, the marriage of—"

And then the poor guy blew it. He said, "Sonny and Cherie."

That snapped me out of the daze I was in.

It was New Year's Eve, the very last day of 1981. Snow was falling outside, which was not especially unusual for Aspen at that time of year. But the momentary chill that descended upon the chapel was.

"Who's Cherie?" asked Susie.

"Oh my God," I muttered under my breath.

The reverend was justifiably red-faced. But after a stunned, awkward second, everybody cracked up and, in true show-biz spirit, the ceremony went on. Hoping that I had made the right decision, I found it easier to not think about it. Just let it happen, I thought. I smiled at Susie, who radiated a serene happiness, albeit in a sexy, white-lace wedding dress slit revealingly down to her navel. The bridesmaids, including Chas, actress Mimi Rogers, and Liz Treadwell, wore red-and-ivory tunics. Soprano Heide Nitze gave the ceremony a seasonal flavor by singing, "Hark, the Herald Angels Sing" and "The First Noel."

Susie and I had decided to marry while vacationing in Aspen just the previous month. Until then, marriage had been a touchy, if not taboo, subject. Why? I had proposed earlier in the year, but Susie exploded when I suggested— not demanded but suggested—she sign a prenuptial agreement. After what I had been through with Cher I did not think it was out of line. But Susie was insulted, and she fled to Europe, where she did some modeling work. The distance cooled our relationship and scared the hell out of me.

When she returned I transformed myself into an attentive Romeo. I dropped my request for a prenuptial agreement, and wedding invitations were subsequently sent out to our families and friends.

Though I wasn't sure about marriage again, I couldn't help but get caught up in the ceremony. As I said "I do," my eyes were filled with tears and my voice was cracking with emotion. In top hat and tails, I escorted Susie, whose head was covered by a fur-lined hood, out of the chapel and past a line of friends carrying long, elegant candles. The wedding was a show of sorts, a chance for both Susie and me to get dressed up and perform in front of our friends. They were the best parts either of us had been offered all year.

The staging was ultraglamorous, but because of the cold outside, we bypassed a romantic horse-drawn carriage and jumped instead into the back of a heated limo. At a champagne reception we were showered with congratulations by Tatum O'Neal, Joan Kennedy, Andy Warhol, and Cathy Lee Crosby.

After honeymooning in Europe, Susie and I fell back into the same routine as before—vamping and waiting for something exciting to happen. In mid '82 I got a small spot in the film *Airplane II*. The work, like all the acting I did, was enjoyable, but it didn't satisfy my desire to be involved in more substantial projects. Once you've stood on top of the mountain, it's hard to accept any other view.

In the meantime, I'd thought about Cher's and my relationship till I had turned myself inside out. I'd examined myself more thoroughly than any doctor ever had. But I was compelled to do one last thing. I wanted to face off with Cher in person.

Cher and I were in one of our more distant periods then. We'd made it through the divorce as friends and remained cordial for several years after that. But in the wake of her divorce from Gregg, Cher severed her ties to me. She withdrew almost completely. I knew it was her way of searching for the next move. What I didn't understand, though, was why she felt so angry toward me. Every time I picked up an interview, Cher was criticizing me—not Gregg or any of the high-priced people that advised her.

No, Cher was still playing the victim, and despite the fact that there had been many other men as well as many years separating us, she still saw me as the bad guy in her life, the Svengali who almost strangled her to death.

I couldn't get through to her at the time—not even when I wanted to talk about Chas. If Cher didn't want to talk, there was no reaching her. She was protected by layers of people. When she wanted to isolate, she made herself very, very alone. The little I knew of her life I learned from Chastity, and the news wasn't comforting. Despite Cher's public show of strength and success, Chas painted a picture of a strange, troubled woman. Cher feared going outside. She worried about being poisoned and hired food tasters. She lapsed into uncontrollable, seemingly irrational crying jags. She wandered around her house lonely and depressed. She looked to astrologers for advice.

I sympathized. I felt bad about whatever Cher was going through, but I didn't want to feel guilty. I was through accepting responsibility for her life.

Sometime around late 1982 I learned that Cher was going to be in Las Vegas performing at Caesar's Palace. I phoned and emphasized to the minions who surrounded her that I needed to talk to Cher. I got through and told her I wanted to speak to her. It was important. She hemmed and hawed. I could hear the reluctance in the long, silent pauses that punctuated her strained voice. Finally she agreed.

I flew to Vegas and took the elevator up to Cher's enormous suite. I felt like a fallen subject who had been granted one final audience with the queen. Cher was polite and pleasant but extremely reserved. She hoarded her words as if they were food that she was saving for a long, severe winter. I didn't let it bother me. I wasn't going to buy into her game. If she wanted to feel that she was in control, then fine. I had my own agenda.

We sat down opposite each other in the living room. Cher raised her eyebrows as if to say, So? She was doing her best to appear relaxed, but I knew Cher was uptight, if only because she had no idea what I wanted to talk about.

"Cher, I really need to clean the slate with you," I said in slow, measured words. "I've reached a point in my life where I want to go on and let go of the past. Not the good stuff, but all the anger and hard feelings. I wanted to do this in person."

"Well, what are you trying to say, Son?" she said. "That you're not mad at me anymore?"

"No, no, not at all," I said. "No, all I want to say to you is that I'm sorry. I'm sorry for whatever I've done that's pissed you off. I still pick up on a lot of anger from you that I don't really understand. But hey, I'm sorry. I really am. And I hope that my apologizing will get rid of the bitterness still between us."

Cher had sat stoically and been unresponsive throughout my little speech. She absorbed it all and said nothing in return. Now that I had finished, she had no choice but to reply. She had to say something, and she did.

"I appreciate it," she said. "I heard what you said and I know that you really mean it."

I thought, Okay. In this sort of situation, one person apologizes and then the other person apologizes for whatever they did. A relationship is a two-way street. Only in rare instances is one person accountable for all the wrongs, and our relationship wasn't one of those. I didn't get an apology from Cher that day. But it was all right. That wasn't why I was there. I felt good about what I had said. I no longer needed anything from her.

Back home I felt a tremendous weight lifted from my shoulders. For the first time in longer than I remembered, I was free and clean emotionally. I accepted myself for who I was, not who I had been. I quit treating myself as a victim. I stopped punishing myself and thinking I was a failure, and acknowledged instead all that I had accomplished, which wasn't bad. I took responsibility for the present and future and that, by itself, proved empowering. I was ready to go on with my life, a step I hadn't been ready to make till now.

It was as if my eyes suddenly opened after being closed for the past decade. I smiled at people. I had more patience with life. I noticed things that I'd previously let pass. While filming *Airplane II,* for instance, I drove back and forth to Paramount along Melrose Avenue. Every day I passed the intersection at Melrose and La Cienega, where there was an odd little building on a small, triangular lot.

The building, formerly a burger joint and now a turquoise-and-pink Mexican eatery called Chicken Olé, had obviously gone through a number of metamorphoses, but it still retained lots of character. Passing by, I never failed to notice the "For Lease" sign displayed in the window. Why I noticed, I don't know. It was like a magnet, an enticement I couldn't resist. I had no plans to go into any kind of business that would require a building, but something about the place struck a positive chord in my imagination.

One day I stopped to look the place over. I can't say why I did that. But I peered through the windows and surveyed the grounds. I rapped on the back door and checked the foundation; I did everything short of calling for a termite inspection. It was as if I was pulled by an unseen force like the mysterious voice in the movie *Field of Dreams* that says, "If you build it, he will come."

I was definitely interested, even though I couldn't say in what. Walking around to the front of the building, I tried the front door. It was locked. I felt the need to get inside so I jotted down the phone number on the rental sign. Later that afternoon I called and talked to the building's owner, who told me that a woman had already made a serious inquiry.

"She's going to take the place?" I said.

"Yeah, that's what she says," the man replied.

"What's she going to do with it?"

"I'm told she's going to make it a French restaurant of some sort."

"Jesus," I said, reacting as if I had a plan for the place. "That won't work."

"It won't?"

"No," I said. "Too elegant, too restrained. This would make a great trattoria."

I found out the square footage, the building's age, various other facts, including the rent, which dropped into the conversation as casually as a basil leaf into marinara sauce. The more I talked, the more excited I got.

"Listen," I said quite spontaneously, "send me the sheet on your place and don't accept any offer until you hear from me."

As sure as I had once been when writing hit songs, I suddenly knew that I was going into the restaurant business. I'd be a restaurateur. The idea stuck in my head like the hook of "I Got You Babe." I couldn't shake it. I couldn't concentrate on anything else but that restaurant.

After Susie went to sleep, I sat up and planned the entire restaurant. I saw the look. I sketched the dining-room layout. I smelled the garlic simmering, the sauces, the long, thick loaves of Italian bread in the oven, the olive oil, and the din of animated conversation. I thought about it until the place seemed real.

Early the next morning I called the landlord and took the lease. The prospect of starting a new career was exciting. Drawing up plans and thinking of concepts reminded me of when I was hustling to launch Sonny and Cher. I wanted the keys immediately and the landlord and I agreed to meet at the building later that afternoon.

He had just one question for me, though.

"Have you ever owned a restaurant before?" he asked.

"No," I said. "But I have a history of doing OK in things I know nothing about."

"Well, good luck."

By the time the lease was signed I was telling myself that I had always wanted to own a restaurant. One of life's phenomena is that everybody, at some time or another in their life, wants to be either an actor or a singer and they also want to own a restaurant. Why that gets tossed in there I haven't the foggiest. I suppose people either fantasize about being the life of the party every night or they have been affected in a big way by *Casablanca*.

I was guilty on both counts. But I also really loved to cook and I always had. I had always cooked at home when entertaining friends, and I don't want to sound conceited, but the compliments rivaled the number of cleaned plates. Going into a venture blind, as I was, having such confidence did not hurt in the least. I started visualizing myself in the restaurant, this cozy, irresistibly aromatic trattoria, strolling around with a smile on my face, passing out greetings to satisfied customers, socializing—basically hosting one groovy party after another.

It took about six months and somewhere between five hundred thousand and one million dollars to rebuild and renovate the building, adding and changing the plan at every stage as advice streamed in from people who knew the restaurant business. Although it was like taking a cram course, nothing anybody said prepared me for running a restaurant, which, I would soon discover, was like being tossed into combat with only a linen napkin and your smile for weapons.

People warned me. I was constantly asked, "You're giving up show business?" I was extremely hesitant about telling the truth. If I said yes, I was admitting that I was switching gears. It was tantamount to waving a white flag. But I had to surrender one part of myself to discover another part. My friends, looking out for my reputation, advised, "Whatever you do, don't put your name on it."

I understood. Owning a restaurant was not as glamorous as being a performer. If I hung my name out front, I was advertising to Hollywood that I was out of the game. And they'd think, Well, that's the end of him.

But I was enthusiastic. At that point, I was ready to say, So what!

People win and lose. That is life. If I lost, so what? I'd start over again. I'd learned that once you fear taking a chance on yourself, you automatically lose. You give up any chance of winning. If you worry more about what other people are going to think rather than about your ability to do a job, you might as well not even try.

I shrugged at the odds against me, like I did when I was a kid shopping songs to Johnny Otis. The odds were stacked against me then too. I was a white Italian kid from the suburbs writing rhythm-and-blues songs and trying to sell them to black radio. Then and now I told myself, Sonny, you are who you are and don't worry about anything else.

The restaurant, having been transformed from taco stand to trattoria, opened in February 1983. The bubble gum—colored Mexican exterior had been replaced by sophisticated moss greens, terra-cotta hues, and off-white Mediterranean shades. I called it Bono's. By opening night I was exhausted but bursting with pride. I was full of the optimism of hard work. With my luck, though, it rained our first night of business.

According to *People* magazine's description of the first night, "The rain fell harder and faster than the ratings" of my last TV series, but the party was hot. Those who showed up to sip champagne, nibble, and wish me "bono appétit" included Tony Curtis, Bert Convy, Dick Van Patten, Donna Mills, Valerie Perrine, and Cher, who told reporters, "When we were together, he made all the food."

One by one, as people slapped me on the back, I confessed, "I don't know what the hell I'm doing." Nobody believed me. Little did I suspect that the highlight of owning a restaurant would be opening night.

But the truth came out as the hangover I had tied on during the gala celebration wore off. Starting on the second night of business, I got a crash course in the food business, and the reality was frightening—stopped-up sewers and toilets, merchandise disappearing out the back door, cooks and waiters screwing up, customers complaining about everything from cold soup to a nervous waiter spilling hot coffee on them.

However, Bono's hit the ground running. For the first three months it was the hottest hangout in L.A. We actually turned away business. People called to book tables two and three weeks in advance. I was working harder, longer hours than I had ever put in during my show business career, but I was having a ball. In the midst of this roll, a wheeler-dealer Texan, a guy who had just sold a restaurant he owned in Houston, came in and talked me into opening a Bono's down there.

That sounded like fun. I was riding high, and the thought of shuttling back and forth between states seemed adventurous. Money was raised quickly and a second Bono's outfitted. Coincidentally, just as the sister restaurant opened, Houston's economy collapsed as the oil business went bust. The restaurant sputtered along for little more than six months. Finally, stressed-out by the travel and the declining business, I sold out to my partner.

By then—early 1984 and past my year anniversary in the business, I was more knowledgeable about running a restaurant. I knew that in order to be successful, I had to choose one place and be there all the time.

Unfortunately, I did not have such an option in my marriage to Susie, which was following the same path as the Houston Bono's. The relationship had been on shaky ground for more than a year, but sometimes when a marriage collapses, and you have been through that disaster before, you cling to the second relationship even more tenaciously, reluctant to go through all the pain and insecurity that you've come to know surround a divorce. At least that was my perception of events. I was not trying to preserve a precious love as much as I was telling myself, Oh no, you can't go through another loss again. You can't survive another failure.

However, the more I questioned myself, evaluated the situation, and assessed my goals, I found, for the first time in my life, that I was able to accept what was happening. My marriage was on the rocks. If I wanted my life to continue functioning smoothly, I had to deal with that. It was a signal of real, tangible personal growth on my part.

Susie agreed that the marriage was beyond salvaging. The problem? If I had to put my finger on one specific thing, I would have to say show business. Our relationship was based more on the pursuit of a career than on romance. Susie wanted to make it as an actress, while I was set on putting in my twelve-hour day at Bono's. Susie and I had been together long enough to realize what made us happy, and neither of us had the incentive to change our priorities.

We started pursuing distinctly separate lives late in 1983 and separated for good in June 1984.

However, we wanted to resolve the various differences and part without any lingering resentment and anger. Both of us wanted to lay the issues on the table and to take responsibility for our actions and feelings. It is a very adult response to a relationship gone awry. Because of this, Susie and I have always been able to remain good friends.

As Susie and I were going through this process, two things happened.

First, the heat that made Bono's hip for its first three or four months disappeared. That wasn't surprising. All but a few of the most successful restaurants in a city like L.A., where eating out is a popular form of entertainment and going to a new restaurant is like seeing a new movie, succumb to a similar fate. After everyone sees the film and talks about it, only a handful of diehards see it again. Bono's had been seen and discussed, and within a matter of months the buzz disappeared.

Not surprisingly, so did my interest in running it, but for now Bono's was the only game in town, the only marquee on which I got star billing.

Then I fell in love.

And so a whole new chapter in my life began.

It was a cool night in late May. I was at the restaurant and I spotted a beautiful, dark-haired young woman sitting at a table with another woman. They were talking animatedly and seemed to be having a good time. The woman was alluring. I kept looking—casually, slyly—and then the look turned into a stare. Her smile was bright. Her eyes danced in the light. While strolling around the dining room, I caught a trickle of laughter and knew instantly that she had spirit.

I noticed that there was a bottle of champagne in an ice bucket beside the girls; they were clearly celebrating something.

Lots of attractive women came into Bono's and I never gave them a second glance, but something about this girl, some inexplicable charm wafting through the air, made me determined to meet her. I pointed her out to the restaurant's manager, Wick Phillips. We sat down at the adjoining table.

I played it cool. A glance, a look, then a smile. After she returned my smile, I started to flirt. I cracked a joke, started a conversation, and before long, Wick and I were seated at their table.

Her name was Mary Whitaker. She was twenty-two, and she had just graduated from USC with a degree in art history.

Mary wasted no time in turning the conversation from witty but superficial small talk into a knowledgeable, indepth discussion of the restaurant business. Her questions kept me on my toes. We talked for three hours and ended on a very L.A. note. Both of us worked out daily. Before Mary left, I asked her if she wanted to work out together the following afternoon. She did, and we exchanged phone numbers.

"Call me, OK?" I said as the valet brought her car up.

"Yeah, I will." She smiled.

The next day came and went. Mary didn't call.

Mary's no patsy. I'm sure she thought that our chat was fun and nothing more. She probably scoffed about my taking her phone number and felt bad having given it to me. She probably thought I engaged in this sort of thing all the time. Little did she know that my designs were on the up-and-up. I really wanted to know her better. She was truly surprised when I called her. She was also happy. We spoke for more than an hour.

"Look, I'm going to keep calling you," I said. "I mean, I'd like to take you out and get to know you."

"That would be nice," she said. "Yeah, it would. I'd like that."

We had a terrific time when we got together for a lunch date, but in the course of conversation, I learned that Mary had a boyfriend with whom she was living. It was over, she explained, which was good news. *Dianetics* had taught me to deal with interpersonal ethics exactly like this. For instance, if someone is involved with another person, as Mary was, you do not encroach upon their relationship. If they are splitting in a month, then you say, "Fine, but handle that first and then we'll deal with each other."

So I told Mary, "If you're really serious about seeing me, then you're going to have to tell the guy that you like me. You have to let him know that you are pursuing this. Basically, you have to let him go and wrap up that relationship before we start anything."

That was a lot to dump on someone I was just getting to know, but Mary handled it. A week later we were dating regularly. That was ironic, for after making a clean break with Susie, I had intended to explore life as a bachelor. After all, I had not been single since I married Donna at age nineteen. I was now fifty years old. For thirty-one years, I had been involved with either Donna or Cher or Connie or Susie. This time I decided I was not going to jump into anything.

I told Mary that, and she said OK.

"We can both date whomever," I said. "I mean, I want to see you. I want to see you a lot. But I also want to leave things open."

"Sure, I understand," said Mary. "That's OK."

Naturally, that was a lot of fluff and backpedaling, because the more we dated, the more we wanted to date only each other. Not only was Mary beautiful, she was smart and direct, qualities that attracted me to her. She also found herself attracted to me. She liked my frankness, the tenacious and creative way I approached life. We grew close quickly, quicker than either one of us would've predicted. It was quite natural—except for one bit of awkwardness: the difference in our ages.

I was more than twice Mary's age. She was twenty-two; I was fifty. When I questioned her about it, Mary said that it wasn't a factor. However, she added an interesting twist that showed the character and directness that I fell in love with. Mary told me that she wanted a family, children, and if that was not a priority with me, she said, then that was more of a problem than our ages.

Strangely, that wasn't a problem, which surprised the hell out of me. Until then I didn't know I was interested in having a family again. But Mary's sudden mention of children opened up facets of myself that I didn't know still existed. I had thought I was long past the stage of rearing children, but now I realized that a family was exactly what

I wanted. I was ready to live the life that I was always too hip or too busy to have.

Mary had a uniquely comforting effect on me. Until I'd met her I'd known only actresses and models. Mary was different, though. She'd graduated from college. She had ambition and spunk. She was working two waitressing jobs. I'd never admired a woman as much as Mary, especially since I was then waiting on tables myself and liked the feeling of real work. It planted my feet on the ground.

I attributed so much of that feeling to Mary. She gave it to me without even knowing it. She was just such a solid person. Through her I saw a completely different set of values than I was used to, values that were rational and sane. She dealt with the basics, like health and love, rather than hinging everything on whether or not she got a commercial or was invited to the right party. It was so damn refreshing.

In September we spent a long, restful, and romantic weekend together in Palm Springs. Palm Springs was my oasis. I'd kept a home there for fifteen years. I wanted to take Mary down there and unwind. That Saturday we were walking down the main street, Palm Canyon Boulevard, window-shopping. The wind was blowing. Our spirits soared. I asked Mary to close her eyes for a moment and hold out her hands.

"What are you doing?" she asked.

"Nothing," I said as I fished in my pocket, pulled out a tiny box, and put it into her hands.

Not a nanosecond passed before Mary opened her eyes.

"What's this?" she exclaimed, opening the box and removing the diamond ring.

"My proposal." I smiled. "I, ah, it's my way of asking you to marry me."

Mary burst into tears. A crowd gathered as we stood in the center of the busy sidewalk, hugging and kissing.

"Yes," Mary whispered into my ear.

It sounds like a cliché, but I knew beyond any doubt that this marriage was . . . charmed.

15

IT'S THE LITTLE THINGS

I'd never been happier in any relationship, but planning a future with Mary, especially a future that included children, brought feelings I'd suppressed for years boiling to the surface. They had nothing to do with Cher. After apologizing to her several years earlier I'd been able to make a clean break from her. But I realized that wasn't enough. There were still some things that troubled me from my past, including a touchy area that thus far I'd been unable to admit to.

I'd failed in the area where I'd vowed not to fail. I'd failed as a father.

My children, Christy and Chas, had never been as high a priority to me as my career.

If I was going to continue to be happy, I had to deal with that situation. If I was going to think about having more children at some point, I had to confront my failings with Christy and Chas so that I wouldn't repeat them. Though it was impossible to make amends, I had to do what I'd so assiduously avoided up until now: I had to own up to the fact.

One day I called Christy. I was so nervous that it took me a couple of hours just to work up the courage to dial her phone number. At the time she owned a small restaurant in Santa Monica, had married, and was doing well for herself.

I hadn't planned what I was going to say and still hadn't when I heard her voice. We traded idle chitchat; I knew that I was stalling.

"Listen, Christy," I said. "I don't know quite how to say this. I'm kind of uncomfortable."

"What are you talking about?" she asked.

"Look." I paused and took a breath. "I know that I wasn't the type of father that I would've liked to be."

"Dad—" she tried interrupting. I could hear Christy's voice cracking.

"No, let me finish," I said in a voice that was also strained by emotion. "I didn't do all the things that I should have as a father. I don't feel as if I did any. But I want you to know that now I would take on any and all responsibilities."

I was barely able to get the words out. Both of us sobbed openly.

"I'm crying," she said. "But I'm happy to hear what you're saying. It's good to know that you're there. I mean I probably knew it, but—"

"But it's good that I can say it," I said. "And I mean it. I really do."

Afterward I was drained, emotionally exhausted, but I felt good about having cleared the air and broken the ground for a better relationship with my oldest daughter. I was proud of her. Christy had a restaurant, a husband, and she'd adopted a baby. She'd always had a father, but now she knew that she had a father who cared about her.

I had much more communication with Chastity than I ever had with Christy. I felt close to Chas, and I knew that we had a solid relationship. But Chas has never been a real talkative person. She inherited that from Cher. Like many parents, Cher and I never sat down and told Chas about our divorce. We never hashed it out. We all lived through it and avoided discussion. I believe Cher filled Chas in on Sonny and Cher, told her whatever stories she thought worth telling.

Not all of it was complimentary, though. I can attest to that.

"Why does Mom say not to trust you?" Chas, then nine

or ten years old, asked me one day when we were driving back to Los Angeles from a weekend in Palm Springs.

"What do you mean?" I asked, startled.

"Mom always says about you, 'I don't trust him.' She says it a lot."

"Well, Chas." I kinda laughed. "I don't know what she's talking about. I hope you know you can always trust me."

Sometimes Chas was extremely close to Cher, other times she wasn't. The same went for me. We had no problem expressing our feelings to each other, though. When Chas was sixteen, she wrote and performed a song in a show her acting class put on in Santa Monica. Mary and I sat in the front row. Chas sang her heart out. I don't think I'd ever been more nervous or more touched in my life.

"What'd you think, Dad?" she asked afterward.

"I think I love you," I said. "I think I love you, and I don't know what else to say."

Chas was one of the first people I told about my engagement to Mary. She was excited, and that reaction pleased me.

"I sold the house," I told her.

"Where're you going to live?" she asked.

Chas had never had roots. Cher lived everywhere—L.A., New York, Santa Fe, Aspen. I'd always been in Bel Air or Beverly Hills, and I sensed that Chas didn't want me to give up the familiarity of the neighborhood. That just happened to be the plan, too. After selling my old house, Mary and I selected a lot in Beverly Hills where we planned to construct a dream house.

In the meantime, though, we needed a place to live.

"This is only a suggestion," I said to Mary one day. "But why don't we move down to Palm Springs until the house is finished?"

Mary went for the idea, and we moved into my longtime Palm Springs home. The peaceful desert town had been a second home to me for so many years that I immediately felt settled. I loved the sun, the quiet, the solitude of a desert night, the picturesque landscape, and the tranquillity. The only downside of living in Palm Springs was the one hundred twenty–mile commute I made several times a week back to the restaurant in L.A., a drive that grew less and less attractive to me.

Since I still enjoyed the restaurant business, Mary helped me find a little restaurant in Palm Springs. I imagined owning a charming little trattoria, high-quality but low-pressure, a place where I could ease into semiretirement and devote the bulk of my time to raising a family.

At the end of 1985 we found just such a restaurant toward the north end of Palm Springs, a stone's throw from Palm Canyon Boulevard, which is the main business strip. The building had character and quaintness. It was part of a tennis club, so it was still surrounded by tennis courts. I leased it from the guys who owned the tennis courts and went to work remodeling, turning the former clubhouse into a laidback version of Bono's, to the tune of one hundred thousand dollars.

In January 1986 Bono's opened for business. The setup was much different than it had been in L.A. The scale was smaller and less frantic. How much? Well, instead of a gala celebrity bash covered by hordes of media, when the new Bono's opened we had two waiters, two kitchen assistants, Mary working as the hostess, and I was on line as the cook. For the first few inaugural weeks, Bono's was a roll-up-your-sleeves, do-it-yourself operation, but it was homey and it worked and Mary and I had fun.

By this time construction on our new house in Los Angeles was so far behind schedule, and Mary and I found ourselves enjoying Palm Springs so much, that we began to question whether or not we wanted to live in L.A. Palm Springs suited our pace. It had a small-town feel. The people were friendly; the access to stores was easier, and so was life in general. The restaurant was doing well. I actually felt myself relaxing.

It was no accident that I was enjoying life for the first time in God knows how long. The answer was simple. Mary. I loved her with a consuming passion. I knew that I was supposed to be with this woman. But the stronger my love grew and the more assured I was that we belonged together, the more frightened I became that somehow I'd blow the relationship. After all, I didn't have the greatest track record. I began reading everything I could lay my hands on that concerned relationships and making them work. That became my number-one priority. I didn't want another one, especially one this special, to go astray.

What I learned from all that reading and discovery was the importance of never losing your admiration for that other person. Relationships have to be maintained with the same care and sensitivity a watchmaker gives a fragile, antique, jewel-encrusted watch. Long relationships, I determined, have a lot more to do with mechanics than with the emotion that fuels them. Love and passion are primary; you can't have a meaningful relationship without them. But you also have to constantly fine-tune, clean, paint, and repair the little things.

Smarter and more confident of myself, I found myself anxious to take the plunge. Fortunately, Mary felt the same way.

We were married in Palm Springs in late February 1986. The ceremony took play in a traditional, nondenominational chapel. It was an intimate and joyous affair. The only celebrities in attendance were our relatives. Mary's parents, Dr. Clay Whitaker and his wife, Karen, and her ninety-year-old grandmother, flew in from their home in North Carolina. My daughter Christy also attended. Mary had never looked more beautiful. I'd muttered "I do" several times before, but when I looked into Mary's eyes, I said it with conviction, and felt a stirring deep within my soul.

When I wrote songs I always knew if I was on to something that was great. I could just tell. I felt that way about being with Mary. I knew it was great.

The ceremony cemented our decision to make Palm Springs our permanent residence. Soon after the wedding I sold the restaurant in L.A. and concentrated on Bono's in Palm Springs.

Then I was offered a part in the movie *Troll*, which was being filmed in Italy. Unlike past acting jobs, which were approached as career moves, I took the part as a lark, an opportunity to have an all-expense-paid vacation in Italy. Mary and I had a great time.

However, we returned home to face a crisis. The guys who had leased us the restaurant had gone broke, and that put me in a predicament. Either I had to buy the whole property—the building and all twenty tennis courts—or I had to eat my one hundred thousand–dollar investment in Bono's. Mary and I discussed the dilemma, though it seemed clear that we had only one choice. So, like Zorba the Greek, we bought "the whole catastrophe."

With our community roots spreading wider and deeper, Mary and I went looking for a new home and bought an old, run-down, Spanish-style mansion in the Mesa area, which was an older, stately residential part of Palm Springs whose once grand homes had seen better days. But in the course of remodeling the disheveled property, I began to see City Hall as a tired complex of unfair contradictions.

First the city shut down construction for lack of a permit. Once that was acquired, they stopped work for lack of an inspector. Then, in trying to meet the building requirements, I spent ten thousand dollars on a wall surrounding my property that had to be finished on both sides. Yet I could stand on my lawn and point to my neighbor's new wall, which was finished only on one side. Why? That was all I wanted to know. Similarly, when I wanted to add a second story, I was told two-story homes were against ordinances. Yet my other neighbor's home was a two-story number. Again, why?

But then I got into another wrangle with the boys downtown when I tried to replace the sign at the entry of Bono's with another, larger sign. My intention was simple: I wanted to let people know where the restaurant was. However, I was informed that the property was zoned residential. Why, then, was a commercial building allowed to go up there in the first place? It was another question without an answer.

And why were neighboring businesses allowed to hang signs and I was not? Again, when I investigated the issue, there were no answers.

These puzzling questions brought me into conflict with the town's leaders, who I quickly realized were entrenched in an abuse of power, like the pudgy bullies one encountered in grammar school. They were elitist. They had an attitude that Palm Springs was their town, and damn whatever anybody else thought; they were going to run the place exactly as they wanted to. As a businessman, taxpayer, and resident, that did not strike me as fair. Nor was it democratic.

Pissed off, I went to see the mayor, Frank Bogart, a jovial, leather-faced cowboy, who is now a friend of mine. We were fairly good buddies, having met on many occasions, but Bogart's long-standing membership in the town's good-old-boy network did not bode well for my complaints. Nonetheless, during our talk, I unloaded on the planning director and other bureaucrats who had stymied my attempts to invest in the town's economy.

My argument was that Palm Springs' sagging economy needed new investments like mine. The town was a sleeper, I said. I just wanted to contribute. I believed the city would be proud of both my house and my business, and I felt these sorts of improvements needed to be encouraged rather than discouraged. Palm Springs relied on tourism, yet, as far I could tell, the stodgy old guard had driven the once glittery desert oasis straight into economic torpor.

Mayor Bogart listened patiently, smiled, laughed when it was appropriate, offered to buy me a drink, and then gave me an avuncular slap on the back as I was leaving. He told me not to worry, and I believed him. I thought he would provide the green light I needed to proceed. But unknown to him, a few of the city's more enlightened bureaucrats came down even harder on me and plied me with stricter building constraints. It was a case of abuse of power.

For more than fifty years Palm Springs had been a luxurious playground for Hollywood's elite, a less uptight Palm Beach. Only a two-hour drive from L.A., the desert town boasted streets named after Bob Hope, Gerald Ford, and Frank Sinatra, all longtime residents. Mere mention of the city conjured up images of cool swimming pools, streets lined with palm trees, golf courses, jasmine-scented night air, and wealth beyond words.

Yet the city's billion-dollar image was no longer reality reflected on the town's main drag. A new and vital effort was needed to lure high-fashion resorts and stores. I was concerned that the town's glamour was slowly moving elsewhere, a danger when your number-one industry is tourism.

I went on an endless tirade, sounding like a broken record. If I wasn't decrying the city's failures to friends, I was complaining to Mary. The more I thought about the problems facing Palm Springs, the more I began thinking of ways to inject new life into Palm Springs. I likened the situation to show biz. The city was a good concept in need of a rewrite.

Like most Average Joes, though, I accepted the old cliché: You can't fight city hall. That was especially true in Palm Springs. It was also terribly frustrating, considering that there were bulldozers sitting idly on my back lawn and empty tables in my restaurant. I felt like the protagonist in a bad TV movie. I wanted to take action. I'd never been a guy who rolled over without putting up a fight. There had to be a way, I thought, to fight back.

Late one night toward the end of 1987 Mary and I were seated at the kitchen table, the site of so many meetings and decisions. Privately, I had spent the past few weeks mulling over one of the strangest-sounding ideas that had ever popped into my head. I couldn't contain it anymore. It was time to test how far out my thinking was.

"What do you think about my running for mayor?" I asked.

Mary was shocked. She gave me a penetrating look. It looked as though Mary's mind had gone out of focus and she was trying to clear it up. I laughed nervously.

"Are you crazy?" she said.

"Maybe," I said. "But what do you think?"

"Well, I'd vote for you." She laughed.

That was good. I had solidarity at home. Even better, I had another vote besides my own. Mary continued talking; but I had no idea what she was saying. With only two certain votes, I had to start thinking about my campaign.

Phil Spector had taught me the value of shocking the public, but nothing I learned from him prepared me for the public's reaction to my candidacy. As far as they were concerned, my declaration to run for mayor of Palm Springs was the best joke I had told in years.

By March 1988, though, the April 12 election was one month off, and plenty of people were nervous. Why? Because I had a good shot at winning. No one was more surprised than I was.

My campaign was hard fought, and strictly unorthodox from the get-go. It began with Mary announcing that she was pregnant; her due date was five days after the election. I then took time out from the campaign to film that John Waters movie *Hairspray*. It turned out to be a kick, but when the role was offered to me, I didn't know John Waters from Joan Rivers. I asked the kid who was managing Bono's if he'd ever heard of the director.

"Wow, man! Are you kidding?" he responded.

"No," I said. "Who is he?"

"Have you ever heard of *Pink Flamingos*?" he asked.

"No," I said.

"Oh, man, that's my all-time favorite movie," he said.

"Yeah? What's it about?"

"It's the grossest thing ever filmed," he said. "I mean, it's got this transvestite named Divine who eats real dog shit at the end of the movie."

"You're kidding." I grimaced.

"No. It's so cool."

By the time I finished asking people about this director, I had a pretty good idea of the personal vision and dementia of John Waters. *Hairspray*, though, had a pretty funny script, a kind of ode to the dance craze of the sixties as experienced by a fat girl who wants to be a dancer on a Baltimore TV show. I loved the music and I understood that the story was intentionally bad. But the grossness that was Waters's trademark was missing when I read the script. So I called him up.

"Look, John," I said. "Is there something you're not telling me? I mean, how are you shooting this thing?"

He did not understand what I was after.

"I'm running for mayor," I explained, "and I can't be in a freaky, weird movie right now."

"I don't think you get it," he said. "The minute I wrote the script, I thought of you. You're perfect for the father role. I mean, I want *you* to play that guy."

"Okay, but what about the script?" I asked.

"What you're reading is what you'll see," he said.

"That's cool," I said. "I'm not trying to undermine you in any way. But I can't be in one of *those* films."

"No, no," he laughed. "You don't have to worry. No dogs on the set."

Filmed on location in Baltimore, the site of all Waters's movies, I worked with Pia Zadora and Riki Lake and Blondie's Debbie Harry, and had a ball. The only thing that topped making the movie was the premiere, which was held in a dilapidated theater in downtown L.A. Fans of Waters, thousands of wild-looking kids, packed the theater. They loved it. As the credits rolled, the audience's reaction made me realize that after all the movies I'd done, I was finally in a hit.

The local Palm Springs paper gave *Hairspray* a good review. My performance was called "a welcome comedy role." By that time, though, the campaign was the biggest show in town, and it was far more humorous than the movie. "I think it's amazing that this little guy who looks like an aging hippie has people come up to him and ask for his autograph," said realtor Eli Birer, the city's vice mayor and one of my opponents. "I would not ask for his autograph even if he dressed like a human being."

Hadn't I heard that before? Like twenty-five years ago when Cher and I used to go into Martoni's? Times changed, but people rarely did. I got a good laugh out of that.

Needless to say, of eight candidates vying for the four-year job, which carried an annual salary of fifteen thousand dollars, mine was the most diverse résumé. Yet only I, Birer, and certified public accountant Lloyd Maryanov were considered front-runners, and the polls showed me running way ahead. I couldn't believe it, but I was delighted.

Not everyone was happy about that, though. It bugged the hell out of the city's political fathers that I was the front-runner. Frank Bogart, the incumbent mayor and a friend of mine, was among the first to take aim at me. He called me every name in the book, from a hippie to a son of a bitch to a squirrel, and then some. Birer and Maryanov chose the more obvious tack. They accused me of being a star on the skids and using Palm Springs to gain publicity for myself.

My skin was thick. More important, I'd done my homework and was prepared. I could rattle off the issues with clarity and confidence. All the city's growth had gone "down valley," into neighboring resort communities like Rancho Mirage and Palm Desert; the city was suffering from a 2.8-million-dollar deficit, resulting in cuts in city services, including the police and fire departments. I charged that the old-boy network that ran Palm Springs like a friendly card game had been setting itself up for years with sweetheart deals at the city's expense.

Local merchants embraced my ideas of promoting tourism, the city's primary industry, with glamorous events like a film festival. Developers, I said, needed new incentives. While locals warmed to my candidacy, outsiders were slow to take me seriously. The press pigeonholed me as a copycat intimating the career leaps of Ronald Reagan and Clint Eastwood. My opponents chided me for it.

"Sonny ain't no Clint," said Mayor Bogart. "Clint's a big star, while Sonny's a big nothing. And comparing the two is like comparing chicken shit to chicken salad."

Mary lost sleep over the name-calling, but I relished the battle. If they were calling me names, I figured I must be hitting them in the right places. In truth, the old guard saw me as their worst nightmare. Why? I did not play by the established rules. I was a rabble-rouser, a troublemaker. I was also Joe Q. Citizen—an honest, ordinary, but frustrated businessman, and I was not afraid to say what I thought. Though perceived as the liberal, I was a registered Republican who had voted for Reagan in the '84 election.

When my experience was questioned, I maintained that running a restaurant and politics were pretty similar. Both were production-oriented with high dynamics. "But compared to politics," I said, "show business is kindergarten. I think I've entered the second-oldest profession."

Mine was strictly a grass-roots campaign, staffed by friends and volunteers and plotted by Mary. The coffers were filled by selling T-shirts, buttons, and bumper stickers; the campaign was fueled, as are all campaigns, by gallons of coffee and tens of thousands of calories' worth of doughnuts. I shook thousands of hands, gave out as many autographs, and kissed more babies than I'd ever seen in my life. If Mary and I were not campaigning we were sprinting back and forth to Bono's, trying to keep the restaurant working smoothly.

It was a crazed time, but I knew that voters, primed for a change in leadership, were listening to what I had to say. Nobody cared that I'd been famous once. I was a local merchant. I was fighting their battles. They saw me reveling in the spit and vinegar that went into a small-town campaign, which was never dull. Confrontations were always around the corner. One afternoon Greg MacDonald, one of my campaign managers, and I had lunch at Paul D'Amico's steak house. D'Amico was Birer's campaign treasurer and I jokingly referred to his restaurant as the "enemy camp."

"Hello, Sonny," said Paul, setting a few menus on our table. "What can I do for you?"

"Well, Paul," I said, "I've been thinking about these paper placemats here. And look, here's a little mention of Eli. I was wondering if I might be able to take out a half-page ad? Or perhaps a full page? Whatever's available."

"Oh, you really know how to zing 'em." Paul chuckled. "You really are something."

To those guys I was something. They just could not figure out what. The old guard had no idea what to make of me. Throughout the campaign, there were more forums for candidates to discuss the issues than at any level of government in the country. I scored major points in a February forum when I accused both Maryanov and Birer of violating a city ordinance prohibiting candidates from posting signs until thirty days before an election. Both denied it. Then I held up photos.

"They were put up by overenthusiastic supporters," Birer argued. "I don't know a thing about it. But they'll be taken down right away."

"I know," I said. "I already took the sign down for you."

On the other hand, I figured I had blown the entire campaign during the last forum, which was held about two weeks before the election. Up until that point, I had run a flawless, albeit unexpectedly successful, race and was leading by a comfortable margin. The junior chamber of commerce was sponsoring this last forum and the local ABC affiliate had decided to televise it live, which elevated the debate to a real media event—at least for Palm Springs.

But the morning of the forum Mary came down with a severe case of the flu. I drove her to the doctor. He detected some possible complications and checked her into the hospital. I called the group putting on the forum, the press, and my campaign people and told everybody that Mary was having some contractions, she was in the hospital, and I was going to stay with her and cancel the forum. Everybody agreed that I was making the right decision.

Later that night in Mary's hospital room I turned on the TV to watch the forum. As they introduced the candidates, they mentioned that I had canceled at the last moment. I screamed at the television set, "Tell 'em why I'm not there!" But no additional explanation was given. I stomped across the hospital room, snarling at the people on TV. Mary told me not to get excited. The nurse told Mary not to get excited, and then she turned to me.

"Can you please keep your voice down?" she said.

"Yes," I whispered as loudly as I had been talking. "But can you tell me why they aren't announcing why I'm not there?"

I called the network. I called over to Maxim's hotel where the forum was taking place and managed to speak with somebody connected to the forum.

"Look, I'm not there because I'm here at the hospital with my wife, Mary," I explained. "Now can you announce that on television? Can you tell them what I'm doing? I'm watching the debate here with Mary. Announce it!"

A few moments later I saw someone hand a note to the moderator, Ed Kibby, a man who disliked me. He studied the note and then looked up at the audience.

"I have a note here," he read, "that says Sonny Bono isn't going to appear. He has other matters."

I turned away from the TV in disgust.

"Jesus Christ, they're sandbagging me," I said.

The nurse asked me to keep my voice down.

"I'm going over there, Mary," I said. "I've got to go there and explain."

"Don't go," she said.

"I'm going." I shook my head. "I'm going. I'll be right back."

The ten-minute drive to the hotel took me five minutes. I jumped out of the car and dashed into the room where the forum was being held. It must have looked as if I was going to run straight onto the stage, because the program director jumped out and grabbed me.

"Why don't you guys tell them what's up?" I snapped.

"Why don't you go on and tell everyone yourself?" he said.

"OK," I said.

"Just a minute," the program director said, "and we'll mike you up."

A note was sent up to the stage, telling the moderator that I was heading onstage. Ed Kibby, trying to be as nasty as possible, sent word back, "OK, but he has to participate in the forum just like the others." Of course, they failed to relay that part back to me. So I strode onto the stage to explain why I hadn't been there. I planned to make a brief announcement and then race back to Mary. But the moment I started to speak, Kibby interrupted me.

"Mr. Bono," he said, "you're out of order."

"But I just—"

"Mr. Bono, you are out of order!"

"I just want to explain why I wasn't here."

"You're out of order, Mr. Bono. If I have to reprimand you one more time, I'll—"

"Just a minute," I snapped, frustrated. "I may be out of order, but I want to explain why I wasn't here. You won't explain. I just thought some people may be interested in the truth."

The audience was full of people supporting every candidate there except for me, since my people were informed that I had canceled. Above the confusion I heard a few hoots, insults, and catcalls.

"Mr. Bono, you are out of order," Kibby exclaimed.

That happened maybe half a dozen more times: I started to speak and this jerk told me I was breaking some rule. Exasperated, I finally lost control.

"You know, Ed," I growled, "you are not my mother. Don't tell me what the hell I can do and what I can't do.

Now I am going to tell everybody why I was not here for the forum and then I am going to leave. But at least they'll know what you purposely failed to tell them."

I drew a breath and tried to explain, but I was so frazzled that everything I said came out wrong. It was a colossal disaster, and the press as well as my opponents made the most of the spectacle. I went straight to the hospital.

"I told you not to go," Mary said.

"How are you feeling?" I asked.

"Better than you," she smiled. "They've been repeating that scene endlessly."

All that night and the following morning my phone rang off the hook. From what people said, if you were just watching television, it appeared that I had stormed out of the audience, gone onstage and exploded, then left. It had been a combustible moment that made no sense. I called a press conference and attempted to explain my way out of the situation, but none of the stations ran it. The newspaper carried a small but incomplete item.

I might as well have driven my car off a cliff. That is how convinced I was that the election was over, that I had blown everything. Nobody offered any comforting words, either. There was nothing to say. I had said it all. The only bit of good advice was to wait it out: let the voters digest the incident and make sense of it themselves.

A few days passed and the word of mouth that filtered back was better than anybody expected. Instead of thinking me a hothead, a lot of people applauded the fact that I had stepped up and fought for something that I believed in, especially a pregnant wife.

With the election a week off, Mary was allowed to return home, and both of us approached the big day in better shape than we had anticipated.

It was the night before the election, and Mary and I were watching the Academy Awards. Cher was among the nominees vying for the Best Actress Oscar, a tribute to her excellent work in *Moonstruck*. I was expected to be elected mayor of Palm Springs the next day, testimony to the dumb tenacity that had always guided me through life. As my very pregnant wife and I sat in front of the television, I thought back to the "Late Night with David Letterman" show on which Cher and I had appeared.

I'm sure Cher would agree that life has its charms. That both of us were surfacing as winners some twenty-five years after we'd started in show business—and more than a decade after our divorce—was one of them. Yet there was inescapable irony to the timing. Earlier that day I had felt the need to connect with Cher, and somehow I'd gotten through to her on the phone.

"Cher," I said, "I know you're going to win tonight. Don't worry. I know you're going to win."

"Well, I hope you're right," she said.

"How're you doing?"

"I'm pretty nervous," she said.

"Don't be," I said. "You've got it. Cinch."

How was I so sure?

Because deep down I was afraid that God had to play one more sick little existential joke on me. Just when I was feeling free of my ties to my past life with Cher, just when I was comfortable being ordinary Sonny Bono, entertainer turned restaurateur turned who knew what, He was going to have Cher win the Academy Award, and all the old anguish and feelings of inadequacy were going to tumble down like a landslide—especially if I lost the election the next day.

If that happened, I told Mary, we were going to have to leave the country.

I wasn't kidding, either.

If Cher won an Oscar and Sonny lost his bid to become mayor of Palm Springs, people would be publishing Sonny Bono joke books. That stuff would be devastating. I tried to put that out of my mind. Then Cher won the Academy Award. I immediately flipped off the TV. I didn't have to be nervous for her anymore. Only one thing occupied my mind—the election. I couldn't sleep. I got up and paced the house. After about half an hour, I sat down at the kitchen table and remained there until morning.

As expected, Cher's name was headline news in that day's *Los Angeles Times*. I knew that the next day's paper was going to mention me—one way or another. Oddly, now that the moment of truth had arrived, I found myself much less anxious than the previous night. I had come to peace with myself. Whether or not I received the most votes really didn't matter. I knew that I was a winner.

I had a beautiful wife, whom I loved very much. In a few days I was going to become a father. There was a contentment to my life that had never been there before, and I attributed a great deal of that to Mary. She loved me for who I was, not what I could do for her. My relationship with Cher never had the balance it did with Mary. I had put everything I had behind Cher and saved nothing for myself. That wasn't healthy. I should've found out who I was and put at least as much effort into that as I did into Cher.

I had no such worries now, though. Mary and I were so mutually supportive. I knew that if I woke up one morning and said to Mary, "Let's sell the house and move to Tahiti," she'd say, "OK. Give me a week to pack up and get the kids together." As it was, Mary woke up and saw that I was antsy. I didn't want to sell the house, but I definitely wanted to get moving. It was election day.

"Come on, Mare," I said, putting down my coffee mug. "Let's go vote."

EPILOGUE

THE BEAT GOES ON

It was the biggest landslide victory in the city's history. After the votes were all counted, Palm Springs had a new mayor and I had a new career.

Mayor Bono.

I repeated the title to myself over and over again, trying to get used to the sound. It was impossible.

I enjoyed the victory. I savored the thrill. I relived it from start to finish. It was tremendously humbling to realize that people had voted for me because of what I stood for. They'd believed in my ideas. I realized the election was one of the first achievements since the sale of my earliest songs that I'd been able to enjoy fully. Cher had never enjoyed the triumphs of Sonny and Cher. She'd always wanted more. It made the whole deal an empty experience for her, and the emptiness rubbed off on me.

That was then, though. The glow of winning had barely begun to fade when Mary went into labor. Shortly after the election, my son was born. In keeping with the *Ch* theme I'd started with Christy and Chastity, Mary and I named the newest member of our family Chesare. I received a lot of congratulations from well-wishers, a lot of back slaps and smiles as I walked around town. But none was more meaningful than the gummy little grin Chesy flashed his pop from his crib.

As Chesare grew, fatherhood took on an entirely new meaning for me. The responsibility became clearer. Though I didn't deserve good marks in raising Christy or Chastity, I'd grown up a lot since then. I knew it was OK to be emotional with him. I made sure to kiss and hug him a lot. I told him that I loved him and made sure he heard those magic words. I also vowed to spend a lot of time with him and to be the hands-on dad I'd never been before.

"You know, Dad," said Chastity, "you're cute. It's weird to see you with a little baby. But it's cute."

I remembered New Year's Eve, 1987. Chas, who had come out from New York, where she was living with Cher, was getting set to make her stage debut. I was headlining a gala New Year's Eve blowout at the recently completed Palm Springs Convention Center and had invited Chas to perform with me. Only a few months earlier I'd been in New York and Chastity had told me that she was writing songs. When I asked to hear some, she belted out three or four and gave me a grin.

"You wrote those?" I asked.

"Yeah," she said.

"Well, the talent's there," I said. "The rest just depends on what kind of horsepower you've got inside and how badly you want to pull it off."

Chas and I spent a few days rehearsing all the old Sonny and Cher songs, and she did great. She was doing all of Cher's parts, and those weren't easy shoes to fill. But Chas never said a word about being nervous. She downplayed everything but her salary. Getting paid for a gig was a big deal to her, as it should've been. Otherwise, she was cool. I was the one who was a wreck. We stood onstage together, sang, and traded several quips. It was when we began singing "I Got You Babe," and I looked into her eyes, that I got all weepy myself. At that moment, her entire life flashed in front of me. I saw Chas as a baby. I remembered holding her in my arms, and I found it difficult to believe that so much time had passed.

Suddenly—or so it seemed—Chas had turned into a

young woman. She was standing next to me, looking great, and it was a thrill I'd never imagined. We were singing a rock-and-roll love song to each other. I'd written it twenty-five years earlier for her mother, yet I found that the words held as much meaning for me and Chas—perhaps a little more.

About a year later Mary and I were in New York City. Both Cher and Chas were going through hell. Cher had recently broken up with her younger boyfriend Rob Camilletti—though that was old news by then. The much bigger story concerned Chas. For the second week in a row Chastity was plastered across the cover of a supermarket tabloid. It was one thing for Cher or, to a lesser extent me, to be on the cover of a gossip rag. But it made me sick to see my daughter there, and I could only believe it was worse for Chas. When she was younger seeing stories about her mother had upset her; now they were going after her.

As always when I was in New York, I took Chas shopping for clothes. With Mary, we trudged through the Village. Chas knew every clothing store in lower Manhattan, and Mary's and my feet were paying the price. The three of us had been together several hours and I sensed that Chas was preoccupied by the turmoil the tabloid had generated. Seeing her so upset got me even more upset. I wanted to strangle the guy who had written the story.

The tabloids were just something that Chas was going to have to get used to. She was now emerging as a singer in her own right, and the rag sheets would be coming after her personally.

"Chas, listen, those papers really print a bunch of garbage. You've seen all of the lies they've made up about me and your mom. Try not to let it bother you."

I saw a bit of relief come across her face. She started to realize she wasn't the first or the last person to be attacked in such a hurtful fashion.

Whoever said you can't please all the people all the time must've been in politics. He or she was right.

By my second year in office, I had survived both insults—Mayor Bonehead and Sonny Boneaparte—and a meager recall attempt led by fringe personalities who chose to operate in the dark and not reveal themselves. I didn't let it bother me. After a shaky first twelve months, I developed into a facile and competent mayor, presiding over weekly study sessions and council meetings. The second year was even smoother.

Unlike a lot of politicians, I did what I said I'd do in my campaign. I injected life into the city's tired bloodstream. Apathy was replaced with energy. The city's sluggish economy was stimulated by a marathon, a vintage-car race, a Grand Prix bicycle race, and the Palm Springs Film Festival, which has become one of the country's more prestigious cinema showcases and a launching pad for Academy Award winners such as *Cinema Paradiso*. The entrepreneurial climate has improved. The city is marketing itself better. Palm Springs is alive.

The rewards of being mayor are immense. Far beyond any money I earned as an entertainer. They're far beyond measure. Why? Because the job has to do with the larger issues of life and the welfare of mankind. Most people never get beyond thinking about themselves, their families, how much money they make, where they're going to vacation, whether or not they have food on the table and a roof over their head. Those same concerns had comprised most of my adult life.

It's great to hear people still humming songs I wrote many years ago, songs that still inspire smiles and whistles. However, when I think that my work as mayor might someday affect a child who is not yet born, I get more excited. I have a shot at contributing to the world, which offers something more meaningful and substantial. It offers something I feel is unparalleled. I'm at a point in my life when I'm supposed to be winding down. But my dreams are getting bigger . . . perhaps re-election . . . perhaps the U.S. Senate.

Only a few things can compete with the satisfaction of public service, and one such thing happened to me just as I was completing this chapter of my life. On February 2, 1991, Mary gave birth to our second child, a daughter whom we named Chianna.

Mary and I brought her home just as I was searching for a sage ending to this book. I was struck by the irony and the symbolism. A new life was beginning as I was trying to sum mine up.

Then it hit me. I didn't need an end as much as I needed a way to begin again. I had never articulated it, but that philosophy had been true my entire life. I'd been knocked down countless times, but I'd never tired of getting back up and trying again. My career was as checkered as a tablecloth. I'd poured cement, delivered meat, written hit songs, made movies, operated a restaurant, and now I was mayor. It was a good life, a fortunate life. The key? As I thought about it, I realized that I never looked on failure as a defeat but rather as an opportunity to start again.

For me, the end of one thing has always led to the beginning of something else.

The beat goes on. Yeah, the beat goes on . . .